D0894987

The Player's Passion

The Player's Passion

Studies in the Science of Acting

Joseph R. Roach

Newark: University of Delaware Press
London and Toronto: Associated University Presses

LC

© 1985 by Associated University Presses, Inc.

Associated University Presses
440 Forsgate Drive
Cranbury, NJ 08512

Associated University Presses
25 Sicilian Avenue
London WC1A 2QH, England

Associated University Presses
2133 Royal Windsor Drive
Unit 1
Mississauga, Ontario
Canada L5J 1K5

The paper used in this publication meets the minimum requirements of the
American National Standard for Permanence of Paper for Printed Library
Materials Z39.48-1984.

Library of Congress Cataloging in Publication Data

Roach, Joseph R., 1947–
  The player's passion.

  Bibliography: p.
  Includes index.
  1. Acting—Psychological aspects. 2. Acting—
Philosophy. 3. Theater—History—Philosophy. I. Title.
PN2071.P78R6 1985   792'.028   84-40059
ISBN 0-87413-265-7 (alk. paper)

Printed in the United States of America

4-23-86

For Janice

Playing is a science, and is to be studied as a science; and he who, with all that nature ever did, or can do for a man, expects to succeed wholly without the effects of that study, deceives himself extremely.

—John Hill, *The Actor* (1755)

It will be asked: "Can there exist a system for the creative process? Has it really got laws that have been established for all time?" In certain parts of the system, like the physiological and psychological, such laws exist for all, forever, and in all creative processes. They are indubitable, completely conscious, tried by science and found true, and binding on all. Each actor must know them. He does not dare to excuse himself because of his ignorance of these laws, which are created by nature herself.

—Constantin Stanislavski, *My Life in Art* (1924)

Contents

List of Illustrations   9

Preface   11

Acknowledgments   19

1   Changeling Proteus: Rhetoric and the Passions in the
    Seventeenth Century   23

2   Nature Still, But Nature Mechanized   58

3   Vitalism and the Crisis of Sensibility   93

4   Diderot   116

5   Second Nature: Mechanism and Organicism from Goethe to
    Lewes   160

6   The *Paradoxe* as Paradigm: The Structure of a Russian
    Revolution   195

Epilogue: The Vitalist Twilight   218

Notes   227

Works Consulted   234

Index   248

Illustrations

Illustration from the *Works* of Terence — 28
Title page from Bulwer's *Chironomia* — 35
Chirograms from Bulwer's *Chirologia* — 36
Chirogram (detail). *Ploro* — 37
Frontispiece to Kirkman's *The Wits* (detail) — 51
Chirogram (detail). *Despero* — 51
Rubens, *Decius Mus Addressing the Legions* — 54
The nervous system according to Descartes — 63
Six universal passions according to Le Brun — 67
Three gestural *points* from Lange, *Dissertatio de actione scenica* — 70
Terror according to Le Brun — 72
Notation of gesture according to Jelgerhuis — 75
Terror according to Engel — 77
Apprehension according to Siddons — 77
David Garrick as Hamlet — 88
Awe with astonishment according to Le Brun — 88
Astonishment and *Dread* according to Jelgerhuis — 90
Five universal passions according to Buffon — 140
Hogarth, *Strolling Actresses* (detail) — 156
Mrs. Siddons — 175
Bell, *Depascentes* — 175
George Frederick Cooke — 176
Bell, *Ringentes* — 176
Terror according to Darwin — 178
Four expressions from Darwin, *Expression of the Emotions* — 180
Meyerhold, Biomechanical exercises — 200

Preface

The actor's body constitutes his instrument, his medium, his chief means of creative expression—that is a commonplace on which performers and spectators alike have readily agreed. A corollary to this point, however, the one that I propose to examine here, is less obvious, but equally pertinent: conceptions of the human body drawn from physiology and psychology have dominated theories of acting from antiquity to the present. The nature of the body, its structure, its inner and outer dynamics, and its relationship to the larger world that it inhabits have been the subject of diverse speculation and debate. At the center of this ongoing controversy stands the question of emotion. Even when the special complications raised by theatrical representation are set aside, the question of emotion tends to defy settled conclusions. Emotions are common to everyone's experience, yet they are notoriously difficult to define. As William James put it in the title of a celebrated essay, "What is an Emotion?" In the history of science, substantially different answers have been proposed to James's question as theories have changed to fit new psychophysiological discoveries. The following chapters explore the revolutionary influences that these changes have exerted on theatrical theory from the Galenic physiology of the passions in the seventeenth century to the conditioned reflex of the twentieth.

My larger purpose is to broaden the framework in which theater historians generally conceive of their discipline. The history of the theater is a history of ideas. In that respect, it need not defer to the history of art, music, or science. When an actor takes his place on a stage, even in the most apparently trivial vehicle, and his audience begins to respond to his performance, together they concentrate the complex values of a culture with an intensity that less immediate transactions cannot rival. They embody its shared language of spoken words and expressive gestures, its social expectations and psychological commonplaces, its conventions of

11

truth and beauty, its nuances of prejudice and fear, its erotic fascinations, and frequently its sense of humor. Whenever this isn't so, the actor will fail. The theater exists at the center of civilized life, not at its peripheries. Specialists in other fields acknowledge this centrality. When a social historian such as Richard Sennett writes *The Fall of Public Man* or an art historian such as Michael Fried brings forth *Absorption and Theatricality*, he demonstrates the crucial importance of the theater in the intellectual history of his own discipline. Theater historians would do well to exhibit such confidence. No fact or set of facts in theater history—this bit of business in that theater on such-and-such a date—can have meaning in isolation. It didn't at the time, and it can't possibly now. One challenge for the historian, then, is to present the relevant evidence in a coherent argument that does not cut the theater off from its larger historical context.

A history of the theatricalization of the human body, which this study aims to be, could be approached from several points of view. The influence of art, fashion, religious mores, etiquette, deportment, each might be fruitfully considered in establishing what Lichtenberg called a "semiotics of affects" for the theater of a given period. I have deliberately narrowed this field by concentrating on how the inner workings of the actor's body have been variously understood by critics and theorists who knew something about the physiology of emotion. My argument often turns on the language of the theorist himself because his phraseology reveals the scientific source of his assumptions, and for this reason I have had to quote extensively, often from apparently remote disciplines.

Although some of the issues that I address will seem familiar, they need to be reevaluated in the context provided by the sciences. Historians of the seventeenth-century theater, for instance, have long recognized the importance of rhetoric and oratory in relation to the actor's art, but they have yet to grasp the full significance of the relation between rhetorical doctrines of expressiveness and ancient medicine. Historians have also documented extensively the revolution in acting effected by David Garrick. Previous accounts of the genesis of his style, however, need to be revised in light of the scientific revolution of which his celebrated naturalness was a direct consequence and expression.

Garrick, indeed, lived at the decisive moment in the development of theatrical theory. The modernization of the physical sciences, their subsequent disentanglement from ancient authority, helped eighteenth-century theorists for the first time to interpret the actor's emotion from outside the framework of classical rhetoric. At the same time the growing secularization of enlightened science extricated empirical investigations of vitality from obfuscating issues like *soul*. The time-honored philosophical and scientific issue of the relationship of mind and body—whether answered by interactive dualists, occasionalists, parallelists, or monists—underlies crucial questions of daily professional significance to the actor, among them movement, gesture, characterization, motivation, concentration, imagination, and memory. I want to demonstrate how the revolutionary achievements of eighteenth-century theory, outstandingly those of Denis Diderot, seemed to promise answers to those questions by approaching the actor's body as a physical instrument, like a piano or a clock, whose capacities and limitations can be objectively analyzed and whose mind and body comprise a material continuum, subject to physical laws in its entirety.

In assessing the impact of eighteenth-century science on subsequent theories of acting, I have been guided by Thomas Kuhn's seminal study of the sociology of scientific ideas, *The Structure of Scientific Revolutions* (1962; rev. ed., 1970) and Michel Foucault's *Les mots et les choses* (1966), translated as *The Order of Things* (1970). I apply Kuhn's concept of a *paradigm* and Foucault's of an *episteme* in a general way without claiming that the actor's art is per se a science, though many of the actors and theorists discussed here have made that claim. Rather, scientific models have so thoroughly permeated acting theory that its history has inevitably developed in ways analogous to the structure that Kuhn outlines for the history of science and that Foucault develops for the history of knowledge generally.

Kuhn and Foucault reject the view that knowledge steadily progresses by accretion. Kuhn describes instead a revolutionary process whereby long prevailing theoretical networks are replaced by incompatible new ones. Ptolemaic astronomy, for instance, was such a paradigm of the cosmos until the Copernican revolution supplanted it by positing a new location for the sun. Any paradigm has *anomalies*—facts which refuse to fit the theory. As a group of *practitioners* in any field continues its investigations, anomalies tend to proliferate. When such unsolved *puzzles* have multiplied to the point at which they subvert confidence in the paradigm, a *crisis* will develop. If, at this time, there appears a competing paradigm which will resolve the anomalies, accounting for more of the known facts, then the old paradigm will collapse and the new one will be adopted. This new model then becomes the basis of *normal science*, whose puzzles will occupy its practitioners indefinitely or at least until the next crisis occurs. Foucault, though differing in important respects, shares with Kuhn the idea that the history of science is discontinuous. He views it as a succession of essentially isolated episodes, each internally dominated by a network of theories, interests, and problems, by a way of knowing the world.

Theater historians have much to learn from this way of looking at intellectual history, emphasizing as it does not only what authorities in the past thought about nature, but how they thought about it. When Foucault differentiates between the mechanistic science of the eighteenth century and the discontinuous *episteme* that followed it and that still dominates our thinking today, he issues a most thought-provoking warning: "Historians want to write histories of biology in the eighteenth century; but they do not realize that biology did not exist then, and that the pattern of knowledge that has been familiar to us for a hundred and fifty years is not valid for a previous period. And that, if biology was unknown, there was a very simple reason for it: that life itself did not exist." Foucault points out that the word *biology* did not come into existence—that life as we think of it simply could not exist as a mental category—until the early nineteenth century. If nature as we define it did not exist in the eighteenth century, the theater historian is bound to ask what Garrick's critics actually meant when they described his acting as natural.

Also of particular interest to students of theatrical theory is Kuhn's idea of a paradigmatic text. In the early phases of the development of a scientific theory, he explains, a paradigm may emerge from a single work, which therefore dominates a field for generations. Such books, among which Kuhn numbers Aristotle's *Physica*, Newton's *Principia* and *Opticks*, Lavoisier's *Chemistry*, and Lyell's *Geology*, take the place of present-day science textbooks in performing the role of transmitting a paradigm. These works show two characteristics. First, they are sufficiently powerful to deflect a group of practitioners away from competing theories and methods of investigation. Second, they are open-ended enough to create a whole new set of problems "for the redefined group of practitioners to resolve." When one views Constantin Stanislavski's *An Actor Prepares* (1936) in this light, with its American proponents of Method Acting serving as the redefined group of practitioners and *emotion memory* providing the puzzling anamoly, one can see why Kuhn's description of communities of scientific knowledge might provide an illuminating analogy for the history of acting theory. But Stanislavski's work, as I hope to demonstrate, is only one case in a much larger movement, the major impulse of which was Diderot's *Paradoxe sur le comédien* (1773).

On the subject of standard scientific textbooks, Kuhn further suggests just how much theater historians could learn from historians of science. He points out that modern texts reflect a distinct historical bias toward the paradigm that they promote. Telescopic discussions of the history of the discipline tend to present it as a triumphant march toward the certainties of the present day, as if the practitioners in centuries past were always at work on the same set of problems, making contributions to the ultimate solution, which is now at hand. Scientists who welcome the accumulation of facts of other kinds, Kuhn trenchantly observes, tend to ignore or suppress historical facts which belong to discredited paradigms. This is Whig history, written by the victors, or at least by the victors of the moment. In such texts historical instances featuring the "right" answers predominate massively over the "wrong" ones, even if the latter were by far the more important to contemporaries. Such procedures may perhaps promote good science, but they make for wildly distorted history.

The vision of theater historians has been blurred by the same sort of parallax view. Theorists beginning with those in Greek antiquity have been analyzed and understood only in relationship to the degree to which they "anticipated Stanislavski," despite the fact that when they said that the actor should be inspired and possessed by his role, they meant something quite different from "building a character" and "creating a role." In our general understanding of acting theory, the smug present tyrannizes over the past. In *The Empty Space* (1968), Peter Brook stated a common view when he referred to the "great system of Stanislavsky, which for the first time approached the whole art of acting from the point of view of science," implying either that science had no influence on acting theory until the 1920s and 30s, or that, even if it did have an influence, it was wrong and therefore not really science at all. Historians of science can help us to move beyond our ingrained attitude that "scientific" and "correct" are synonymous. They can help us to challenge our assumption—nurtured by omissions from the historical sections of our school science texts—that the accepted verities of the present are so secure that we need not understand the discarded verities of the past.

What is true of the history of scientific thinking is true also of the history of theatrical theories. If each age prides itself on having attained the right answers about how the world works, it prides itself equally on being able to view theatrical exhibitions of human feeling that are more realistic and natural than those of the previous age. In fact, each acting style and the theories that explain and justify it are right and natural for the historical period in which they are developed and during which they are accepted. In order to understand historical styles of acting in the context of their contemporary settings, we must therefore restore the meaning of outmoded terminology and explanatory principles. Before we label an acting style artificial, we should have at least made an effort to understand what its practitioners meant by *natural*. Unless we know how Thomas Heywood's use of the term *animal spirits* in 1612 differed from

Aaron Hill's in 1735, what the word *sensibility* actually signified to Sainte-Albine and John Hill, what Diderot meant when he referred to the human body as a *machine*, what G. H. Lewes understood by *fluctuating spontaneity*, what William Archer meant by *innervation*, Vsevolod Meyerhold by *reflex inhibition*, and Jerzy Grotowski by *canalizing the stimulus*—unless we have a clear understanding of all these issues and the science that stands behind them, we cannot hope to know what these theorists actually thought about the complex psychophysiological event that takes place on the stage. These terms and concepts do not add up to anything approaching complete answers to the problems posed by the actor's art, then or now. That we still regard the creative process and the performance event as miracles of a sort is credit to their fugitive nature and to the fascination that their contradictions continue to exert upon us. But the history of the scientific languages in which acting has been described can shed new light upon how such contradictions were viewed in the times of the actors whose memories we most revere and whose performances we would most like to attend if leaps through time were possible. It can even send us back to the theater with a heightened appreciation of the fact that our era too has its own style of expression, that today's actors have also learned a special code that links our general preconceptions of the natural order of life to their specific embodiments of it.

The idea of approaching theatrical history from this theoretical perspective came to me gradually as I experienced and shared with young performers the frustrations and startling self-discoveries inherent in acting. Not the least of these discoveries is the paradoxical nature of theatrical spontaneity—the immediate presence of the body to itself—which inevitably raises questions about the nature of the physical bases of all human behavior. The central issues of psychology and physiology, by whatever names they are known, are not remote abstractions to the performer, but literally matters of flesh and blood. In the early stages of an actor's efforts—either as a beginner or at the start of rehearsals for a new role—his body resists his will: his gestures die stillborn, words fail him, his rhythms sputter and lurch like a new machine whose parts do not quite fit. As he repeats himself in rehearsals and exercises, however, testing the pulses of his imagination, probing his physical and mental limits, these hesitancies tend to fall away one by one; his assurance generates energy, until he seems more thoroughly alive than ever before. The paradox is evident: the actor's spontaneous vitality seems to depend on the extent to which his actions and thoughts have been automatized, made second nature. This process may be easily observed in dancers, but it occurs with greater psychological significance in the work of actresses and actors. Performance gives the same paradox an added twist. Every night the words, gestures, and movements that the actor embodies are so nearly the same as to be indistinguishable from those of the night before. Vague notions that a given performance is "up" or "down" do not nullify the fact that, barring a major stage emergency or blunder, the actor replicates his performance each night, however violent the passions that he enacts may be, with an astonishing precision of emphasis, reactivating in time and space ornate sequences that have been absorbed into muscles and nerves. Yet every night the actor's experience of his performance is somewhat different; as its vitality fluctuates, the delicate instrument of his mind and body must sense the slightest realignment of forces and adjust accordingly. Thus every actor's experience gives new pertinence to the question that has persisted through the ages: What is the nature of this extraordinary instrument—its memory, its imagination, its capacity for sensation and reflection—that it can accommodate the diversified and even contradictory demands imposed upon it by the art of acting? Some of the most provocative answers to this question, proposed by theatrical theorists in the light of science, are the subject of the following pages.

Acknowledgments

The initial research for this book was supported by a grant from the Mednick Memorial Fund of the Virginia Foundation for Independent Colleges and by Sweet Briar College. The staffs of the Mary Helen Cochran Library at Sweet Briar, the Alderman Library at the University of Virginia, the Library of Congress, the Folger Shakespeare Library, and the Olin Library at Washington University in St. Louis rendered valuable assistance at every stage of the project. Some of the material incorporated into Chapters 2, 4 and 5 first appeared in *Theatre Journal* (32 [1980]: 312–28; 34 [1982]: 431–40) and *Theatre Survey* (22 [1981]: 51–68). Various sections and drafts of the manuscript were read by Professors Marvin Carlson, Helen Krich Chinoy, Lawrence Ross, Robert Benedetti, Brooks McNamara, and Laura T. Buckham. Their thoughtful criticisms and suggestions saved me from many errors and infelicities, but those that remain are entirely my own. For her editorial scrutiny, I thank Elizabeth R. Mansfield. Above all, this project could not have carried through without the patient help and encouragement of my wife, Janice Carlisle.

The Player's Passion

1

Changeling Proteus:
Rhetoric and the Passions
in the Seventeenth Century

Passions are *Nature's* never-failing *Rhetorick,* and the only *Orators* that can master our *Affections.*
—*The English Theophrastus* (1708)

In a passage of excruciating intimacy, Marcus Fabius Quintilianus, Latin rhetor in the rule of Vespasian, prefaces Book 6 of his *Institutio Oratoria* by recounting the death of his family. He first tells how his wife, whom he loved not only as a mate but as a daughter, succumbed at the age of nineteen, leaving him with two sons. The younger boy, who devoted "all his love to me, preferring me to his nurses [and] to his grandmother who brought him up," lived just past his fifth birthday. "After these calamities," the narrative continues, "all my hopes, all my delight were centered on my little Quintilian, and he might have sufficed to console me." By the age of eleven this first-born son had demonstrated such brilliance in his studies and such noble qualities of mind as to inspire the first five books of the *Institutio*, intended by his father as a guide to educate especially promising youths towards the goal of eloquence, the most highly esteemed attainment in ancient public life. Even during the terrible pain of his final illness, the boy astonished the attending physicians with his courage and dignity, consoling his grieving father as long as he was able. "Even in the wanderings of delirium did his thoughts recur to his lessons and his literary studies, even when his strength was sinking and he was no longer ours to claim." Finally, at the moment the light faded out of the boy's eyes, the father embraced his son's "cold and pale

23

body" to breathe in the "fleeting spirit" from his lips. In the natural
scheme of life, this last rite should have been the child's final duty to his
parent, for it was then the custom for the nearest relative to receive in the
mouth the last breath of the dying in order "to continue the existence of
the spirit."[1]

After having unburdened his soul publicly with this account, Quintilian chills the freshly vulnerable sensibilities of his reader by turning
abruptly to a technical question: How does the speaker most effectively
deliver the peroration, the denouement of the classical address and the
part most highly charged with emotion? By way of an answer, most of the
balance of Book 6 treats the orator's skillful use of *pathos* to elicit a
sympathetic response from his audience. The author's explanation of the
power of manipulating emotions, which at one point he calls *deinosis*,
literally "making terrible" (6.2.24), leads him to reveal some of the "secret principles" of his art. He promises that these are founded on personal
experience and the guidance of nature.

His first principle, however, disappoints in its banality: "the prime
essential for stirring the emotions of others is, in my opinion, first to feel
those emotions oneself" (6.2.26). This hand-me-down had already been
worn threadbare by Aristotle, Horace, and Cicero. Yet Quintilian's complicating premise, while also derivative, casts the question in a different
and far more interesting light. An orator, he says, like an actor, should
employ imaginative identification to "impersonate" and "exhibit" emotions as if they were his own. He urges the orator to "assimilate [himself]
to the emotions of those who are genuinely so affected" (6.2.27), taking
those passions into himself and transforming them into vocal and bodily
eloquence. Emotions should remain felt emotions, but they also become
"impersonations [by which] I mean fictitious speeches." The actor and
the orator face the same problem, and Quintilian invites the reader to
"draw a parallel from the stage, where the actor's voice and delivery
produce greater emotional effects when he is speaking in an assumed role
than when he speaks in his own character" (6.1.26–27). Interesting as it
may be, this answer merely poses another question, one that would be
the source of controversy and debate for centuries to come: "How," the
rhetor asks himself, "are we to generate these emotions in ourselves?"
(6.2.29).

His answer tantalizes the modern reader with its apparent psychological specificity. Affective embodiments overcome both actor and orator in
what Quintilian calls *visiones:* "fantastic . . . daydreams . . . whereby
things absent are presented to our imagination with such extreme
vividness that they seem actually to be before our very eyes" (6.2.29–30).
These visions are obviously linked to the rhetorical ideal of *enargeia*,

supreme animation in language, which Aristotle, in discussing the power of vivid metaphor in his *Rhetoric* (3.11), compared to *kinesis* or "movement." Quintilian's line of thinking is founded on another Aristotelian precept, later compressed in the Latin axiom, *Fortis imaginato generat causum*—"A strong imagination begets the event itself." In *De Anima* (3:7) Aristotle stated that the soul never thinks without a mental picture, the *imago animi*, and that, when these pictures are strongly present in the imagination, the soul is as moved as if the actual objects of desire were present to the senses.[2] Quintilian notes that intense *visiones* naturally nourish the more violent passions, those belonging to the rhetorical category of *pathos*, namely anger, loathing, fear, hatred, grief, and pity. When the actor/orator has strongly "identified" with such passions, his spirit has sufficient power over his body to alter its physical states, inwardly and outwardly: "I have often seen actors . . . leave the theatre still drowned in tears after concluding the performance of some moving role." Quintilian's own experience proved that rhetorical eloquence has its concealed bases in the operations of mind on body, and to this fact of nature he attributed his success as an orator: "I have frequently been so moved while speaking, that I have not merely been wrought upon to tears, but have turned pale and shown all the symptoms of genuine grief" (6.2.35–36). At such moments feigned emotion becomes indistinguishable from genuine feeling.

The full purpose of the threnody with which Book 6 opens is now more readily apparent. Elsewhere in the *Institutio* Quintilian illustrates his precepts before he describes them ("What is more common than to *ask* or *enquire?*" he asks at the head of the section on rhetorical questions [9.2.6]). Thus in his preface to the chapter on working up emotions, he has marked the broken cadences of genuine grief that he wishes his followers to emulate. Yet he seems to have had an even deeper pedagogic design, one more in keeping with the profundity of his self-revelation. The dying son has figuratively as well as literally inspired, breathed spirit into, the father and rhetor, who in turn has offered up his *pathos* to inspirit the "dreams" and "visions" of orators by engaging their imaginative sympathies with his bereavement. Spirit, the breath of life, the transmigration of what the Latins called *anima* or soul from one body to another, stands as a symbol of the oratorical or theatrical act of impersonation, the physical embodiment of one soul, its passions and its actions, by another.

After opening Book 6 with a paean to inspiration, Quintilian turns to an extended discussion of artifice and enumerates the various techniques that the orator can use to render emotion. He therefore whets a double-bladed axe for the historic, continuing, and apparently inexhaustible combat between technique and inspiration in performance theory. Then as now the issue hinges on spontaneity. Quintilian knows that "the method of arousing the emotions depends on our power to represent or imitate the passions," but he insists that excellence in this endeavor requires a delicate balance of spontaneity ("nature") and premeditation ("care, art, polish"). As rhetor he shows himself reluctant to surrender either the presumed sincerity of emotion flowing freely from *visiones* or the regularity and discipline promised by calculation. His advice that a speaker "excite the appropriate feeling" in himself, one that "cannot be distinguished from the truth," concludes paradoxically that true emotion should be deeply felt by the person who is faking it (11.3.156, 10, 61–62). That conclusion, like the other issues Quintilian addresses, leaves ample room for further debate.

The fact that such questions should have been raised by the chief of the classical rhetoricians suggests not only the form that they would take but also the source of their answers at least through the seventeenth century. The rhetoric of the passions, derived from the work of Quintilian and his successors, dominated discussions of acting up until the age of Diderot and Garrick. Like the mimetic and pragmatic theories of art that held similar sway over aesthetics until late in the eighteenth century,[3] rhetorical explanations of expression and expressiveness predominated because they provided satisfying responses to pressing questions. They did so in part because they were based on the contemporaneous understanding of how the human body functions. Giving emotional resonance to such scientific and medical thinking was a bedrock of ancient belief in a spiritual realm that justified man's sense of the commanding forces that work within and upon his body. This concatenation of factors—the discipline of rhetoric, scientific knowledge, and ancient belief—endowed the doctrine of the passions with its longstanding power to explain and illuminate the actor's art.

Quintilian's definition of impersonation as a mode of inspiration and his emphasis on the power of *visiones* both derived from the ancients' understanding of the relationship between breath and states of consciousness and their association of the mind with the lungs. Emotions strongly felt in the chest are part of our common human experience, but the ancients attributed much of this intensity to the reaction of volatile inhalations on the blood, which they believed to be copiously present in the chest around the heart as a congregation of *humours* and *spirits*. Much of the force of this idea depended on its roots in a time when inspiration was a term that comprehended the movements of the gods and the possession and ecstasy of man. Apollo, it was thought, took the form of intoxicating vapors and breathed himself into the mouth or other convenient orifice of the Pythoness of Delphi as she squatted astride the divine tripod; the "Spirit" which then lived in her and spoke through her, moving her lips "as long as she was in frenzy," was the oracular god himself.[4] In Quintilian's time these supernatural manifestations were thought to be inherent in the nature of the body itself. The *praecordia* or diaphragm was viewed as a barometer of the passions; and the association of breath, thought, and blood explained the characteristic physiological manifestations of strong emotion, including the heaving breast, blushing, bulging veins in the neck, choking and purpling with rage, and sighing with grief.[5]

These inspiring forces came literally out of thin air. A vital *pneuma*, imbibed from a universal *aether*, supposedly permeated the blood as spirits, and, radiating outward from the heart and lungs, displayed inward feelings as outward motions. This magical aether was neither fire nor water, air nor earth, but a fifth essence more subtle than any substance. The word *emotion* itself derives from the Latin *emovere* (to move out, to stir up), which assumed the existence of a vital spirit, constantly active and motive, suffused throughout the human frame. This meaning informed Leonardo's call for the depiction of the "movements of the mind" in Renaissance portraiture, but its lineage goes much farther back in time. Quintilian shows its influence, for instance, when he digresses from his discussion of inspired oratorical gesture to note that the principal agent of bodily expression exists in "the blood, which moves in conformity with the emotions that control the mind, causing a blush on a skin that is sensitive, and giving place to icy pallor under the influence of fear" (11.3.78). As prescientific lore, pagan superstition, and astute observation of nature coalesced into classical medical opinion, *pneumatism*, the association of spirits with psychic phenomena, persisted, exerting an influence on Galen (A.D. 130–200) and through him on medieval and Renaissance doctrine.[6]

The rhetoric of the passions that derived from pneumatism endowed the actor's art with three potencies of an enchanted kind. First, the actor possessed the power to act on his own body. Second, he possessed the power to act on the physical space around him. Finally, he was able to act on the bodies of the spectators who shared that space with him. In short, he possessed the power to act. His expressions could transform his physical identity, inwardly and outwardly and so thoroughly that at his best he was known as Proteus. His motions could transform the air through which he moved, animating it in waves of force rippling outward from a center in his soul. His passions, irradiating the bodies of spectators through their eyes and ears, could literally transfer the contents of his heart to theirs, altering their moral natures. The exercise of this power entailed certain dangers. The desperate prejudice against actors in the

FIGURE 1. The actor as orator. From the *Works* of Terence (1561). *(Courtesy of P. M. Arnold Semeiology Collection, Washington University Libraries.)*

seventeenth century was motivated in part by superstitious fears of their unnatural practices on the audience. As we shall see, however, the principal danger was to the actor himself. The same physiological model that explained his powers of bodily self-transformation also demonstrated his acute vulnerability to the forces that he summoned. The word *passion*, derived from the Latin *patior* (to suffer), suggested that emotions seize upon and possess those who suffer them, just as Quintilian's *visiones* penetrate and pervade those experiencing them. How to control and restrain that process became a major question of acting theory well into the eighteenth century.

The close ties between rhetoric and acting were based on more than the obvious similarity of the two activities. Rhetoric had not yet diminished to its modern status as a concern appropriate only to conservative grammarians and speech teachers. It constituted an entire system of analysis, composition, expression, persuasion, and audience psychology. In the *Apology for Actors* (1612), Thomas Heywood attempted to establish the liberality of the player's art by defining it as a species of rhetoric. From Aristotle's work on the subject onward, rhetoric had descended as a

science of persuasion that necessarily incorporated a practical psychology: before the orator can move men, he must know what kind of creatures they are—how they think and feel and why they act the way they
do. One branch of rhetoric, therefore, consisted of the study of the
Passions and Affections of men—terms defined spaciously enough in the
1600s to admit much of what we would term behavioral science. Thomas
Wright, whose rhetorical treatise *The Passions of the Minde* (1604) is
frequently quoted by theater historians in other contexts, propounds a
list of perplexing issues he considers pertinent to his study: "How are the
Soule and body, Spirit and Flesh coupled together, what chaines, what
fetters, imprison a spiritual Substance, an immortal Spirit in so base,
stinking, and corruptible a carkasse. . . . How do humours of the body
stirre up passions. . . .Or, why do Passions engender corporal humors?"[7]
The answers to such questions could be found only in a discipline that
comprehends physiology and psychology as well as aesthetics.

Quintilian remained a dominant authority on such matters. As long as
rhetoric constituted a fundamental subject in school and university cur-
ricula, as it did throughout the eighteenth century, even those with little
Latin and less Greek could scarcely avoid the *Institutio Oratoria.* In the
Renaissance it was "everywhere thought of as a perfect rhetoric"[8] and
thereafter enjoyed a repute summed up by Alexander Pope: "In grave
Quintilian's copious work we find / The justest rules and clearest method
join'd" (*An Essay on Criticism,* 3.110–11). His "justest rules," however,
have been the source of modern skepticism about the usefulness of his
"method." His "rules for delivery," the most reductive and specific to
have come down to us from antiquity, prescribe a decorum which may
strike the modern reader as the most inhibiting and affected sort of
artifice: "It is never correct to employ the left hand alone in gesture";
"instructors in the art of gesture will not permit the hand to be raised
above the level of the eyes"; "Wonder is best expressed as follows: the
hand turns slightly upwards and the fingers are brought into the palm,
one after the other, beginning with the little finger; the hand is then
opened and turned round by a reversal of this motion" (11.3.114, 112,
100–01), and so on through numerous outward significations. Scholars
have examined these restraints under the rubric of decorum, meaning the
fittingness or propriety of action and gesture to character and circumstance. This doctrine has been interpreted as representative of a "classical
concern with a clearly delineated and harmoniously controlled external
form" and "rhetorical acting" as a system of building a generalized
character from the "outside."[9] There is some truth to this view, but it fails
to emphasize the reasons behind the system of decorous gestures and

postures with which Quintilian and his successors filled their texts. It does not show how these forms were understood in terms of physiological function.

To the extent that modern critics and historians have lost sight of the scientific and pseudo-scientific underpinnings of rhetorical theory, our understanding of seventeenth-century actors and acting has been diminished. In consequence, a number of the tantalizingly meagre accounts of contemporary performances seem even less descriptive and substantial than they are in fact. In 1612, for instance, when Thomas Heywood wrote of the "perfect shape to which [an actor] fashioned all his active spirits,"[10] he could assume his reader's comprehension of the Renaissance version of Galen's nerve physiology and its explanation of how thought becomes action—just as an author on theatrical subjects today can safely assume the intelligibility of a reference to conditioned reflexes. B. L. Joseph came closest to stating the issue in historically sensitive terms when he said in the first edition of his *Elizabethan Acting* that the rhetorical principle of *actio* "merely showed through speech and gesture the state of physiological secretions within the body, as well as what went on in the soul," but he did not develop the implications of this observation, nor did he distinguish sharply between the physiology of character as written by the dramatist and the actor's physiology. The tiresome debate over the relative formalism or naturalism of seventeenth-century acting style can be traced to the disinclination of both sides to understand the historic links between acting, rhetoric, and ancient physiological doctrines. The same misunderstandings have been carried over into the study of acting in the Restoration period, the theory of which was no less rhetorically attuned and the popular physiological assumptions no less archaic.[11] The rhetorical theory on which seventeenth-century discussions of acting were based rested not on a foundation of dramaturgy, but on an understanding of how the passions operate on the human body, specifically on the body of one who is actively transforming himself, "fashion[ing] all his active spirits," into some shape he has imagined.

The evidence documenting performance theory and practice in this period must be radically reinterpreted in this light. Such a revision can illuminate comments from those made about Richard Burbage, the leading actor in Shakespeare's company, across the Interregnum to the richer descriptions of Thomas Betterton, the principal London actor from the 1660s until his death in 1710, and finally to James Quin, who carried on the old ways even as David Garrick embodied the new. It is a significant but little appreciated fact that in seventeenth-century England, rhetorical theories of acting still retained their close ties to ancient medicine. Charles Gildon, in his pseudobiography *The Life of Mr. Thomas Better-*

ton (1710), literally plundered earlier oratory texts for material to attribute to Betterton himself. Gildon's plagiarism from an English translation of La Facheur's *Essay Upon the Action of an Orator* has already been documented, but he also perpetrated another theft, from Thomas Wright's treatise on the psychology of emotion, *The Passions of the Minde,* originally published in 1604. Gildon puts the following maxim into Betterton's mouth: "a rolling Eye that is quick and inconstant in its Motion, argues a quick but light Wit; a hot and choleric complexion, with an inconstant and impatient Mind; and in Woman it gives strong Proof of Wantonness and Immodesty." In *The Passions of the Minde,* Wright had used exactly the same argument, terminology, and sentence structure to reach the same conclusion, adding that "such quickness proceedeth from abundance of hot spirits."[12] Aside from this bold-faced plagiarism, which Gildon continues for another page or two of characters, it is significant that he has no qualms about attributing Wright's antique medical doctrines, founded on Galenic humours and spirits, to Thomas Betterton the actor.

Because it stood at the point of intersection between natural and moral philosophy, the question of the physical expression of the passions, the bodily incarnation of the inward mind, pervaded seventeenth-century rhetorics, psychologies, and medical tracts. An age preoccupied with the study of motion of all kinds—in clocks, in planets, in blood—quite naturally found itself drawn to that special movement which constitutes emotion. The passions of the mind were generally thought to be of two types, *concupiscible* or *irascible,* caused either by the desire to attain or to avoid some object or entity: the former draws the body and spirits toward the exciting object, as in love or joy; the latter repels them, as in fear, or churns them up, as in hate. Philosophers differed widely on the number and division of the primary passions. Virtually all authorities agreed, however, that the passions exhibit themselves in regular significations. As Francis Bacon explained in *Sylva Sylvarum* (1627), fear results in pallor, trembling, starting, or screeching, while joy puts a sparkle or "sometimes tears" into the eyes, and wonder reveals itself in immobility or the lifting of the hands and eyes.[13] Passions operate on an all-or-nothing principle, either quiescent or firing full bore like the discharge of a musket. They were presumed to have the power of utterly deflecting the psyche and physique from their natural course. This attribute helps us to understand what Othello means when he says that he is not naturally jealous, but, having fallen into a passion, is very jealous indeed.

Treatises on the passions, cataloguing their inner causes and outer characters, became numerous enough to constitute a minor literary-scientific genre in which it seemed that ever more careful descriptions of outward expressions would somehow explain the inward nature of the phenomena. Perhaps the most exhaustive yet representative work in this tradition was the five-volume compilation of Marin Cureau de la Chambre, *Les caractères des passions* (1640–62), which was only a fragment of a much larger opus, never completed, to be called *L'art de connoistre les hommes.* "Many things more might be said of this matter," confessed Thomas Wright disarmingly after saying more than a few himself, "but I find all bookes and commonplaces, so stuffed with these discourses, that I thought it superfluous to write any more" (*Passions of the Minde*, 41).

The rhetorical concept of *actio* was the nexus of the seventeenth-century ideal of theatrical eloquence. In his *Apology for Actors*, Heywood adopted Tully's five rhetorical categories of invention, disposition, elocution, memory, and pronunciation, but added a sixth, *action*, without which the others would be "nothing" (29). The most widely circulated anecdote on this subject derived from Plutarch's account of Demosthenes, who, after studying deportment and gesture under the actor Andronicus, was asked to name the three most important parts of oratory: "Action," Demosthenes is said to have replied, "Action, and again Action" (*AA*, 14). Citing another version of this same story, Quintilian had proposed a fusion of word and gesture in one unified effort. His maxim was *pronuntiatio a plerisque actio dicitur*—"delivery is often styled action" (*Institutio*, 11.3.1)—implying a continuum of bodily and vocal expression, or, in other words, suiting the action to the word and the word to the action. When Hamlet urges the Player to speak the speech "as I pronounc'd it to you," he refers to the action of which the speech consists as well as the words, for he stresses the need to avoid both mouthing of spoken words and, its kinesthetic counterpart, sawing the air aimlessly in gesture (3.2.1–5). *Pronuntiatio* (delivery) thus constituted a physical act performed by the body as a whole, of which the articulate speaking voice was an important part, but by no means the only important part. In 1615 the author who described the character of "An Excellent Actor," perhaps John Webster, neatly dovetailed the ideas of motion and sound in rhetorical delivery: "Whatever is commendable in the grave orator, is most exquisitely perfect in [the actor]; for by a full and significant action of the body, he charms our attention: sit in a full theatre, and you will think you see so many lines drawn from the circumference of so many ears, while the actor is the center" (*AA*, 88). The actor is the source and focus of a process, an action that begins with his own body and quickly extends beyond it.

What orators and stage players do, then, is to discover the passions of the mind with their bodies—larynx, limbs, torso, and head together—

thereby transforming invisible impulse into spectacle and unspoken feeling into eloquence. In his *Passions of the Minde*, Wright defines action as an "externall image of an internall minde," an image that involves the whole body: "by mouth [the actor] telleth his minde; in countenance he speaketh with a silent voice to the eies; with all the universal life and body hee seemeth to say, Thus we moove, because by the passion thus wee are moved" (176). Following the ancients, Wright recommends both the inward embodiment of the passion and its careful "moderation" or "composition" in outward gesture. Like Hamlet, he seems to urge on the actor a "whirlwind of your passion" qualified in the same breath by a "temperance that will give it smoothness" (3.2.7–9). As they had since antiquity, rhetoricians remained untroubled by this apparent contradiction; indeed, one of the most prolific of them constructed his entire body of work on Quintilian's dichotomy of inner feeling and outer form.

The most systematic theorist in seventeenth-century England to address the issue of expressive motion was John Bulwer, best known for his fraternal treatises, *Chirologia: or the Natural Language of the Hand* and *Chironomia: or the Art of Manual Rhetoric* (bound in one volume, 1644). Bulwer's achievements as a rhetorician are familiar to theater historians, but his medical and scientific credentials have gone unremarked. To understand the full import of his work, it is necessary to appreciate his intellectual background and ambitions. Himself a physician and son of a physician, Bulwer consciously and methodically set out to fulfill Bacon's program for a modern science of gesture. He took from "that great light of learning"[14] not only an aim but a method. A prefatory verse proclaims *Chirologia* "another *Novum Organum*" wherein "Science, crescent like extends her light" (10). Science, for Bacon, meant ordering and classifying natural reality, and his method included the proliferation of instances drawn from all manner of authorities, ancient and modern, reputable and otherwise. Bulwer's methodology closely resembles Bacon's *Sylva Sylvarum* in its range of erudition and curious admixture of empiricism and gullibility. Among his representative references in various works, Bulwer quotes liberally from the rhetorics of Cicero, Quintilian, and Cresollius, Aristotle in his entirety, the histories of Xenophon, Plutarch, and Tacitus, the poems of Ovid and Virgil, the Bible in both testaments, and the patristics; he has fully digested the classical medical doctrines of the Hippocratics and Galen (a "miracle of wit"), and the modern anatomies of Vesalius, Fabricius, Eustachius, Laurentius, Columbus, and Falloppius, as well as the iatrochemical theories of Paracelsus and, of course, the current medical literature in English, including Robert Burton's *Anatomy of Melancholy* and Helkiah Crooke's *Mikrokosmographia, a Description of the Body of Man*. Yet at the same time he makes good his promise in

Chirologia to "annex consultations with nature, affording a gloss of their causes" (6). In his subsequent publications Bulwer styled himself "the Chirosopher," claiming an authority on the subject of manual gesture that embraced the extant literature and observable phenomena.

Bulwer's major treatises reveal his dual loyalty to art and nature. *Chirologia*, best known by its plates (often reprinted out of context), has been widely misunderstood as a chapbook of recondite rhetorical hieroglyphs abstracted from reality. It has been cited to justify a symbolic style of acting on the Elizabethan stage. In fact, Bulwer attempted to essay a *Natural Language of the Hand*, a language in which gestures follow on "unalterable laws and institutes of nature," in which "art hath no hand." Such a language may be comprehended universally by "men in all the regions of the habitable world," even the savages of America (16). Outward significations attain universality, Bulwer believed, because they flow naturally from the inner workings of the body—an undeniable part of the common experience of all humanity. *Chironomia: or the Art of Manuall Rhetorique*, conversely, purports to show how the natural gestures of the hand are regulated by rhetorical conventions. It consciously juxtaposes its art to the nature of *Chirologia*. It offers lessons in the management of manual gesture useful at the bar and in the pulpit as well as in "schools, theatres, and the mansions of the Muses" (151). It demonstrates that its author had copiously "consulted with the oracle of Quintilian" (153) and had assimilated the doctrines of *pronuntiatio*, including the hyperbole that "the tongue, without the hand, can utter nothing but what will come forth lame and impotent" (156–57). *Chironomia* concerns itself primarily with attaining decorous form and the control of expression, in which the stage may be allowed some greater liberties than the court or church, but not many. Raising the hand above the level of the eye or below the belly is, for instance, "accounted [a] vicious misdemeanor" in any forum. Yet for all the apparent legalisms of expression he enumerates, Bulwer advises his readers to "shun affectation": "others are most moved with our actions when they perceive all things to flow, as it were, out of the liquid current of nature" (241, 244).

Gestus 3 of *Chirologia*, marked *Ploro* ("I weep"), shows how Bulwer's concept of nature, his medical knowledge of the physiology of the passions, stands squarely behind his chirology. Weeping, he explains, by citing Bacon, "the elegant expositor of nature," is a "natural expression of excessive grief": "by wringing of the mind, tears, the sad expressions of the eyes, . . . are produced and caused by the contradiction [contraction] of the spirits of the brain," and tears therefore flow from the eyes. Similarly, this "compression of the brain" causes "the hard wringing of the hands which is a gesture of expression of moisture" (32). Bulwer goes on

FIGURE 2. The rhetorical fraternity of actors and orators: Demosthenes, Andronicus, Roscius, and Cicero. Title page of *Chironomia* (1644) by John Bulwer, M.D. *(Courtesy of P. M. Arnold Semeiology Collection, Washington University Libraries.)*

FIGURE 3. Chirograms from John Bulwer's *Chirologia* (1644). *(Courtesy of P. M. Arnold Semeiology Collection, Washington University Libraries.)*

to fortify his explanation with historic instances of hand-wringing cited in Cresollius, Apuleius, Chrysostom, and St. Gregory of Nazianzus, among others.

To the extent that the gestures Bulwer describes and the causes he imputes to them are not still part of our everyday experience, the dramas of his time provide ample illustration. *Ploro* appears at least once in Shakespeare when Hamlet orders a weeping Gertrude, "Leave wringing of your hands. Peace!" (3.4.34), and perhaps again in a more subtle form during the sleepwalking scene in *Macbeth*. For this "great perturbation in nature," the more readily applicable gesture from Bulwer would seem to be Gestus II, *Innocentiam ostendo* ("I display innocence"): "To imitate the posture of washing the hands by rubbing the back of one in the hollow of the other with a kind of detersive motion is a gesture sometimes

C *Ploro* .

FIGURE 4. Chirogram (detail). *Ploro.* (*Courtesy of P. M. Arnold Semeiology Collections, Washington University Libraries.*)

used by those would profess their innocency and declare they have no hand in that foul business" (40). To perform this gesture Mrs. Siddons set down her candlestick, and that choice is amply justified by the Gentle-woman's line, "It is an accustomed action with her, to seem thus washing her hands." But the theme of guilt on which the first part of the scene is constructed seems to change to one of overwhelming sorrow at Lady Macbeth's outburst, "Oh, oh, oh!" and the Doctor's observation and diagnosis, "What a sigh is there! The heart is sorely charg'd" (5.1.32, 59–60).

In Galenic medicine the strain of grief on the heart was thought to be caused by the morbid congregation there of bodily substances. As Bulwer noted in *Pathomyotomia* (1649), his treatise on facial expressions, "Sad-nesse is a certaine Contraction of the heat and spirits toward their Princi-ple";[15] it was certainly considered one of the most lethal of emotions. The body needs to "expel" the surfeited fluids from the chest and head (Ba-con, *Works* 2:568)—hence tears, sighs, and hand-wringing. When Mac-beth taunts the Doctor of Physic about his inability to "minister to a mind diseas'd," he challenges him to "Pluck from the memory a rooted sorrow" and to "cleanse the stuff'd bosom of that perilous stuff / Which weighs upon the heart" (5.3.40–44). This, the Doctor replies, the patient must do for herself, purging the healthful spirits along with the foul. In his description of *Ploro,* Bulwer observed that sorrow "diminisheth the body" (32), a physical wastage ultimately culminating in death. In a play otherwise marked by violent death, such an idea would explain the bloodless demise of the grieving queen.

The essential idea behind each Gestus Bulwer presents is that every bodily motion springs directly from a discoverable cause within the hu-man frame. This assumption was shared by Wright, Heywood, Gildon, Bacon, and indeed by rhetoricians generally. Their understanding of how the human frame was constructed, however, radically separates their view of nature from those that followed.

There are three points to keep in mind about the rhetoricians' under-standing of the body: they did not distinguish sharply or consistently between cardiovascular and nervous functions in emotions; they were divided on whether to place the seat of the soul in the brain, the motive-perceptive center, or in the heart, the locus of the primary passions; and they did not believe in the circulation of the blood.[16] Under the sway of Galen's authority, the heart was thought to resemble a small combustion chamber in which blood is brought into contact with *pneuma* inhaled through the lungs and burned by a subtle flame—rather like an oil lamp, not at all like a pump. Blood and spirits were thought to emanate away from or retire toward the *vital heat* of the heart under the pressure of certain emotions, hence the cold pallor of fear in ebb tide and the searing flood of rage or shame. Each organ was thought to have an attractive power, which gathers fluids as needed, an assimilating or transforming power, which refines fluids to a state of greater subtlety, and a cathartic power, which expels wastes and residues. *Blood* could refer to one of the four humours, the sanguinary—the others being choleric, melancholic, and phlegmatic; or it could refer to them all mixed together—the *mass of Blood*—as they seep languidly through the body's steamy chambers and viscous channels. Each humour corresponds to both a characteristic passion and an element of nature: choler, like fire, dry and hot, fuels anger; melancholy, like earth, dry and cold, embodies grief; the sanguinary humour, like air, is moist and hot, and leads to amatory passions; the phlegmatic, like water, is wet and cold, and if not inert, shows itself as fear or astonishment. The basis for this system resided in the common-sense idea that the body is made up of the same substances found elsewhere in nature, and that order, as in the world at large, is achieved through equilibrium, balance, and proper mixture *(eukrasia)*. Ideal balance varies somewhat according to the individual *temperament*. Upsets in the blending of the humours *(dyskrasia)* unhinge this delicate psychophysical balance, causing physical illness and mental distress.

Thus the body, which Wright called a "stinking carkasse," resembles a large bag containing juice-filled sponges of various shapes and sizes. Between sponges there is seepage, percolation, and general sloshing about, but not the regular cleansing action of continuous circulation. Equilibrium of these potentially stagnant juices defines health. That is one reason why a surfeit of a humour could be so frightening in its physiological consequences and violent in its psychological effects. In sickness the body resembles a standing pool, clogged and befouled with diverse obstructions, excreta, putrifying humours, and soot from the fire in the heart. Excessive passion can cause the coagulation of humours around the heart, leading to disease, madness, and worse. The black bile of sorrow, for instance, notes Robert Burton in *The Anatomy of Melancholy*, contracts the heart, congeals the blood, hinders all its operations, and causes "melancholy, desperation, and sometimes death itself."[17] It is understandable why medical opinion favored treatment through some sort of drainage—purgation or bleeding.

In received opinion, animal or active spirits accounted for all the functions now alloted to the nerves, motor and sensory. They are the exquisite product of a three-fold refinement. First, gross digestive juices sluice into the liver, which manufactures blood and charges it with *natural spirits* to nourish the body. Second, some of the enriched blood rises into the heart through the right ventricle where combustion occurs with the vital *pneuma*. This fire in the heart causes vital heat, turns blood from a thick, purple ooze to a volatile scarlet, and yields *vital spirits*. Thus clarified of grossness and impurity, the refined blood crosses through the septum, which was believed to be permeable to the newly subtle spirits, and enters the left ventricle, humidifying the left side of the body particularly. Some of the vital spirits then rise into the brain and there, by a final mysterious process called *exhalation*, are transformed into *animal spirits*. In substance animal spirits resemble wind and fire, more subtle than matter, more material than soul. They reside in the ventricles of the brain and from there communicate down the core of the spinal cord, permeating the porous, twig-like extensions of the nerves, penetrating the body, working its muscles, literally animating it, commanding it to life and motion.

Contemporaries attributed to animal spirits a potency of movement and expression recalling the ancient Apollonian forces of inspiration and possession. Spirits mediate between mind and matter—transforming thought into action, shaping what would otherwise be a collapsed bag of pus and bile into a form in God's image. Hamlet describes their effects as "infinite in faculty, in form and moving! How express and admirable in action!" (2.2.316–17). Animating the muscles as if by magic, they fashion the body to fit the soul's design.

To understand the role of the passions in this system, a political metaphor is helpful. The body politic on which rhetoricians based their art reflects a kind of class hierarchy of corporeal substances, rising in refinement toward the head: the plebeian humours, generally sluggish when properly kept down, become dangerous when they rise in revolt, while the animal spirits, quintessential Tories—subtle, sensitive, well-connected—try to run everything. The spirits act as ministers of the sovereign will, as physical extensions of the immaterial soul, which rules by divine right and looks forward to a transcendent existence beyond its earthly clay. Passions, however, cut across class lines. Because they derive from the humours and in turn influence their quantity, disposition, and destination, they are of the body. Because they are called into existence and directed by sensory, mnemonic, or imaginative functions of the mind and spirits, they are of the soul. As Bulwer explained in *Pathomyotomia*, each passion "requireth" or depends on a specific humour, its material form: the "image" in the mind, "excited by Heat and Spirits," is "drawn into Act" by their drying or moistening of the muscles. The face reveals "the affections of the mind" as the body displays the emotions of the heart (102–04). The rhetoric of the passions thus offered a satisfyingly complex definition of the relation between matter and spirit, body and mind.

The Galenic-Renaissance physiology of the passions seconded the Aristotelian view that the *image* in the soul serves as the prime activator of bodily response. Following the theory of eloquence behind Quintilian's *visiones*, rhetoricians and physicians alike believed that the animal spirits can amplify an exciting impulse through the body, stirring the humours up, whether the object is actually present to the senses, remembered, or imagined. In each case, they believed, Joy will heat the spirits and radiate them to the peripheries while Fear will collapse them back upon the heart—in the presence of a lover or merely in the contemplation of her, in the grasp of a bear or merely in his neck of the woods. According to Burton's *Anatomy of Melancholy,* apparitions, sonambulism, hallucinations, bugbears, witches, and all manner of things that go bump in the night stream copiously from the *imago animi.* The body is its principal agent and victim. Many have died by the force of imagination. From Galen onward physicians routinely advised pregnant women to eschew peculiar thoughts or fancies. The Queen of Aethiopia in Heliodurus, seeing a picture of Perseus and Andromeda, gave birth to a white baby, while one of Pope Nicholas the Third's concubines by seeing a bear "was brought to bed of a monster." Thinking about a disease will produce its symptoms. Imagining great heights will make us fall. Agrippa reported that by force of imagination men are turned to wolves, women are turned to men "or men to asses, dogs, or any other shapes" (124–25).

An implied belief in the body's magical powers of instantaneous self-transformation, a fascination with the possibilities of the quicksilver alteration of corporeal shape on command, sets rhetorical theories of acting apart from their successors. As is the case with many theories having historic links to the supernatural, this belief imbedded itself as much in the subtext of the treatises as in the text, but it emerged clearly and persistently in contemporary comparisons of actors to the mythic figure of Proteus, the versatile water spirit who could change his shape at will.

The Protean metaphor implied that the actor possesses not only the power of self-alteration, but also the more mysterious Delphic power of self-abdication in favor of the role. The foremost instance remains Flecknoe's retrospective homage to Richard Burbage as a "delightful Proteus, so wholly transforming himself into his part, and putting off himself with his clothes, as he never (not so much as in the tiring-house) assum'd himself again until the play was done" (*AA,* 91). Flecknoe may have recalled that Thomas Randolph prefaced his *Jealous Lovers* (1632) with a conceit commending the transformations of one Thomas Riley:

> I have seen a Proteus, that can take
> What shape he please, and in an instant make
> Himself to anything: be that or this
> By voluntary metamorphosis.

Not to be outdone, Thomas Heywood remembered Burbage's principal rival, Edward Alleyn, as a "Proteus for shapes, and Roscius for a tonge /

So could he speak, so vary,"[18] while a prefatory verse to Bulwer's *Chirologia* extolled the various uses to which his language of bodily expression might be put, including its theatrical uses: the actor can "portray many forms" and therefore "surpass many a Proteus" (14, Cleary trans.).

In a practical sense, prevailing stage conditions and dramaturgical conventions insured that actors of the stamp of Burbage, Alleyn, and later Betterton were indeed called upon to change shapes with dazzling frequency and swiftness. The constant rotation of the repertoire demanded the personation of far more parts in shorter blocks of time than has been expected of more recent actors. Moreover, within a given role an actor could be expected to effect sudden, highly visible transitions between passions in the length of a speech or even a single line. As modern actors rehearsing the jealousy of Leontes or the lust of Angelo have occasion to note, playwrights demanded that actors depict the passions as sudden and violent metamorphoses. Implied stage directions from late in the seventeenth century suggest that the dramatists continued to rely on the actor's powers of precisely controlling the instantaneous transitions between passions. A number of these were gathered under the entry for "Expressions" in the *Thesaurus Dramaticus* of 1729, an anthology of purple patches from the previous century. Dryden, for instance, stipulated a sudden onstage transformation from Fear to Rage in *Love Triumphant; or, Nature will Prevail* (1693):

> See, the King reddens:
> The fear which seiz'd him at Alphonso's sight
> Is vanished now;
> And a new Tide returns upon his Cheeks,
> And Rage, and Vengeance sparkle in his Eyes.

In *The Orphan: or, The Unhappy Marriage* (1680), Thomas Otway went out of his way to have an actor call attention to his virtuosic physiognomy: "Reads't thou not something in my Face, that speaks / Wonderful change, and Horror from within me."[19] When such flagrant perturbations are compared to the evasive tics called for in modern stage directions, of which Rebecca's "As if surprised" in Ibsen's *Rosmersholm* is not unrepresentative, they attest to the vigorous self-confidence of the rhetorical theater in its powers of expression.

The predilection of the age for Ovidian alterations of bodily state further emphasized the actor's capacity to assume the "perfect shape," as Heywood called it, "to which he had fashioned all his active spirits." Above all Heywood admired the actor who could "qualifie every thing according to the nature of the person personated" (*Apology*, 29). The activity of the "spirits" implied that by "qualifie every thing" he had in mind a physical transformation, an actual change in the actor's bodily shape between passions and between roles. A century later Gildon certainly harbored no doubts about the feasibility of this process. In recommending that an actor study history painting in order to mold his face into "the Character of his Hero," he argued confidently that the diligent student can "vary his Face so much . . . as to appear quite another Face, by raising, or falling, contracting, or extending the Brows; giving a brisk or sullen, sprightly or heavy turn to his Eyes; sharpening or swelling his Nostrils, and various Positions of his Mouth . . . [which] would in every part make him a new Man" (*Life of Betterton*, 62–63). Bulwer's account of the proximity of the facial musculature to the source of the activating spirits (*Pathomyotomia*, 103) reveals the science behind such confidence in the actor's expressive plasticity. *Pathomyotomia* carries a subtitle advertising its discussion of the *"Immediate Organs of the Voluntarie or Impetuous Motions of the Mind."* Voluntary control has more potency in Bulwer's physiological system than the modern reader would expect: "*Muscles* illustrated with the Animal Spirits *obeye*" (14). Thus Riley could be that or this "by voluntary metamorphosis," and Burbage could put off and assume himself at will. Contemporaries believed that the magical force of the spirits, conducted to the appropriate muscles and organs, could effect spectacular physical transformations. In this light Colley Cibber's familiar remarks on Betterton's versatility may be reinterpreted in a literal, physiological sense. He notes specifically the actor's capacity to divert and channel spirits to different organs as the character and circumstance warrant: "A farther Excellence in *Betterton*, was that he could vary his Spirit to the different Characters he acted. Those wild impatient Starts, that fierce flashing Fire, which he threw into *Hotspur*, never came from the unruffled Temper of his Brutus (for I have more than once, seen a *Brutus* as warm as *Hotspur*) when the *Betterton Brutus* was provok'd, in his Dispute with *Cassius*, the Spirit flew only to his Eye. . . ."[20] Cibber attributes to Betterton the kind of magical control over his body that the rhetoricians praised for its expressive effect.

It would be harder in terms of modern physiological doctrine, with its sophisticated tendency to separate systems from one another in specialty of function, to account for the many references in theatrical history to the blood draining from an actor's face or a fire sparkling in his eyes and raging crimson in his cheeks—on instantaneous command and at precisely the proper moment. In 1888 William Archer asserted confidently that any "medical man" knows that the "functions of the 'vaso-motor system' are quite involuntary" (*MF*, 160). In other words, one cannot dilate or contract his blood vessels by conscious choice. Earlier physiology, however, which tended to integrate rather than isolate bodily systems, helped commentators, for instance the anonymous author of *The Laureat* (1740), to account for such bravura perturbations as the reaction of Betterton's Hamlet to the second appearance of the ghost: "his Countenance (which was naturally ruddy and sanguin) . . . thro' the violent and sudden Emotions of Amazement and Horror, turn[ed] instantly on the Sight of his Father's Spirit, as pale as his Neckcloth, when every Article of his Body seem'd to be affected with a Tremor inexpressible; so that, had his Father's Ghost actually risen before him, he could not have been seized with more real Agonies."[21] Here Quintilian's paradoxical ideal of fictitious emotion genuinely felt has found its supreme embodiment. Students of classical medicine and the rhetoric of the passions would classify Betterton's posture and gestures under the categories of Fear, Amazement, and Horror, noted for their symptomatically irascible withdrawal of the blood and spirits from the extremities. These essences were thought to be crucial to both sensation and motion; therefore, if they withdraw or are cut off, everything stops—gesture, expression, voice—until they seep back in again, like juices into a sponge. According to Bulwer in *Pathomyotomia*, an object present to the imagination is sufficient to "move" the *"Appetite,"* which "by a wonderfull providence of Nature moves the *mobile spirits,*" which in turn "flie forth with stupendious obedience to their destinated Organs" (21–23), just as the spirits flew to Betterton's flashing eye. The actor can produce the signs of real fear on demand—manifestations of an emotion that he fully embodies, but at the same time is not really his own. And thus it was that Betterton could match his face to his jabot at will: the act of seeing the ghost, imagining the ghost, and starting in Amazement at the ghost were all conducted by the same semi-miraculous substances, liquid air and fire, shimmering on the margins of thought and action, transforming volition into expression. The outward shapes of the passions, obedient to the animal spirits, are constrained only by the perimeters of the actor's imagination.

The author of *The Laureat* continues his description of Betterton's performance by explaining its effect on the audience. The "Tremor" exhibited by "this excellent Actor" was "felt so strongly by the Audience, that the Blood seemed to shudder in their Veins likewise." Students of classical oratory would immediately classify this reaction as a specimen of *enargeia*, an inspired image in the mind of the speaker so striking that it transforms his actions as if the actual object were present to his senses and thereby communicates its vivid impression to the bodies and minds of the spectators. The spirit moves the actor, who, in the authenticity of his transport, moves the audience. Cibber's description of Betterton's re-cuperative reaction on the first appearance of the ghost defines this pro-cess as clearly as the writer of *The Laureat* does: "he open'd with a Pause of mute Amazement! then rising slowly, to a solemn, trembling Voice, he made the Ghost equally terrible to the Spectator, as to himself!" (61). Betterton's responses could be translated in physical terms to each mem-ber of the audience. As Wright had imagined his actor saying to his listeners, "Thus we moove, because by passion thus wee are moved, and as [passion] hath wrought in us so it ought to worke in you" (*Passions of the Minde*, 176). Hamlet refers to precisely this idea in his second solilo-quy. The Player, "in a fiction, in a dream of passion," can so "force his soul" that tears, pallor, distraction, and a "broken voice" bespeak his grief for Hecuba. Hamlet compares this "conceit" to the potential effects of his own genuine sorrow on an imaginary audience:

> What's Hecuba to him, or he to Hecuba,
> That he should weep for her? What would he do,
> Had he the motive and the cue for passion
> That I have? He would drown the stage with tears
> And cleave the general ear with horrid speech;
> Make mad the guilty and appall the free,
> Confound the ignorant, and amaze indeed
> The very faculties of eyes and ears.
>
> (2.2.585–92)

With the proper cue and motive, say, the penetration by a spirit from beyond the grave, a speaker may induce in his auditors feelings of over-whelming intensity, carrying them to the point of self-abandon, ecstasy, and purgation.

Underlying the powers characteristic of the Protean actor there existed a theoretical substructure of considerable interest: a parapsychological explanation of communication founded on the ancient concept of *pneuma*. It was widely believed that the spirits, agitated by the passions of the imaginer, generate a wave of physical force, rolling through the aether, powerful enough to influence the spirits of others at a distance. This well-traveled idea reappears in the science or pseudo-science of every age, most recently in popular cinematic space fantasies featuring specially sensitized listeners who can feel "a disturbance in the Force" across very great distances indeed. Robert Burton's claims in 1621 were more modest in extent but no less startling in effect: "So diversely doth this fantasy of ours affect, turn, and wind, so imperiously command our bodies, which as another 'Proteus, or a chameleon, can take all shapes; and is of such force (as Ficinus adds), that it can work upon others, as well as ourselves' " (*Anatomy*, 127). The roots of this idea extend back to the powers originally attributed to the divine spirits of the ancient world. As Plato described the creative process in the *Ion*, the "Muse first of all inspires men herself; and from these inspired persons a chain of other persons is suspended who take the inspiration" (*AA*, 7–8). Socrates compares the transmigration of this spirit through physical bodies to the effect of a magnetic force on bits of metal, which penetrates them, transforms them, and irresistibly draws them to itself and together through the medium of themselves: the god inspires the muse, who in turn inspires the poet, who inspires the rhapsode, who, in the authenticity of his transport, inspires the spectator. It is, in the language of physical chemistry, a process of *ionization*.

Bacon entertained a version of this explanation of the sympathetic response to the passions. In his "Experiments . . . touching transmission of spirits and the force of imagination" (*Works* 2 : 641), the great Advancer of Learning divided the power of the imagination into three categories: first, over the "body of the imaginant"; second, over the objects of inanimate nature, including corpses; and third, over "the spirits of men and living creatures." By imagination he meant nothing more or less than "the representation of an individual thought"—so the spirits constituted the active ingredient. He noted that the strength of the passions in the body of the sender determines the force of the transmission. He believed that the strongest points of origin for the signals, as well as the most receptive terminals, are the eyes. Strong emotions "make the spirits more powerful and active; and especially those affections which draw the spirits into the eyes." As lovers gaze longingly into one another's eyes, the spirits, communicating through the aether between, form physical bonds. Corrosive emanations from "the evil eye," intensified by hatred and envy, strike down their victims at considerable distance (2 : 653–54). The attractiveness of this theory of communication to rhetoricians need not be stressed. Oratorical delivery, by definition, orients the speaker face to face with his audience, whose continuous presence he must at least implicitly acknowledge. Quintilian confesses that even in his moments of transporting passion, he keeps an eye on the judge to gauge the impact of his performance. The account of the Oxford *Othello* given by Shakespeare's company in 1610 reveals a similar orientation toward the spectator: "Indeed, Desdemona, killed by her husband, in her death moved us especially when, as she lay in her bed, her face alone implored the pity of the audience."[22] It seems that the boy actor was opened up, facing his audience, to maximize the visual effect of his *pathos*—and, like Quintilian, he kept at least one eye on the judge. Ancient and Renaissance doctrine presumed the primacy of sight among the senses, particularly its efficacy in provoking intense emotional responses. Gildon's Betterton restated this point three times, on each occasion concluding: "And this Fire of their Eyes will easily strike those of their Audience . . . and by a strange sympathetic Infection, it will set them on Fire too with the very same Passion" (*Life of Betterton*, 67, cf. 70, 71). This profound belief, bolstered by ancient authority, provides a key reason why rhetorical delivery required actor and spectator to meet face to face.

The Protean "force of Imagination" then, poised between natural and supernatural explanations of the life of the body in its spirits, allowed rhetorical theorists to assume something that more modern theories of acting have not been able to take for granted: that the actor can embody the passions by a "voluntary metamorphosis," that he enjoys instantaneous command over his means of expression, that, Pegasus-like, the image in his mind will fly to the peripheries of his body and beyond on the wings of his spirit.

The preternatural power allotted to the imagination in rhetorical theory, however, had another, darker side. The same imaginative force that transforms the outward shape pulsates through the inner frame as well. There it necessarily stirs up the humours, which do not possess the same animated malleability as the spirits. Conventional wisdom dictated that once the humours course through the body, they cannot be balanced again without the passage of time or the intervention of physic to restore *eukrasia*. This physical threat clouds the image of the spritely Proteus commanding his body into new shapes at will. The passions are easily summoned from the lower regions, but, like devils, once summoned they are not so easily put back. In this view the actor, like the Sorcerer's Apprentice, toys with enormous forces that he can evoke quickly but not easily subdue. For this reason imagination was both powerful and dangerous. Dramatists joined leading moralists and physicians in bracketing imagination with the dread unreason and its destructive affiliates—passion, fantasy, impatience, lust, heat, choler, fury, heart, and blood—whereas judgment keeps good company with mind, will, coolness, understanding, patience, reason, virtue, and grace.[23] Imagination fuels the most excessively violent passions, the ones actors are, by the nature of dramatic literature, most frequently called upon to depict. As the most vehement of the passions, they are also the most unhealthy. "There is no Passion very vehement," concludes Thomas Wright, "but that it alters some of the foure humours of the bodie; and all Physitions commonly agree, that among diverse other extrinsicall causes of diseases, one, and not the least, is, the excess of some inordinate Passion" (*Passions of the Minde*, 4).

Medicine took particular alarm at the prospect of vapors and fluids from below being forced upward into the heart and brain. There is something primordially descriptive and terrifying about an agent in the guts with a will of its own that rises up out of control to attack and choke its host. This is shown by the persistence in our thought patterns of the need to keep passions "down" and "under" when we mean in control. Physicians called the extreme form of this malady *hysteria* and identified it as a visceral disorder. Hysteria drives the womb or entrails, the *mother*, upwards in the body, suffocating and poisoning the vital organs. Hence King Lear's desperate imprecation directed at his own innards:

> O, how this mother swells up toward my heart!
> *Hysterica passio*, down, thou climbing sorrow,
> Thy element's below!
>
> (2.4.56–58)

In this case, the force of the internal revolt is so great that its victim personifies and objectifies his passion as if it had an independent life of its own. Imagination proves a villain here because of its capacity to agitate the spirits and summon up the humours, instigating and exacerbating the passions beyond control—literally working them "up." To enthusiasts like Heywood and Gildon, each of whom had a public relations task to accomplish on behalf of the theater, such a drawback did not seem worth mentioning. To physicians who had occasion to comment on the subject, however, the dangers, while not cause for panic at the tiring house of the Red Bull or backstage at Drury Lane, were evident.

The most authoritative medical opinion on this issue comes from Edmund Gayton, Bachelor of Physick, Son of Ben, and author of the delightful commentary on Cervantes, *Pleasant Notes upon Don Quixot* (1654). Gayton himself acted in *Love's Hospital* (1636) at St. John's College, Oxford, before taking his medical degree there. During the Interregnum he looked back on the late Caroline theater, and in his *Pleasant Notes* he digresses on his memories of Ben Jonson, of Inigo Jones, of Taylor in the role of Arbaces, and of Swanston as Bussy D'Ambois. Gayton's tone is generally light throughout these memoirs, but it darkens appreciably when he takes up the clinical and pathological details of the actor's profession. Medicine or liquor, he concludes, are the only recourse available to those who have "counterfeited" the passions for any extended period of time: "I have known my selfe, a Tyrant comming from the Scene, not able to reduce himselfe, into the knowledge of himselfe, till Sack made him (which was his present physick) forget he was an Emperour, and renew'd all his old acquaintance to him; and it is not out of most mens observation, that one most admirable Mimicke in our late

Stage, so lively and corporally personated a Changeling, that he could never compose his Face to the figure it had, before he undertook that part."[24] Gayton's anecdotes recall to mind the mime in which Marcel Marceau struggles desperately to tear off the mask his face has become, and they reinforce our sense of how emphatically physiological seventeenth-century psychologies of acting were. They reiterate how malleable the identity of mind and body was thought to be under the physical influence of the passions, how pliantly the outward shape was thought to conform to the actor's inward state of mind.

Gayton's professional remarks represent an early document in the steadily accumulating literature on the unhealthiness of acting as a profession. As one nineteenth-century authority expressed it, the age-old worry was "that fictitious sufferings sometimes lead to real infirmities, and sometimes death."[25] Pliny recorded that an actor once imitated the symptoms of gout with such verisimilitude that he thereby contracted the disease. Seneca related the frightening case history of Gallus Vibius, who went mad while rehearsing the part of a madman. The unfortunate example of Montdory, who out-Heroded Herod to achieve apoplexy and paralysis, was closest at hand, and, significantly, Gayton found French actors particularly uncontrolled in "their loose and apish gestures" (272). In a little-known essay on bodily health entitled *The Art of Longevity,* Gayton amplifies on his prescription of sack for its powers of "making the afflicted forget his grief." Clearly, he valued it for its purifying and cleansing functions, its capacity to purge the recesses of the body of nasty juices surfeited by excessive emotion: "The grosser blood [it] streight dost clarifie," and it "cleansest the purple channell when its foul'd." By terms of this regimen Edmund Kean or George Frederick Cooke should have been the healthiest of actors, but Gayton himself counseled against excess, which will cause dessication of the liver and "trembling Nerves."[26] Speaking to the same point on behalf of the stage, Gildon's Betterton tears a page out of earlier rhetorics in suggesting frequent but moderate exercise of the actor's lungs. This respiratory calisthenic is desirable because it "augments the natural Heat, thins the Blood, cleanses the Veins, opens all the Arteries, prevents every Obstruction, and hinders the gross humours from thickening into Distempers" (*Life of Betterton,* 100).

The figure of Proteus, in myth and metaphor, was thus ambiguous, for he who can assume any shape is in danger of losing his own. Gayton's instance of the mimic who too "corporally personated a Changeling" also had a wider frame of reference than it would seem at first glance. *Changeling* could have one of several meanings in 1654, none of them good. First, it could mean a person given to constant change, fickleness, unreliability. This would seem to link it to the shadowy network of meaning surrounding Proteus, in and out of its theatrical context, which harbored primordial loathings and fears of that which is bodiless, pulpy, amorphous. Secondly, Changeling could mean a person or thing put in exchange for another, implying an irrevocable substitution, a confusion of identities. Thirdly, it could mean an imbecile, particularly one whose idiocy took the form of a spiritless vacancy of mind and limp flexibility of body. "The temper of the braine" was indeed overthrown. The Changeling depicted as a theatrical droll in the frontispiece to Kirkman's *The Wits* (1672) conforms to this type. His hands dangle torpidly before him, dispirited lumps of flesh. There is an illuminating parallel in Gestus 8 of Bulwer's *Chirologia, Despero* ["I despair"]: "To appear with fainting and dejected hands is a posture of fear, abasement of mind, and abject and vanquished courage, and of utter despair" (37). Bulwer elaborates on this type of gesture, which he has observed in those "clowns and men of a most unfaithful memory" who have "leaden hands, together with the arm" and whose movements are so "slow and ponderous . . . that they seem to move a great lump of trembling flesh, reaching their slow right hand out so timorously, as if they gave provender to an elephant" (*Chironomia*, 228). Such "abasement of mind" is one ill effect of the humours that Gayton recognized as "too passionately and sensibly represented" (*Pleasant Notes*, 144–45). The actor who forces his body into the representation of the Changeling becomes physically "dispirited" and "distempered"—unable to command his features, and thus robbed of the only attribute that separates his body from a mass of pulp. Gayton was not the only physician to comment on the perils of habitual self-transformation. John Bulwer's remarkable treatise *Anthropometamorphosis* (1650), subtitled the "Artificial Changeling," takes as its theme the horror of irrevocably forcing the body into unnatural shapes, and it opens with a pointed warning:

> Stay, Changeling Proteus! let me count the rapes
> Made on thy Form, in thy abusive shapes:
> I have observ'd thy Nature-scoffing Art
> Wherewith th'art Schematiz'd in every part.[27]

On several grounds the actor's lot was not to be envied. A seventeenth-century physician, steeped in ageless anxieties of bodily penetration by vapors from below, could not but notice the unsettling resemblance between inspiration and disease.

Rhetoric thus imbibed from physiology two contrasting, even contradictory interpretations of the body. Learned opinion viewed the body as an instantly malleable, highly volatile concoction of dangerous es-

FIGURE 5. *Changling* from Kirkman's *The Wits* (detail). *(Courtesy of Washington University Libraries.)*

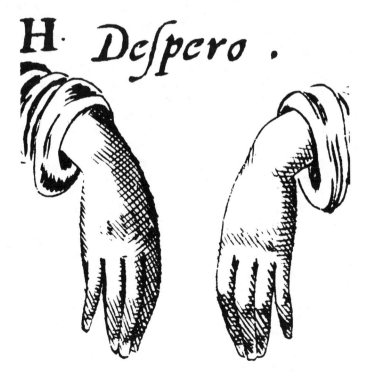

FIGURE 6. Chirogram (detail). *Despero.* *(Courtesy of P. M. Arnold Collection, Washington University Libraries.)*

sences: like a spirited horse, it responds swiftly to firm commands but can easily get out of control. Learned opinion, however, also regarded the body as a mass of sludge, inclining to dissolution and decay. The actor's art, therefore, requires him to discover a *via media* between the Scylla of spirit and the Charybdis of humours. His art requires him to set his bodily instrument in expressive motion, not by freeing his actions, but by confining them in direction, purpose, and shape. He has to keep his flammable inner mixtures stable even in the heat of passion. As we have seen, he has good reason to keep the *force of Imagination* on a tight rein, to keep it "down," to hold it "under." Emotion, passion, transport, ecstasy—these he can take for granted—like mercy, they rain down from heaven; but to attain restraint, control over these copious and powerful energies, represents both artistic challenge and preventive medicine. Alumni of modern-day acting classes have a difficult time grasping this essential fact, though all the best evidence we have points toward it: the actor/orator of the seventeenth century sought to acquire inhibitions.

As long as rhetorical theories of acting prevailed, the esteem in which an actor was held by his public seems to have depended on the degree to which he was perceived as capable of keeping his bodily powers in check. Of course he had to experience the passions he enacted—deeply, physically, vividly—but in theory almost anyone could do that. Plop a periwig on the pate of an average fellow, and he can tear a passion to tatters, but only a skilled player can tailor the same passion to adhere to his own body with a smooth fit. Hamlet's advice to the Player drew upon the presumption that a "very torrent, tempest . . . and whirlwind" (3.2.7–9) lay within reach of anyone who could summon up a strong mental image; the player's art was to keep the resulting passion within the bounds of what Heywood called "a smooth and formal motion" (*Apology for Actors*, 29) and what Thomas Wright called a "prudent mediocritie [which] best may be marked in stage players" (*Passions of the Minde*, 179). Heywood argued that a principal goal of *actio* in academic rhetoric was to insure that in the heat of the moment the scholar did not "buffet his deske like a mad man" (*Apology*, 29). Gildon seconded this point when he said that "tho the Passions are very beautiful in their proper *Gestures*, yet they ought never to be so extravagantly immoderate, as to transport the Speaker out of himself . . . [into] Madness" (*Life of Betterton*, 86–87). So the greatness of a player stemmed from the forms he gave to his conceits. A witness to Powell's ill-advised attempts at Bettertonian roles recalled that he "*out-rav'd all Probability; while Betterton* kept his Passion under, and shew'd it most (as Fume smoaks most, when stifled)."[28] This metaphor is a telling comment on the advantages of controlling the passions: the restraint itself, the stifling, results in a more forceful evocation of the fires of passion.

The criticism of every period contains cautions against scenery-chewing and overacting tricks, but rarely does it offer the kind of specific guidelines available from the rhetorics. One such rule, the prohibition against gesturing with the left hand alone, demonstrates how concepts of art and nature were coordinated to justify gestures that may seem to us to be merely quaintly arbitrary and esoteric hieroglyphs. Rhetoricians speak as one in decreeing that the left hand may gesture in support of the right, but that it must not take the lead and certainly must not act alone: "The left hand of itself alone is most incompetent to the performance of any perfect action" (*Chironomia*, 247). Bulwer assembles an impressive array of authority against the "sinister" left hand. He also reviews the Hellenic military tradition—sword or spear held in the attacking right hand; shield strapped on the left arm and held close to the left side of the body for defense of the heart and liver—a convention so inflexible that the Spartans considered left-handedness a deformity. Bulwer's clinching argument, however, is strictly physiological, founded on Aristotle and Galen.

Ancient medicine taught that the vital spirits, exiting through the left ventricle, permeate and humidify the left side of the body. This renders the left arm harder to control, more pliant, more tractable—rather like a limp noodle. It can more easily and naturally conform to the gestures of the right, which enjoys a less congested traffic with the propelling animal spirits, than initiate controlled actions on its own. Bulwer quotes two passages from Aristotle's *Problemata Physica* and cites one from Quintilian (*Institutio*, 11.3.114) to bolster this rationale: "The best way (therefore) that the left hand can be employed is in attendance on the right which by the course of nature hath the priority, as the more proper and propense, and apter to make good in its actions by a more handsome diligence, as being planted nearer the fountain of the blood. And, verily, the left hand seems to be born to an obsequious compliance with the right." Though Bulwer frankly admits perplexity as to what to do with an orator who is left-handed by nature, he still insists that "acting with the left hand in chief be an error so gross that we cannot [get] away with it even in a picture where the imitation of speech is expressed" (*Chironomia*, 235–37). It makes an interesting study to apply this observation to the rhetorically correct compositions of French classicist painters like Poussin or of Rubens's painting of Decius Mus addressing his legions. Their figures gesture with the right hand when depicted in the act of speaking. This is particularly evident in figures who occupy the "stage right" portion of the canvasses and who must thus close themselves off by

FIGURE 7. Peter Paul Rubens. *Decius Mus Addressing the Legions* (c. 1617). *(Courtesy of the National Gallery of Art, Washington, D.C., Samuel H. Kress Collection, 1957.)*

gesturing with their downstage hand. In the theater the tendency of actors to open out to the audience would have circumvented this problem. How completely actors subscribed to the doctrine and acted predominantly with their right hands we shall never know for certain, but Aston's *Brief Supplement,* with its eye-witness description of Thomas Betterton in performance, provides a substantial clue: "His Left Hand frequently lodg'd in his Breast, between his Coat and Waistcoat, while, with his Right, he prepared his Speech" (215).

The elaborate network of inhibitions called theatrical decorum, then, should not be understood as a capricious etiquette imposed by some bloodless notion of style. As applied to acting, it should be interpreted as a coherent physiological system designed to regulate the great natural forces of the body for artistic and hygenic effect. Without such regulation anarchy reigns. If the actor gestures vehemently with his left hand alone, the agitated vital spirits explode out of the left ventricle, and he loses expressive control. If he possesses himself of a passion with unrestrained spirits and imagination, the surfeited humours will choke out the fire in his heart and poison his brain. At best he will resemble a lunatic; at worst he will become one. Far from denying natural inspiration in acting by substituting disembodied hieroglyphs for truthful gestures, the rhetoric of the passions proposed a means of harnessing inspiration's inexorable synergistic effects. Rhetors saw the body of the actor "fallen into a passion" as brimming over with emotions in need of channeling into properly regulated conduits—hence the rules for gesture, posture, deportment, voice, physiognomy, and expression that fill so many pages in our earliest acting textbooks. A passion, once unleashed, cannot be suppressed, but it can be shaped into outwardly expressive forms. An oratorical gesture, a prescribed pattern of action, serves as a pre-existing mold into which this molten passion can be poured.

In theory at least, an actor/orator can master the system of inhibition by diligent practice and exercise. We have seen how Gildon's Betterton recommended vocal exercises to prevent the humours from thickening into "Distempers." He also recommended extensive practice before a mirror to perfect "the whole Body likewise in all its Postures and Motions." If you do not have a looking glass at hand, he advises, rehearse your passions before a friend of judgment and delicacy of taste whose reactions will supply the same effect—security of self-control (*Life of Betterton*, 55). Bulwer vigorously endorses the mirror also, but goes on to elaborate more specific measures:

> Use exercise . . . . Bend and wrest your arm and hands to the right, to the left, and to every part, that having made them obediant unto you, upon a sudden and the least signification of the mind, you may show the glittering orbs of heaven and the gaping jaws of earth. . . . Sometimes lifting up your hands, threaten and denounce punishment; or with a rejecting posture, abominate; sometimes shake and brandish your hand as the lance of elocution; that so you may be ready for all variety of speech and attain . . . [that] facility for action, with decorum and beauty of decent motion, which excels both that of the colors and proportion. (*Chironomia*, 246–47)

Bulwer's advice clearly did not answer all the questions about acting that Quintilian raised in his *Institutio*, but it did offer a theory that could be readily put into practice. A synthesis in the unresolved dialectic of inspiration and artifice continued to elude the grasp of rhetoricians, but not their reach. To say that certain inhibitions of the body are themselves necessary for natural equilibrium does not bridge the distance between mask and face, a character's persona and the actor's body. It simply implies that there is a proper way for the mask to be constructed and kept in place without harm to the wearer.

By the eighteenth century, however, this theoretical formulation had reached the end of its usefulness and, therefore, of its dominance. Just as Betterton, the premier actor of his day, had mastered the rhetorical mode, Garrick epitomized its successor. It was immediately apparent to all factions, pro and con, that the kind of acting he offered up at his debut in 1741 broke decisively with the past. Garrick reputedly substituted speed, agility, and variety for the apparent heaviness and monotony of the reigning oratorical style. As the principal surviving exponent of the superannuated system, James Quin saw that the two styles were mutually exclusive: "If this young fellow is right," he remarked at Garrick's debut, "then we have all been wrong" (*AA*, 131). For purposes of direct comparison, we are fortunate in having the eye-witness account of Richard Cumberland, who saw Garrick as Lothario in Rowe's *Fair Penitent* opposite the Horatio of Quin. At curtain's rise Cumberland discovered Quin garbed in an old-fashioned periwig and square-toed shoes, chanting out the cadences in a sing-song tone, and "sawing" the air with his gestures. His action "had more of the senate than of the stage," and no doubt he strongly favored his right hand. But when Garrick "bounded" onstage:

> ——heavens, what a transition!—it seemed as if a whole century had been swept over in the transition of a single scene; old things were done away with, and a new order at once brought forward, bright and luminous, and clearly destined to dispel the barbarisms and bigotry of a tasteless age, too long attached to the prejudices of custom, and superstitiously devoted to the illusions of imposing declamation.[29]

Not only does Cumberland reject the rhetorical style as obsolete; he also correctly perceives that Garrick's style is something quite modern, something neither custom-bound nor superstitious.

I propose that this response records a theatrical version of what historians of science would term a revolutionary paradigm shift. In its purest form, such a shift of belief and practice comes about with the clarity and instantaneous completeness of a Gestalt switch, when, for instance, the figure that we always thought was a vase suddenly reveals itself as two faces juxtaposed. In Cumberland's account of *The Fair Penitent*, the terms of understanding and appreciation have irrevocably altered; one system of assumptions has been supplanted by a competing view based on radically altered presuppositions and expectations. Quin's inherited vocabulary of rhetorical gesture, founded on ancient physiological theory, has ceased to convey meaning; *actio* and *pronuntiatio* are on their way to join the epicycles of Ptolemaic astronomy in the boneyard of dead ideas. Hence Garrick, entering at the right historical moment, renovated theatrical semiotics, founding his vocabulary of expressive gesture on a new order of understanding, a revised concept of what nature is and means.

Part of the reason for the obsolescence of the rhetorical mode can be found in the scientific developments that were taking place during the era of its prominence. The emerging thought of the seventeenth century, steadily liberating itself from ancient authority and received opinion, assured the theorist with ever-increasing confidence that formality and regularity of motion, far from being artificial in the negative sense of unnatural, corresponded to the most beautiful and fundamental of natural phenomena, the physical laws of the universe itself. These laws, moreover, seemed to be subject to verification through reason and experience, not by appeal to ancient authority. They are knowable to the rational intellect, requiring no leaps of superstitious faith in animating spirits. Thus, while rhetoricians were still busily elaborating a theory of performance on what was essentially the same model of the body available to Quintilian, a profound paradigm shift was under way in physiology, particularly in the explanation of the relationship between the nervous system and emotional responses. This revolution would not only overturn the ancient authorities on which the rhetoric of the passions had rested its case, but also remove many of its ambiguities by proposing a far more streamlined model of the human body and its passions: the machine.

2

Nature Still, But Nature Mechanized

> Given the least principle of motion, animated bodies will have all that is necessary for moving, feeling, thinking, repenting, and in a word for conducting themselves in the physical realm, and in the moral realm which depends on it . . . . Let us then conclude boldly that man is a machine and that in the whole universe there is but a single substance variously modified.
> —Julien Offray de la Mettrie, *L'homme machine* (1747)

The name of one Perkins, hair-dresser and wig-maker, enters into the history of the eighteenth-century stage on the strength of a technical contribution to David Garrick's Hamlet. The actor employed his services to enliven the Prince's first encounter with his father's ghost, a scene in which Garrick's start made Lichtenberg's flesh creep, set poor Partridge's knees to knocking, and moved Dr. Johnson to express concern over the effect of the shock on the ghost. When other spectators marveled that Hamlet's hair actually seemed to stand on end as the ghost appeared, they testified to a fact. The ingenious Perkins had engineered a mechanical wig to simulate the precise physiognomy of mortal dread. On the line "Look, my lord, it comes," the hairs of this remarkable appliance rose up obligingly at the actor's command. Hamlet, Prince of Denmark, flipped his wig. This sudden perturbation astonished Garrick's audiences and has embarrassed his biographers, who have found in Perkins's fright wig a cause for baffled amusement and apologetic muddle—just the sort of claptrap that the actor was, alas, "not above."[1]

Although it may be hard to think of Perkins's device as anything more than an amusing sidelight on theater history, it does pertain to the most celebrated scene played by the greatest actor of his time, perhaps of all time, in a tragic role by the poet he professed to revere. Historians must entertain the possibility that Garrick took this mechanical wig seriously as a means of heightening his expressive effect. At least one contemporary believed that the actor took himself too seriously on this point: *The Monitor* carped that Garrick "introduced stage tricks and gestures, as *scientific*, which were originally the motions of mountebanks, merry-andrews, and harlequins at Bartholomew-fair, to make the people laugh."[2] Garrick himself in his early *Essay on Acting* (1744) had recommended "science"—"natural, metaphysical, and consequential deductions"—as the actor's authority. In a telling formulation, he explained that such analysis could help the actor "discover the workings of spirit (or what other physical terms you please to call it) upon the different modifications of matter." Garrick spoke of a particular human body as a "moving statue"; in his view, the "spirit" that activates the body might or might not have a physical existence. As a commentator on his art, he set out to answer the question, "how are the different members of the body to be agitated?" (*AA*, 134–35). Here, when he is discussing his interpretation of terror in works by Shakespeare and Ben Jonson, his words hardly suggest a disposition to frivolity.

Clearly, however, they do suggest an understanding of nature different from our own, and it would be difficult to overemphasize how radical that difference is. Today we tend to use *natural* and *organic* as synonyms, but in Garrick's day Romanticism, Naturalism, and Darwinism had yet to proclaim that we have more in common with the scum on the pond than with the statue in the park. In this respect we are the intellectual heirs of nineteenth-century science and its invention of the concept of biology, and when we try to gauge the ramifications of eighteenth-century scientific thought on theatrical practice and theory, we can do no better than heed Michel Foucault's warning that our own "pattern of knowledge" is simply "not valid" for that period.[3] But once we try to liberate ourselves from our own limiting perspective and ask what kind of *nature* was known and understood by Garrick and his contemporaries, a number of puzzling phenomena begin to make sense. The seminal interplay between the plastic arts and theatrical theory—in particular, the actor's fascination with pictures and statues—corresponds directly, as we shall see, to the interaction between art and science that encouraged the most advanced thinking in the period. In turn, the theatrical theorist's tendency to enumerate the physical signs of the passions and his desire to notate their transitions stemmed logically from current developments in physiology and psychology. So also did the characteristically eighteenth-century definition of acting as the alternation between periods of action and moments of static tableaux. Moreover, the fact that Garrick's acting was based on a new paradigm, a new concept of what nature is and means, revitalizes the truth behind the cliché that his "naturalness" re-formed the old-fashioned declamatory style of James Quin. Finally, and most importantly, the overriding interest in the relation of mind and body, as it appears in the work of such contemporaries of Garrick's as Aaron Hill and G. E. Lessing, reveals itself as a necessary and inevitable concern for anyone interested in the expression of emotion—and that at least is one interest that would continue to animate discussions of acting theory throughout the next two centuries. By reconstructing the intellec-tual issues of Garrick's age, we might even be able to see why that actor thought of Perkins's fright wig as an appropriate enrichment of his own physique.

Indeed, this device and other specimens of eighteenth-century theatri-cal practice that resemble it in kind if not degree take on a new meaning when confronted in their proper context, one that includes the hypothesis La Mettrie boldly set forth: "man is a machine." If the human body can be viewed as a machine, and its external emotional expressions analyzed as the mechanical effects of internal physical causes, much like hours showing on the face of a clock, then an apparatus such as that designed by Perkins simply extends a comprehensive metaphor. Its motions are no more or less ludicrous than those of the host machine, the body, which propels it.

In *L'homme machine* of 1747, La Mettrie carried to its radical conclu-sion a scientific revolution begun over a hundred years before. This revo-lution emerged from the struggle of the new science to view the world afresh, to cast down the idols of received opinion and ancient authority. Its new policy was self-consciously dramatized by the uncompromising motto adopted by the Royal Society in 1662—*nullius in verba*, "on the word of no one." The so-called "mechanization of the world picture," which was the collective achievement of seventeenth-century science and philosophy, presented the universe as matter in motion, as a large ma-chine busily populated by many smaller machines, human and animal, constructed of the same substances as other bodies, subject to the same physical laws.[4] In the universe depicted by Galileo and Newton, the words *mechanical* and *natural* did indeed become synonyms. In the mechanization of the biosphere as envisioned by René Descartes, earlier interpretations of physical processes were revised in the new light of universal natural law. Descartes believed that the human body is a ma-chine, a "moving statue," but, unlike other machines such as animals and water-wheels, it is guided by an immaterial force without extension in space called the "rational soul," just as a clock keeps time by an invisible agent pulling on its counterweighted mechanism. According to this view, the bodily dispositions of machines extended in space seem reducible to the same principles that govern the orbit of a planet or the swing of a pendulum. Physics and psychology intersect in the study of the human body, identifying emotion with motion.

This trend in scientific thinking found some of its seminal cues in the world of the theater. The history of science reveals that physiological knowledge has more than once progressed by means of metaphor, the mode of imaginative understanding native to poetry. Galen, who presided as physician at gladitorial combats, ostensibly knew as much as William Harvey about the relationship between blood and the internal organs. What Galen did not have readily at hand, however, was a practical pump to suggest how liquids could be continually circulated by mechanical means. By the time Harvey began his study of the motion of the blood in the 1620s, pumps were commonly used in mining operations and in fire-fighting, and they provided a model for his radically revised explanation of the action of the heart.[5] In casting about for an analogy to explain their materialization of animate motion, the pioneers of modern nerve physiology pressed into service the actor's historic analogue and his most bitterly resented rival—the mechanical puppet.

Metaphors of toy-theatrical automata proved particularly appropriate. The development of systematic and scientific anatomy from Leonardo to Vesalius had amply demonstrated the mutual interdependence of science and fine art in the investigation of the human body through dissection and illustration. Two-dimensional depictions of dead organs had been adequate for the study of anatomical structure. The extension of the alliance of the arts and science into the physiological realm, however, posited the need for models capable of showing processes: locomotion, circulation, nervous impulse, respiration, and emotions in expressive transitions—all actions of bodies in time and space, the special province of simulacra moving in three dimensions. Mechanical theaters, which enjoyed a much longer and richer history than one might casually suppose, thus provided seventeenth- and eighteenth-century physiology with a profusion of analogues.

Fascination with theatrical automata, which perhaps more readily brings to mind Futurism, Juenger's 1923 novel *The Glass Bees,* or the mechanical ballets at the Bauhaus, actually dates back at least to the automatic theater invented by Heron of Alexandria in the first century A.D. As described in his *Peri Automatopoietikes,* Heron's mechanical entertainment presented a five-act tragedy on the legend of Nauplius, featuring changeable scenery and robot actors who entered, declaimed, gesticulated, and exited by remote control. The entire *mise en scène,* including the actors, was kept in motion by a slowly sinking counterweight clutched into interlocking systems of pulleys, levers, reels, strings, and cogs[6]—as if, by some magical anachronism, Giacomo Torelli had been commissioned to execute a production conceived by Edward Gordon Craig. Indeed, the fabulous development of baroque stage machinery by Torelli and others represented a direct application of modern mechanics to Heron's ancient concept. Heron's treatise on pneumatics was translated in 1589 by Giovanni Battista Aleotti, best known as a theater architect and early pioneer of changeable scenery. He initiated and Torelli brought to perfection a system of scene-shifting that operated off counterweights, drive shafts, cams, ropes, and pulleys. As an elaborate network of force and material, mechanical advantage and dynamic motion, this system epitomized the triumph of the machine in the service of magic and allegory, a miniature cosmos with its own gods and clouds. During the 1660s Paris supported the Salle des Machines, a theater predicated on the entertainment value of tangible objects propelled into motion by unseen physical forces.

Complex and fanciful mechanical theaters, including speaking automata, also enjoyed considerable popularity as garden follies in the baroque courts, only here they were powered by water pressure supplied by the same hydraulic systems that made the fountains play. In the park of Schloss Hellbrunn near Salzburg, for example, a specimen survives in which one hundred and nineteen automata powered by hydraulic machinery enact a day in the life of a village and court—soldiers march, gentlemen bow, ladies rustle their fans, and carpenters saw—a microcosm of the world in automated dance.[7] In the royal gardens of Saint-Germain-en-Laye, as depicted by Salomon de Caus in *Les raisons des forces mouvantes avec diverses machines* (1615), six spacious and eerily lit grottoes housed numerous mechanical statues cunningly constructed so as to enact mythological scenes with apparent spontaneity. Their limbs and even their faces were laced with hydraulic tubes, shaping their features and gestures. The visitor unwittingly activated these automata by stepping on springs concealed under the floor tiles. At his approach a bathing Diana first modestly hid herself among the reeds, then a particularly testy Neptune, brandishing a trident, menaced the spectator from a sea-shell chariot, after which a monster rose up from the deep and spewed water in his face.

The theatrical toys of St. Germain have special interest because, as a young man, Descartes frequented their grottoes as he strolled home along the banks of the Seine. Later, in the *Traité de l'homme* (written 1633, published 1666), he seized upon such automata as the functional analogues of the human body and nervous system. Here water acts the part of a spring in a double sense: as a reservoir and as a medium of propul-

 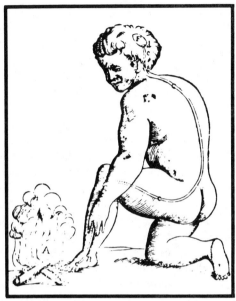

FIGURE 8. The nervous system of the human machine: pineal gland, tubes, and animal spirits in action. From Descartes, *Treatise of Man* (1666). *(Courtesy of Alderman Library, University of Virginia.)*

sion. It symbolizes the hidden mechanical cause of the visible effect, the means whereby "this statue" or "terrestial machine"—for that is how Descartes conventionally referred to the body—moves and emotes.[8] When the spring is pushed, the machine stirs. The "rational soul" pushes on a gland in the center of the human brain, and the nerves, which resemble hollow tubes, convey this pressure by a subtle fluid or current called animal spirits. The "will" or the "imagination," both functions of the soul, presses the gland, which presses the muscles throughout the entire body and makes them swell and contract as needed—in very much the same manner as that of an hydraulic brake system in an automobile. Descartes's rational soul became known as the "ghost in the machine," which, like a driver or operator, directs the flow of animal spirits to the right tubes at the right time. But certain rudimentary responses, such as the withdrawal of one's hand from a flame, can be effected by the body acting alone without the participation of the rational soul. Such an idea is the forerunner of our concept of reflex action.

For the purposes of the subsequent development of aesthetic theory, *Les passions de l'âme* of 1649, in which Descartes focused his mechanical philosophy on the question of emotional experience and expression, exerted a decisive influence. Though *Pathomyotomia* appeared in the same year, Bulwer's Babel of phrases, derived from ancient and modern authorities from Galen and Vesalius to Burton, seems to belong to another century as well as another mode of scientific discourse. Descartes opened his treatise on the passions by summarily dismissing all previous work on the subject and, particularly, that of the ancients, as "so slight, and for the most part so far from credible, that I am unable to entertain any hope of approximating to the truth excepting by shunning the paths which they followed."⁹ As a machine-soul dualist, Descartes was most interested in the passions for the light they shed on the relationship between spirit and matter—how the soul acts on the flesh and vice versa. He identified six primary passions of the soul—wonder, love, hatred, desire, joy, and sadness—all of which are materialized by mechanical actions within the body, then communicated automatically into the outward features. Through the power of imagination, the ghost can alter the bodily machine, inside and out, by forming an Idea of the passion and triggering a release of animal spirits to the appropriate organs (Articles 43–45). The Cartesian division of experience into body and soul, moving machine and thinking ghost, is thus called interactive dualism.

Though Descartes sneered at *Les caractères des passions* for its aridly meticulous descriptions, he agreed with Cureau de la Chambre on a fundamental premise: each passion, as a cause, may be identified by its effects, a set of bodily postures and physiognomical manifestations.¹⁰ "There is no passion," for instance, "that is not evidenced by some particular action of the eyes." Although these rapid and subtle manifestations are very difficult to describe separately, "the result of their conjunction is very easily observed" (Article 113). Even the dullest servant knows his master's anger by looking at his eyes.

In advancing a mechanical physiology of expression, Descartes seems to picture the physical manifestations of the passions as ideal templates, matrices, into which the animal spirits, automatically reacting to outer stimuli or inner imagination, mold the body. Astonishment, for instance, a compound passion intensified by wonder, makes the animal spirits pool at the site of the impression of the perceived object so "that it sometimes thrusts them all there, and causes them to be so much occupied in preserving this impression that there are none which pass from thence into the muscles . . . and this causes the whole body to remain immobile as a statue" (Article 73). Desire and joy, by contrast, make the body more mobile by increasing the outward flow of animal spirits to the limbs (Article 111). Lively motion represents a rippling expansion of hydraulic impulse from the center to the periphery; stillness and silence stem from the inward contractions of the spirits, a deprivation of the fluid needed to power the automaton.

Though the concept of animal spirits has ancient roots, Descartes divested it of its magical properties and integrated it into a physical system of force and matter. He deflected subsequent practitioners by radically streamlining the model of the relation of mind and body. Perhaps most importantly, this model localized emotions primarily in the nervous system, itself now squarely anchored in the brain as the seat of the soul. *Heart* and *blood* no longer served as the principal loci of the passions. The complex role of the humours no longer explained affective phenomena. The fact or metaphor of mechanical causation allowed scientists such as Robert Hooke, Thomas Willis, Jan Swammerdam, Giovanni Borelli, Hermann Boerhaave, and later Albrecht von Haller to bypass tradition-bound modes of physiological explanation and to concentrate on the body as a reactive nervous mechanism. Medical opinion was perhaps the most powerful source of the popular diffusion of such interpretations of the body, for Cartesianism exerted a considerable influence on medical science, particularly in England and Holland.[11] As the English physician George Cheyne, intellectual heir to Willis and Sydenham, put it in 1733: "Feeling is nothing but the Impulse, Motion or Action of Bodies, gently or violently impressing the Extremities or Sides of the Nerves, of the Skin or other parts of the Body, which by their Structure and *Mechanism,* convey this Motion to the *Sentient* Principle in the Brain."[12]

As the mechanization of physiology took hold, an important and influential treatise on aesthetics, *Réflexions critiques sur la poésie et sur la peinture* (1719) by Abbé Du Bos, led the reader through detailed accounts of Cartesian and Newtonian mechanics, Harvey's explanation of the circulation of the blood, and Torricelli's demonstration of air pressure. Du Bos then posited a mechanical conception of artistic temperament and creative mood based on the idea that our minds react to the air in exactly the same fashion as do barometers and thermometers.[13] The emphasis no longer falls on air as a magical, inspiriting *pneuma,* but on the capacity of the bodily instrument to react mechanically to physical pressure or temperature. Such formulations of Cartesian opinion ultimately emerged in popularizations like the "physical terms" to which Garrick referred in his explanation of how the members of the body become agitated.

In the eighteenth century automata continued to assume a special role in symbolizing the man-machine. Robot actors with moveable parts found heroic employment as doubles in dangerous flying machines and as miniatures in perspective vistas. Loutherbourg's *Eidophusikon,* for instance, could house only toy actors scaled down to aggrandize the larger machine of nature in violent transition. Human automata, androids, attained an apogee of mechanical complexity in the work of Jacques Vaucanson (1709–82). Although his most famous creation consisted of a *bête machine*—an automatic duck, which could paddle, eat, and excrete—his *chef d'oeuvre* was a robot flutist who could play a variety of pieces, not only sounding the notes but also shaping his lips and placing his fingers in the correct positions. The performing automata of the eighteenth century must not be viewed with a post-industrial bias against the poisonous engines that have blighted the modern landscape and dehumanized modern relations. They attained the level of exquisitely and uniquely crafted works of art—as delicately beautiful as the most intricate clocks and the finest musical instruments of the period. In that role they exerted a powerful metaphoric appeal. In exorcising the Cartesian ghost, the immortal soul, from the *homme machine*, La Mettrie took his text from Vaucanson. The difference between animal and man parallels the difference between mechanical duck and mechanical flutist: the latter's organization is more complex; he contains more cogs, more gears, more beauty. *Soul* for La Mettrie was thus a matter of physical organization. The human mind and body resemble not only a self-winding watch, but also a fine musical instrument, an automatic harpsichord, mechanically registering stimuli on its keyboard and reproducing chords of thought and feeling.[14]

Cartesianism, as a physiological doctrine, entered into eighteenth-century theatrical theory by a circuitous route. The painter Charles Le Brun first appropriated the *Passions de l'âme* to the fine arts. His illustrated text, *Méthode pour apprendre à dessiner les passions* (French ed., 1702; English trans., 1734), which depicted the physiognomy of the Cartesian passions in clinical detail, served as the manual Hogarth knew as "the common drawing-book" of Le Brun and as a reference guide for "painting the passions" as late as the Davidian school.[15] The idea that the expression of the passions in nature could be academized and systematized hardly broke new ground. Giambattista della Porta, the Renaissance naturalist, had anticipated Le Brun's comparative physiognomical methods in *De humana physiognomonia* (1586), and we have already seen how thoroughly rhetoricians anatomized the passions. Le Brun stayed safely within the bounds of neoclassical generality and ideal nature, already epitomized by Poussin, by showing the lips parted in astonishment, the brow furrowed in anger, and the eyes bulging with fear. But Le Brun's treatise drew on more than the observation of nature, neoclassical theorizing, or appeals to ancient precedent. Cartesian physiology stood firmly behind it, a fact long recognized by historians of art.[16] Descartes's authority, coupled with Le Brun's lucid drawings and easily

FIGURE 9. Six universal passions as depicted by Charles Le Brun: *Horror, Fright, Sadness, Astonishment, Ravishment, Awe.* From *Encyclopedia of World Art.* (*Courtesy of McGraw-Hill.*)

followed descriptions (which seem indebted to Cureau de la Chambre for details), helped to foster the idea, later abetted by the acting textbooks of the eighteenth century, that the study of the passions involves contemplating graphic representations of idealized characters. This improved on the abstract descriptions of the rhetorics by proposing a modern body of visual literature on which the actor could draw: the painter's representation of the passions.

As early as 1710, Charles Gildon, in his *Life of Betterton*, expressed his desire that actors should, "like Le Brun, observe Nature" wherever it could "contribute to their Perfection" (37). But Gildon also proposed a model standing at a greater remove from nature when he urged the actor "not to be a Stranger to Painting and Sculpture, imitating their graces so masterly, as not to fall short of a Raphael Urbin, a Michel Angelo, &c" (139). He analysed in detail the variations in the "characters" of grief in the *Deposition* of Jordaens. Although he emphasized the "wonderful Variety" rather than the uniformity of facial "lineaments" and bodily postures in the expression of grief, he clearly stamped each as a refined template of its general type. Gildon premised his entire recommendation on the actor's need to study "Moral Philosophy" (i.e., psychology), the passions of men and their physical manifestations according to their different effects on matter, "for they produce various Appearances in the Looks and Actions, according to their various Mixtures" (36–37). As the century progressed, these ideas provided the basis not only for the style but also for the plots of contemporary performances. Such commonplace entertainments as Rameau's popular opera-ballet *Pygmalion* (1748) or Aaron Hill's knockabout farce *The Walking Statue* (c. 1746), featuring the escapades of Sir Timothy Touch, simply returned to the theater a recurring metaphor of Enlightenment physiology and psychology: the human body is a statue mechanically endowed with motion, as if limbs and features shaped from inanimate matter could somehow be vibrated into sentience and reactive vitality by an unseen force as eerily penetrating as Mozart's trombones.

Just as the *homme machine* confronts today's reader with a recondite physiological paradigm, so the conventions of eighteenth-century performance challenge his capacity for imaginative assent to a radically alien treatment of the human body. Rarely is the power of historical empathy more severely tested than by the fabulous international success of the *castrati* or male sopranos. Their bodies were maimed to fulfill the demands of an erudite public for an even more exquisite mode of theatrical expressiveness. The best of the *castrati*, or *musici* as they were called, were superb actors as well as singers. Even though they performed exclusively in Italian, English audiences could expect their expressions and poses to convey the passions with the kind of precision and vivid effect favored by contemporary mechanical sciences and the fine arts.

One *musico* in particular, Cavaliere Nicolini Grimaldi (1673–1732), known as Nicolino, epitomized the interconnections between the plastic arts and stage performance. He was trained by one of the rigorous Italian *conservatori* in a curriculum designed to prepare singer-actors for the stage. He brought to the theater, which had no comparable schools, a virtuosity born of physical technique. His art was frankly mechanical. In addition to exacting repetition of musical exercises—scales, counterpoint, improvisation—his preparation included at least an hour each day exercising his body in front of a mirror "to practice deportment and gesture."[17] His training also embraced the study of sculpture. Statuary provided a repository of ideal types from which he could draw images of the theatrical passions. His style of representing the passions consisted of a sequence of actions culminating in a series of carefully calculated tableaux. Contemporary descriptions of his body as a "statue" are therefore particularly apt. He gestured deliberately and majestically until a strong accent or climax in the score required him to stand motionless for a moment in an exceptionally expressive pose, and he held this attitude until he had made his *point.*

Nicolino's phenomenal success in London during the season of 1708–09, coming just at the end of Betterton's career, marks a significant moment in the development of eighteenth-century acting. He spoke a new language of the passions that made the vocabulary of English actors seem old-fashioned. The significance of the change he represented can be measured by the enthusiastic commentary on his acting style offered by the contemporary English critics Addison and Steele, who otherwise had nothing good to say about the Italian opera. They found in this one singer, however, a mastery of physical expression that the best English actors, even Betterton, had yet to rival. They knew that Nicolino offered something revolutionary, and they urged his innovations on their countrymen. "I have often wished that our tragedians would copy after this great master in action," Addison admonished; "could they make the same use of their arms and legs, and inform their faces with as significant looks and passions," then English spoken tragedy might appear passionately "glorious" next to the "cold conceits" of operatic libretti (*Spectator,* no. 13, 15 March 1711). Steele elaborated on the theory behind Nicolino's powers of expression. He noted that the *musico* could manipulate his body with the precision of a moving statue: "Every limb and every finger contributes to the part he acts, insomuch that a deaf man may go along with him in the sense of it. There is scarce a beautiful posture in an old statue which he does not plant himself in, as the different circumstances of the story give occasion for it" (*Tatler,* no. 115, 3 January 1709/10). Steele admired Nicolino's mechanical ability to move, to cease moving, and to move again with dignity and exactitude, a requisite capacity in establishing one tableau and preparing smoothly for the next.

A similarly structured sequence of passions, accented by moments in which the actors held a climactic tableau indefinitely, became the signature of eighteenth-century acting style. Admiring references to the animate statue likewise recurred in the theatrical criticism of the period. Garrick himself was praised, as we shall see, for his physical command over "trains" of passions. He was a favorite subject for artists, and the preponderance of paintings and engravings depict him poised at a climactic moment, frozen in a statuesque attitude, as if waiting for the applause to die down. Although it may seem odd to identify an Italian opera singer as the forerunner to the English actor who is remembered above all for his naturalness, both Nicolino and Garrick represented a view of nature based on a physiology alien to our own. The unnatural or

FIGURE 10. Three *points* from Franciscus Lange, *Dissertatio de actione scenica* (1727): issuing a command, entering with a message, expressing the emotions silently. *(Courtesy of Alderman Library, University of Virginia.)*

supernatural virtuosity of the *castrati,* who reigned in popularity throughout the first half of the century, suggests another and rather chilling variation on the theme of performing automata. Setting such streamlined bodies into motion may represent the ultimate mechanical version of theatrical expressiveness—singing machines to delight the emperor and his ladies.

The concept that the generalities of expression, pose, and gesture governing drama derive their validity from the plastic arts pervades works as widely dispersed in time and place as Franciscus Lange's *Dissertatio de actione scenica* (Munich, 1727), François Riccoboni's *L'art du thèâtre* (Paris, 1750), Roger Pickering's *Reflections upon Theatrical Expression in Tragedy* (London, 1755), and Goethe's *Regeln für Schauspieler* (Weimar, 1803). Substantial evidence exists to show that the liaison of fine and performing arts on the subject of bodily representation went beyond airy theorizing. In extending practical advice to the actor, Thomas Wilkes in *A General View of the Stage* (London, 1759) liberally paraphrases from the 1734 translation of Le Brun's *Méthod.*[18] Most of the theatrical prints or paintings of the period, even those as reliably realistic as Hogarth's, show the actor posed. Individual actors had already become identified with this technique. Barton Booth, for instance, who for a time shared the stage with Nicolino at the Haymarket, made a reputation as an actor who enriched his expressive vocabulary by drawing on the fine arts. Booth was especially noted for his taste in sculpture and painting. He kept on hand a collection of prints of famous works from which he studiously derived poses and expressions. His mastery of these "Attitudes" and the "Easy Transitions" between them was so carefully rehearsed that his admirers claimed to be unable to distinguish them from spontaneous reactions.[19]

Booth's attitudinizing reinforced and extended over the entire body the post-Cartesian assumption, codified by Le Brun's heads, that the passions impress themselves on the human form as ideal templates, which can be successfully imitated by meticulous description, careful draughtsmanship, or study before a mirror. The thoroughness of recent scholarship on this subject confirms what mechanical philosophy might lead us to suspect: the classification of the passions by gestural and postural stereotypes presented the actor's body as a dead mechanism from which parts may be detached for separate treatment.[20] An illustrated acting text such as Lange's *Dissertatio de actione scenica* even shows a curious and not altogether attractive similarity to the military manuals of the period. The inventors of the new art of close-order drill used positional drawings to inculcate a uniformity of motion in the appendages of well-trained grenadiers, any one of whom could stand in for another should a sudden vacancy in the ranks occur. The concept of the interchangeability of parts thus has a pre-industrial history in both military science and the arts.

Indeed, the very proliferation of images of the universal passions in eighteenth-century acting texts reflects a mechanistic view of nature. The notion that the management of the face, limbs, and torso should conform to certain ideal patterns, set in motion by pre-existing Ideas, derives from the successful methodology of physics. Mechanization objectified and exteriorized the passions, draining them of their subjective content. A physical theory of the passions devoid of psychology was possible as long as the soul could be regarded as transcendent. Since machines lack individuality, except by terms of the most clear-cut classification into objective types, signs of psychological eccentricity could be overlooked. It is certainly not coincidental that eighteenth-century science was characterized by great advances in botanical and zoological classifications. Phylogeny poses less daunting problems to the taxonomist who views creatures as static forms cast from what La Mettrie called "a single substance variously modified" and what Garrick termed the "different modifications of matter." In urging the "philosophical knowledge of the passions" on actors, Charles Macklin confidently assured them that the passions "are all to be distinguished into *genus, species,* and individual characteristics, like dogs, fowl, apples, plums, and the like" (*AA*, 121). To

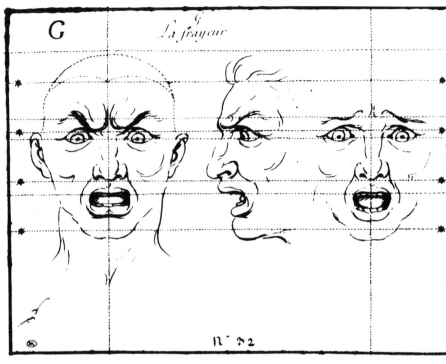

FIGURE 11. La Frayeur. Le Brun's schematization of terror from *The Method for Learning to Design the Passions* (1734). *(Courtesy of Washington University Libraries.)*

Macklin a body or a passion is a thing like a bird or a stone. They are all laid upon the same taxonomic "grid," to borrow Foucault's term, a grid which calibrates the fixed variations of lifeless matter. Hence the success of Le Brun's catalogue of the passions, the specimens of which are mounted like butterflies under glass.

What many theatrical theorists in the eighteenth century overlooked was that Descartes portrayed the passions as sequences of bodily functions, manifestations of a moving machine propelled by its own physical springs and guided by its ghostly soul. The Cartesian templates depict a process, not a picture. Le Brun arrested the motion of the face to fix each passion by its superficial signs in a still moment of time. This suited the needs of the history painters well enough, but it offered the actors only static images of dynamic events. Since Le Brun's heads were intended for painters and sculptors, he naturally omitted Bulwer's sensible *caveat* about his illustrations to *Chirologia:* "The necessary defect of the Chirograms in point of motion and percussion, which Art cannot expresse, must be supplied with imagination" (114). In the parlance of the modern study of kinesics, graphic representation of the passions following Le Brun is at best "digital," proceeding by fixed steps, whereas complete representation of expressive motion must be "analogic," flowing continuously in time.[21]

This was a topic of considerable urgency in eighteenth-century aesthetics. To his famous treatise on the limits of painting and poetry, *Laöcoon* (1766), Gotthold Ephraim Lessing projected a sequel that would have explained drama as the point of intersection between the arts in time (music, poetry) and arts in space (sculpture, painting). Though he never completed the larger tome, he took up the problem of the tension between tableaux and continuous action in the fifth number of the *Hamburg Dramaturgy* (1767):

> The art of the actor here stands midway between the plastic arts and poetry. As visible painting beauty must be its highest law, but as transitory painting it need not always give to its postures the calm dignity that makes ancient sculpture so imposing. It may, it must at times permit to itself the wildness of a Tempesta, the insolence of a Bernini; and they have in this art all that which is expressive and peculiar without the offensive element that arises in the plastic arts through their permanent posture. Only it must not remain in them too long, it must prepare for them gradually by previous movements, and must resolve them again into the general tone of the conventional.[22]

The tableau was equivalent to the cinematic stop frame. The actor's challenge was therefore to manage the transitions in and out of striking poses. Like Barton Booth, with his "Attitudes" and "Easy Transitions," Lessing's ideal *Schauspieler* had to master the arrest of analogic action in a frozen moment, a stop frame, a digit in time, wherein an imposing posture could be held; he had then to effect the artful resumption of its continuous motion. Like Pygmalion, Lessing seems to have wanted his statues to move, to stop, and to move again automatically on command— a characteristic ability of machines. This was also the technique at which David Garrick excelled.

Garrick offered a glimpse of his thinking on what art critics in his time called the "fruitful moment" in a letter to the illustrator Francis Hayman, concerning "that point of Time in the last Act" of *Othello* when the "Whole Catastrophe of the play is unravell'd." Disclosing many interesting details about his ideas of composition and the physiognomical templates of the passions, Garrick stages the scene for Hayman, more than once promising to give him the full effect by assuming each attitude and expression the next time he visits: "Othello (ye Principal) upon ye right hand (I believe) must be thunderstruck with Horror, his Whole figure extended, wth his Eyes turn'd up to Heav'n & his Frame sinking"; and he offers a similarly detailed description for each of the assembled characters.[23] As an actor and stage director, Garrick vivifies Lessing's vague instructions about how to manage the tableau, and yet his words obviously fall frustratingly short of his physical conception. Even his ideas for composing a still must be demonstrated before the eyes of the beholder, as a choreographer demonstrates a new dance step, because he lacks—as we still lack—a system of notation to convey the theatrical passions graphically.

The problem of notating continuous motion for the stage occupied theorists in the eighteenth century as it still fascinates us today. The invention of the motion picture camera permits kinesiologists and choreographers to analyze gesture digitally, frame by frame, or continuously at approximately twenty-four frames per second, the point at which the human eye sees an unflickering, analogic flow of motion. In searching for a pre-cinematic graphic medium to depict movement, eighteenth-century aesthetics produced some ingenious though largely impractical suggestions. William Hogarth, for instance, in the *Analysis of Beauty* (1753), tentatively proposed a linear schematization of stage movement based on his undulating "line of beauty." Later Gilbert Austin in his *Chironomia; or a Treatise on Rhetorical Delivery* (1806) surrounded the actor's body with a globe and recorded the trajectory of his gestures in relationship to the three-dimensional perimeter of the sphere. But linear representation, continuously turning figure eights like the afterimage of a traffic policeman's baton or circling the points of the compass, quickly exhausts its ability to depict coherently the scope and variety of animated gesture. Some determined pedagogues, notably Johannes Jelgerhuis in *Theoretische Lessen over de Gesticulatie en Mimiek* (1827), attempted to overcome this difficulty by simultaneously representing the limbs and features in multiple positions, but the resulting cacophony of gestures seems to perplex more than it edifies.

Other, more subtle thinkers—including Jean Georges Noverre with his concept of *ballet pantomime* or *danse d'action*—dreamed about the feasibility of a complex language of gesture, complete with its own vocabulary and grammar, which could parallel and supplement the spoken languages but excel them in expressing the passions. Noverre's insistence that ballet should "represent on the stage the different passions with that variety of shades which is peculiar to each of them" returned the passions to the realm of analogic action and placed them in the hands of the choreographer. The metaphor Noverre employed to describe the *ballet d'action*

Pl. 22.

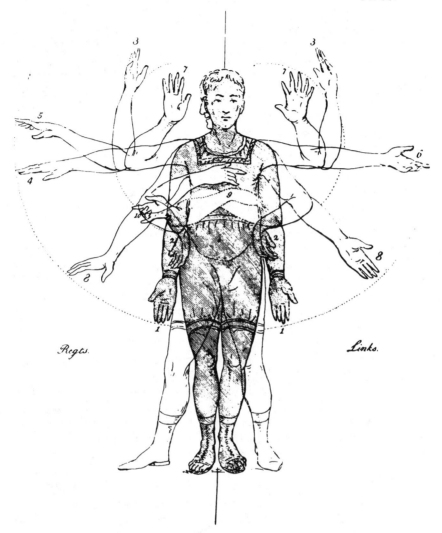

FIGURE 12. Notating gesture. From J. Jelgerhuis, *Theoretische Lessen* (1827). *(Courtesy of Washington University Libraries.)*

hints that the trend of his thought was toward a linguistics of expression based on the physics of sequential motion. His description of the balletic ensemble resembles the modern biomechanical concept of *effort shapes*, in which the body is comprehended as a sequence of measurable forces in motion, a machine in time:

> What is a Ballet but a piece of more or less complicated machinery, which strikes or surprises the beholder by its various effects, only in proportion as those are diversified and sudden? That chain and connection of figures, those motions succeeding each other with rapidity, those various forms turning contrary ways, that mixture of different incidents, the ensemble and harmony which mark the steps and accompany the exertion of the dancers; do not all these give you the idea of a mechanism most ingeniously contrived?[24]

But in the absence of a system of notation much beyond the floor patterns of dance steps depicted in R. A. Feuillet's *Choréographie* (1700), there appeared no latter-day Aeschylus or Newton who could write, *ab ovo*, the first grammar of the language of the unspoken passions.

Still, there were attempts to describe what such a grammar would be like, if it could be had. Condillac, Du Bos, and Lessing speculated on the nature of the lost poetic-pantomimic language of the ancient theater, and Rousseau evoked the power of unadorned gesture as the most primitive natural language, one fitted to express the deepest feelings without dissimulation or deceit. Diderot probably came closer than anyone in the eighteenth century to a practical demonstration of a gestural language of the passions in his stage directions for *Le fils naturel* (1757). In the more malleable realm of theory, flesh could still be fashioned into more or less complete systems. Johann Casper Lavater, in his *Essays on Physiognomy* (1775–78), believed he had found "the science or knowledge of the correspondence between the external and internal man."[25] Johann Jakob Engel's *Ideen zu Einer Mimik* (1785, best known through Henry Siddons's translation and adaptation of 1822) proposed a "science" of expressive gesture modeled on the Linnaean system of botanical classification for "the study of natural history." Such an ambition seems somewhat less imposing when Engel reveals how much of this science would have consisted of common sense inflated into natural law: "the man who strives to avoid a danger which is very near, for instance, that of being bit by a venomous serpent ready to fly at him, will save himself with his feet greatly elevated from the ground."[26]

The systematization of the theatrical passions reached its apogee in the treatises of the eighteenth-century elocutionists, James Burgh and John Walker. In *The Art of Speaking* (1761), Burgh first catalogues the passions

FIGURE 13. The passions classified. *Terror.* From J. J. Engel, *Ideen zu Einer Mimik* (1785). *(Courtesy of P. M. Arnold Semeiology Collection, Washington University Libraries.)*

FIGURE 14. Apprehension. From H. Siddons, *Rhetorical Gesture and Action* (1822). *(Courtesy of P. M. Arnold Semeiology Collection, Washington University Libraries.)*

according to their mechanical signs. He then offers a series of "Lessons" in which he annotates scenes and speeches from plays and poems. His marginal notations refer back to the standardized passions drawn from his compendious taxonomy. In effect, Burgh creates in the margins a line of action, which the actor can read as a series of cues. It resembles a crude musical score, paralleling and reinforcing the text, throughout which the passions proceed in a sequence of "affects," as in the progression "Awe—Horror—Fear." In the same spirit, Walker appended *A Complete System of the Passions* to his *Elements of Elocution* (1787).[27]

There was, however, another, more promising application of post-Cartesian science to the art of acting. It drew upon the mechanical paradigm to account for the inner psychophysiological processes behind the passions rather than simply to enumerate exhaustively their external signs. Abbé Du Bos, attempting to refine and explicate ancient oratorical verities in the context of modern science, was the first to grasp the theatrical implications of the inner mechanization of the passions: "I apprehend therefore, that the genius requisite to form an excellent declaimer, consists in a sensibility of heart, which makes him enter mechanically, but with affection, into the sentiments of the personage he acts. It consists in a mechanic disposition to be actuated easily by all those passions, which he has occasion to represent" (*Reflections* 1:338). By separating mechanics and affections into parallel but mutually supporting tracks, Du Bos bends Descartes's interactive dualism of mind and body to the actor's purposes. Efficiency of emotion represents a function of the corporeal machine, but the machine is driven by a mental spring. Du Bos did not pursue this issue to its logical theatrical ends, but two subsequent theorists did: Aaron Hill, founder of the theatrical paper called *The Prompter* (1734–36), and Lessing in the third number of the *Hamburg Dramaturgy*. By construing the mechanization of the body in light of its implications for the actor, Hill and Lessing liberated themselves from superstition and mystification and probed basic issues that have retained their currency to this day: does the actor's emotion begin inwardly, mentally, and then work its effect on the body or does the simple performance of the outer bodily actions associated with the emotion adequately produce the feeling itself?

Aaron Hill developed his "system" of acting—for that is what he called it—piecemeal in a number of journal articles, essays, letters, and poems. His career spanned Nicolino's triumph in Handel's *Rinaldo* (1711), for which Hill wrote the libretto, the fall of James Quin, and the rise of Garrick and Charles Macklin. Throughout his writings on the theater, he seemed anxious to argue for the newness of his approach and to demonstrate its foundation in science and natural law. He pugnaciously signed his *Prompter* articles "B" for "Broomstick" because he meant to sweep the stage clean of worn-out conventions. In the Quarrel of the Ancients and Moderns, his allegiance was stridently partisan. He specifically denounced those who would formulate rules of acting based on the old rhetorical principles, "for instead of examining nature, they look to Quintilian, . . . falling into mistakes and absurdities which are so much the more ridiculous by that pretense of authority whereon they would ground their establishment." Hill noted that Quintilian arbitrarily proscribed the raising of the hands above the level of the eyes—a superstitious pedantry, Hill thought, in view of the several dramatic instances in which this gesture must naturally, indeed, mechanically, occur: falling backward into a posture of astonishment, pleading to a higher authority, praying to the heavens. "Thus narrow or thus blind," he concluded, "are almost all our stage maxims."[28] *Nullius in verba.* Aaron Hill's progressiveness influenced even elocutionists such as Burgh and Walker, the latter of whom cited him specifically, and their replacement of Quintilian with the modern science of the mechanical passions suggests how far the paradigm shift in physiology had gone to transform the theoretical basis of expressiveness.

This direct assault on the ancient authority enshrined in the *Institutio Oratoria*, however, did not occasion an immediate actors' revolt against what Hill viewed as the tradition-bound and the theoretically threadbare. As late as 1815 Leigh Hunt was still grumbling about "declamation" and the "puttings forth of the old oratorical right hand," well over a century after the physiology that supported this gesture had supposedly been rendered obsolete. The precepts of Cicero and Quintilian enjoyed a long and active old age and in fact are still drawing breath today. But Hill's dismissal of classical rhetoric cleared the way for him to offer "a justification of [the actor's] Mechanism, . . . by demonstrating its foundation on clear natural causes" so that he could ascertain in full "the *natural foundation* of that mechanism, in the art described, whereby the springs are moved, to represent the passions, outwardly."[29] Once these causes were known and fully understood, Hill assumed, they would clearly establish the "universality of the system" (*Prompter*, no. 118, 26 December 1735, 141). He depicts the actor's art as a mechanical process of inwardly experiencing the passions at the will's command. He seems to share the seventeenth-century view on the volubility of the emotions, but he harbors no lingering doubts about the certainty of their obedience to the rational soul. Nor does he demonstrate any apparent fear of the physical consequences of intensely sustained imagination. Hill divides acting into four clear steps, resembling those in an operator's manual accompanying a new appliance. As he understood it, the player's passion was "no more than a connected deduction of these plain and natural consequences":

> 1st.—The *imagination* assumes the idea.
> 2dly.—Its marks and characteristical impressions appear first in the face, because nearest to the seat of imagination.
> 3dly.—Thence, impelled by the will, a commissioned detachment of the *animal spirits* descending into the dependent organization of the muscles, and swelling and adapting them in its progress, bends and stimulates their elastic powers into a position apt to execute the purpose (or to express the warmth of) the idea.
> 4thly.—Thus the look, air, voice, and action proper to a passion, preconceived in the imagination, become a mere and *mechanic necessity,* without perplexity, study, or difficulty. (*Prompter,* no. 118, 140, emphasis added)

Hill took from Cartesian physiology a number of important ideas: imagination plays a crucial role in establishing the mind's power over the body; the passions make "characteristical impressions" on the physiognomy; and the ever-useful animal spirits puff up the muscles in meticulously engineered sequences so as to move the body hydraulically or pneumatically. Here, also in an immediately recognizable form, is Descartes's idea that the body functions by "mechanic necessity" and with quite astonishing efficiency when it operates under the proper supervision of its ghost. Hill's originality resides in the way he applied this interactive dualism to the actor's means of expression, particularly in his emphasis on the actor's inner affective and imaginative processes. The "spirits" of which he speaks are enlightened spirits, far removed from the animism out of which they emerged, now deemed capable of possessing the nerves and brain of only the machine that contained them. The four humours have evaporated like mists at sunrise and, with them, the need for a system of protective inhibitions. In short, mechanism has supplanted magic in the interior as well as the exterior world, and the expression of an emotion is itself a "mechanic necessity" of the actor who calls it to mind.

In setting forth the inner process of the passions, Hill specifically enjoins actors from indulging those "tedious and laborious schemes of adjusting their gesture to looking-glasses" or from "calling in the painters to their assistance" in a futile attempt "to succeed by observation of certain lineal and expressive distinctions of the passions as they vary on the visage" (*Prompter,* no. 118, 141). In place of such external methods, Hill specifies that a strong imagination should fix the *Idea* of the passion in the mind, thus dispatching the animal spirits through the hollow nerves on their way to shape the facial muscles into the proper expression and the body into the proper posture. Richard Steele had previously touched on this subject when he advised Mr. Mills on playing in Wilkes's *Hamlet* that "the way to action was not to study gesture, for the behavior would follow the sentiments of the mind" (*Tatler*, no. 201, 22 July 1710). Luigi Riccoboni had argued along the same vaguely dualistic lines in his essay on declamation when he observed that "our soul is the *Agent*, and our Members and Organ[s] the *Ministers* she employs. . . . We can declaim only in the accents of the Soul, and . . . without these there can be no Action."[30] Hill took the same principle, dismissed Steele's "sentiments" and Riccoboni's vague "accents" in favor of the mechanic imagination, and supplied the process with a physical basis. He believed that the actor's willed image or Idea of the passion exerts an actual physical pressure or push, which moves the spirits and muscles to conform. Hill called this facility the "plastic imagination" (*Prompter*, no. 66, 27 June 1735, 85). Its principal activity consists of printing the Idea of the passion on the brain and nerves as a letter press imprints ink on wet paper. In a poem called "The Art of Acting" (1746), Hill explained that the impassioned performance and the willed Idea follow one another as mechanically as thunder follows lightning (*Works* 3:395). He versifies Descartes thus:

> Previous to art's first act—(till then, *all vain*)
> Print the *ideal pathos*, on the *brain:*
> Feel the thought's image on the *eyeball* roll;
> Behind that *window*, sits th' attentive *SOUL:*
> Wing'd, at *her* beck, th' obediant MUSCLES fly,
> *Bent*, or *relaxing*, to the varied *eye:*
> Press'd, moderate, lenient, *VOICE*'s organ'd sound,
> To each felt impulse, tones the tuneful round:
> Form'd to the *nerves*, concurring *MEIN* partakes,
> So, the *mov'd* actor *Moves*—and passion shakes.
>
> (*Works* 3:408)

Thus the embodiment of an emotion flows effortlessly from "ideal" to physical manifestation; as Hill notes simply, "the *mov'd* actor *Moves*."

Hill urged the study of the passions on the actor as a means of acquiring mental images to reinforce his "ideal pathos." Here the use of prints and paintings was permissible to increase the actor's store of Ideas—not to copy but to suggest by association or, as Descartes put it, to influence the bodily emotions "indirectly by the representation of things which are usually united to the passions which we desire to have" (*Passions*, Article 45). Hill began by defining six "capital dramatics"—joy, sorrow, fear, scorn, anger, amazement—which are roughly equivalent to Descartes's six primary passions. He also recognized that numerous "auxiliary" passions, such as jealousy, revenge, love, and pity, could be compounded from two or more of the "capitals" (*Prompter*, no. 66, 84). Later Hill expanded the primary passions to include pity, hatred, jealousy, and love. In the "soft passions," such as love, the spirits allegedly flow through the nerves languidly. In a rage they gush about turbulently, causing fits and starts and popping veins, but in the "passive passions," such as fear and grief, the animal spirits reverse their outward emanations and pool in the central organs, causing pallor, langour, dejection, muscular collapse, and even paralysis of the extremities (*Prompter*, no. 118, 141).

Although Hill claimed that the passions must be rendered from the inside out, his location of the emotive process in the brain of the actor did not license sendentary brooding. Embodying a passion demands physical labor as exhausting in its way as threshing grain, and Broomstick savaged those overly elegant players who thought that sweat should be left to the stagehands (*Prompter*, no. 66, 85). Hill also held strong views on the need for actors to expend maximum effort at rehearsals and in what we now call physical warm-ups, the purpose of which was and is "to warm, dephlegm, and clarify the thorax, and the wind-pipe, by exerting (the more frequently the better) their fullest power of utterance" (*Works* 4:413). Hill seems to have believed that the actor's machine clogs up from disuse more readily than it wears out from exertion. This *aperçu*, as with everything else in his system, extends from his basic premise concerning the mechanical logic of bodily processes. He was so confident in the scientific rightness of his acting "system" that he cast his nephew, a complete neophyte who had never been near the stage, in the leading part of Osman in his own translation of Voltaire's *Zaire* (1736). So certain was he in the law of "mechanical necessity" that he counted on proper coaching in the Ideas of the passions to insure a triumph.

Lessing's theatrical career ran parallel to Aaron Hill's in interesting and significant ways: both were founders of short-lived theatrical periodicals; both had close managerial ties to the stage and acquaintance with prominent actors; both were active playwrights and translators with particular knowledge of French aesthetics, while they were strongly critical of French literary dominance. Lessing certainly knew Hill through his translation of *Zaire* (*Hamburg Dramaturgy*, no. 15) and probably knew "The Art of Acting" in the edition of 1746, for Konrad Ekhof proposed to translate it for use at the Hamburg National Theatre.[31] In applying the man-machine hypothesis to the act of acting, Lessing drew alternate, though not contradictory, conclusions from the same model of the body available to Hill. Lessing's Cartesianism also owes something perhaps to Du Bos, whose views on the nature of pantomime in antiquity led him to translate the third volume of *Réflexions critiques* for the *Theatralische*

Bibiothek of 1755. No doubt Lessing would have taken up the actor's bodily mechanism in some detail if he had continued the *Laöcoon* as planned or completed an outline headed "The Actor: A Work wherein the Axioms of Complete Bodily Eloquence Will Be Developed." As it happened, he addressed the subject on a smaller scale in the third issue of his theatrical journal by way of a digression on Ekhof's delivery of *sententia*.

The dramaturg begins by stating the Enlightenment's position on emotion, in which animistic, panpsychic, or parapsychic spirits have no stature: "For feeling is something internal of which we can only judge by its external signs" (*Hamburg Dramaturgy*, no. 3, 12). He had previously translated Rémond de Sainte-Albine's *Le comédien* (1747) and François Riccoboni's *L'art du théâtre* (1750). These authorities continued the historic debate begun by Quintilian on the question of inspiration versus technique, but they centered the inspiring agency in the physical and moral fabric of the actor without having recourse to Delphi. Sainte-Albine championed the idea that the player's passion resides "in the entrails."[32] Riccoboni, opposing both Sainte-Albine and his own father, Luigi, defended the view that the actor should represent emotion by external imitation and prior calculation. By 1750 the opposition of external and internal methods was thus firmly entrenched, but it was marked by much greater theoretical complexity than is usually understood. In mediating between these two positions in light of interactive dualism, Lessing came up with something new—emotion felt in the body, eventually perceived by the mind, but not prompted by the imagination.

In the first place, Lessing observed, there may be an actor who feels everything exquisitely inside, but whom we do not believe because his body is inadequate for external expression. Aaron Hill failed to give adequate weight to the possibility that there might be machines of varying efficiency, his nephew for one. On the other hand, Lessing continued, another kind of actor may "have his muscles so easily and quickly at his command" that he may appear "animated with the most intense feeling" when in fact everything he does is "nothing but mechanical imitation" (no. 3, 13). Mechanical imitation represents the opposite extreme from what Hill calls the "Bodied resemblance of a copied mind" (*Works* 3:292), for the *Hamburg Dramaturgy* goes so far as to say that an actor can still act effectively even when he does not mentally understand the passion he portrays (13). In emphasizing the capacity of the machine, as it were, to jump-start an emotion by soulless reflex, Lessing partakes of the Cartesian view of extended nature, which was amusingly illustrated by Du Bos. In *Réflexions critiques*, the Abbé offers an insight gained by the distinguished academician Tournefort while negotiating a tricky steeplechase: "For my part, I abandoned myself entirely to the guidance of my horse, and found it answered better than if I had strove to manage him myself. An automaton that follows naturally the laws of mechanics, conducts itself much better on these occasions, than the most knowing person in mechanics" (2:255). By similar means, the actor, in Lessing's view, may still enact rage and anger even if he cannot "imagine them vividly enough to arouse anger in his soul." He can generate internal passions by first engaging in external activity. He can physically perform the actions and expressions of anger, for instance, copied from "an actor of original feeling." The very activity of mechanically repeating these conventional movements—the impulsive stride, the stamping foot, the gnashing teeth, the strident trembling voice—"will thus infallibly cast on his mind a dim feeling of anger that will react on his body and will produce such changes as do not solely depend upon his will. His face will glow, his eyes sparkle, his muscles will dilate; in short he will seem to be truly furious without being so [i.e., in his soul], without comprehending in the least why he should be so." These mechanical actions thus stimulate "involuntary changes" (13–14).

Descartes laid the foundation for Lessing's view when he spoke of "movements of the body which accompany the passions and do not depend on the soul" and of emotions that "may be excited in the body by the disposition of the organs alone" (*Passions*, Article 38). Indeed, the corporeal machine so governs Descartes's discussion of the passions, and he treats the physical symptoms of emotion in such detail, that he has been interpreted by historians of psychology as anticipating the James-Lange theory of emotion.[33] This theory, which dominates many modern acting systems and which will be encountered in various guises hereafter, maintained in essence that emotions have no real existence apart from their physiological manifestations. Anger, for instance, is not a description of a mental state, but a description of clenched teeth, bulging veins, and trembling hands. The mind's perception of the physiological manifestation is the emotion. "A purely disembodied human emotion is a nonentity," James wrote: "If our theory be true, a necessary corollary of it ought to be that any voluntary arousal of the so-called manifestations of a special emotion ought to give us the emotion itself."[34] Thus we work ourselves physically into a passion and whistle past the cemetery to keep up our courage. Lessing's position certainly resembles twentieth-century applications to acting of the James-Lange theory, a theatrical borrowing from psychophysiology summed up by the acting teacher's familiar admonition: "Do the act, and the feeling will follow."[35] Yet equating ideas formulated so far apart in time would be an oversimplification. For one thing Lessing's confidence that an actor can successfully copy the conventionalized gestures of an "actor of original feeling" offends against the modern romanticization of the creative uniqueness of each artistic organism, especially on the touchy subject of emotion.

More significantly, both Hill and Lessing held Cartesian assumptions about the duality of body and mind that sever their views cleanly from currently prevailing opinion on the nature of the creative process. Neither Descartes in his philosophy nor the authorities on acting who applied his mechanistic view of the passions to the stage recognized the existence of the subconscious or unconscious in any modern sense of those terms. They saw mind, which for them consisted of conscious thought, acting on body, which consisted of matter, and body acting on mind, but they saw little or nothing in between. With hyperbole intended to exalt the "right" answers to which he has access, a modern philosopher of the creative process suggests that this outdated view might be termed "the Cartesian catastrophe"—the division of the world into discrete realms of mind and matter and "the identification of 'mind' with conscious thinking." This allegedly resulted in "an impoverishment of psychology which took it three centuries to remedy even in part."[36] From the point of view of modern acting theory, it was certainly true that Cartesianism did not plumb the mysterious depths and complexity of inner life, the shaping forces of forbidden desire, and the torments of bodily inhibition. Lessing did not unduly complicate his idea of the actor when he wrote that "reason" should mediate between coldness and fire in emotion, which was a bodily affair (*Hamburg Dramaturgy*, no. 3, 14). Nor did Aaron Hill hesitate when he first divided the actor evenly into nonextended force and volumetric moving parts and then reassembled him, piece by piece, as a hydro-dynamic passion mill, all springs, and cogs, pulling strings, and pushing gears:

> Shap'd in *conception's* mould, *nature's* prompt skill
> Bids subject *nerves* obey th' inspiring *Will:*
> Strung to obsequious bend, the musc'ly frame
> *Stamps* the shown image.—*Pleasure, pity, shame,*
> *Anger, grief, terror,* catch th' adaptive *spring*
> While the eye darts it! and the *accents* ring.
>
> (*Works* 3 : 394)

Yet it is the physiological specificity of Hill's system that holds the key to the underlying assumptions behind the acting style of his contemporaries. He illustrated his general precepts with revealing particulars, richly suggestive of the changes that mechanical physiology brought about in theatrical semiotics.

In his culminating *Essay on the Art of Acting* (c. 1749), Hill offers the actor ten "Applications" of the primary passions. Each consists of a definition and a physiological description illustrated by exemplary passages from popular dramatic works. "Wonder," for example, he defines as "inquisitive Fear." Wonder shows two degrees of intensity— "Amazement" and "Astonishment." The first creates "alarm" leading to "involuntary rigour" (*Works* 4:384). The second provokes an even more concussive reaction:

> But, in Astonishment, the recoil of the animal spirits, hurried back in two [*sic*] precipitate a motion, drive the blood upon the heart with such oppressive redundance, as, retarding circulation, almost stagnates the vital progression: and arresting the breath, eyes, gesture, and every power and faculty of the body, occasions an interruption of their several rules, that would bring an actuall cessation—but, that the reason, struggling slowly to relieve the apprehension, gives a kind of hesitative articulation to the utterance, and gradual motion and recovery to the Look, the Limbs, and the Countenance.
>
> (*Works* 4:385)

Hill has paraphrased Article 73 of the *Passions de l'âme* in which Descartes described the sudden evacuation of spirits from the limbs in astonishment. This withdrawal causes the body to freeze momentarily in statuesque immobility, like a hydraulic automaton from which the fluid has been drained. Horripilation, the raising of the hair on the head in fear and awe, along with the widening and bulging of the eyes, was thought to be caused by the sudden rush of the spirits to the head and eyes as they rivet on the object of surprise or dread. Such was the foundation of Perkins's wig in natural law as contemporary physiologists construed it. Furthermore, the passion of astonishment obviously lent itself to the interplay of analogic action and grand tableau.

Hill finds all the aforementioned physiological details in Hamlet's first encounter with his father's ghost at "Angels and Ministers of grace defend us," including both degrees of wonder and the slow recovery to action. He notes first "the starting spring upon the nerves," then the "slow struggling" back to equilibrium, and finally the "resolution of recovered firmness" (*Works* 4:386). His specifications conform with remarkable fidelity to Georg Christoph Lichtenberg's much admired description of the violent start and slow recovery at the appearance of the ghost in Garrick's Hamlet of 1775: "At these words Garrick turns sharply and at the same moment staggers back two or three paces with his knees giving way under him; his hat falls to the ground and both his arms, especially the left, are stretched out nearly to their full length, with the hands as high as his head, the right arm more bent and the hand lower, and the fingers apart; his mouth is open: thus he stands rooted to the spot." Garrick held this tableau for so long that some spectators wondered if he needed prompting, but the physiology of astonishment as described by Descartes and Hill justified a long pause at this point while the statue regained hydrostatic equilibrium. "At last," Lichtenberg concludes, Garrick's thunderstruck machine creaked back into action to follow the ghost offstage, at first moving with visible effort: "Now standing still, and then going on, . . . eyes fixed on the Ghost, hair disordered, and out of breath, until he too is lost to sight."[37] Lessing's ideal of acting as "transitory painting"—a flowing movement stilled for a digit of time and then artfully resumed—could hardly be defined by a more incisive illustration. Nor could Noverre have found a better example of his concept of the *mise en scène* as an intricately designed machine in time. The very structure of Garrick's stage business derived from the action and reaction of two mechanisms: first, the ghost rose up from the trap, sprung by counterweights; then, responding like the hydraulic automata of St. Germain at the approach of an intruder, Hamlet's body turned and extended its limbs in an automatically determined reaction to stimulus. Onstage actions begot equal and opposite reactions, and mechanical responses followed mechanical stimuli as invisible forces pushed bodies into action. The Benjamin Wilson painting of Garrick in his tableau of horror and amazement confirms Lichtenberg's description in all its essentials. In both portraits the actor's physiognomy shows a distinct resemblance to Le Brun's astonished maiden, herself the stepdaughter of Article 73 of the *Passions de l'âme*.

Lichtenberg's testimony on Garrick's acting carries special authority. As Professor of Experimental Physics at the University of Göttingen, leading naturalist and mathematician, Lichtenberg advocated an indisciplinary mode of inquiry founded on the "coherent exposition of physical relationships as preparation for a *future* science of nature."[38] He was acutely interested in the physics of emotional experience and coined the term "Pathognomik" to describe his opposition to the moral and mystical aspects of Lavater's physiognomical theories, which he sharply attacked in *On Physiognomy: Against the Physiognomists*. Using strikingly modern terminology, he claimed that the true science of expression, stripped of cant and mystification, would embrace "the whole semiotics of affects, or the knowledge of the natural signs of emotions in all their degrees and mixtures."[39] The acknowledged value of Lichtenberg's descriptions of Garrick resides in their precision of detail and clarity of notation. The

FIGURE 15. Garrick as Hamlet: engraved by J. McArdell (1754) after the painting by Benjamin Wilson. *(Courtesy of Alderman Library, University of Virginia.)*

FIGURE 16. L'Admiration avec étonnement. Preparatory sketch by Le Brun for *La tente de Darius. (Courtesy of the Musée du Louvre, Cabinet des Dessins.)*

reason for this scrupulousness was his interest in recording theatrical events as organized sequences of expressive signs—the same language of the passions that was the dream and despair of his contemporaries.

Garrick's own *Essay on Acting* shows the extent to which he was aware of current theories of what Lichtenberg called the "physics" of expression and the "semiotics of affects." Good actors in any age seem to digest the salient concepts of contemporary psychological theory. Garrick's knowledge may have been no more profound than that of any literate non-specialist, but it was certainly not superficial. Aaron Hill pestered him with tendentious letters on the science of acting often enough to have communicated his point. Later Garrick was in contact with the materialistic *philosophes*, including Holbach and Diderot, and perhaps his early essay drew some of its language from a currently popular digest of philosophic thought such as the *Bibliothèque raisonnée des ouvrages des savans de l'Europe*, vol. 32 (1744), an immediate precursor to La Mettrie. In any case, the heated argument concerning spirit and matter, prompted by the concept of the *homme machine*, was very much in the air.

The *Essay on Acting* seems to have been written to steal a theoretical march on Garrick's critics as he prepared to revive *Macbeth* in 1744. He assumed the guise of a wit hostile to the forthcoming production and its producer. Within this ironic framework, which demands an extremely complex tone, Garrick promoted his own ideas. If he speaks seriously about anything in the *Essay*, it is the proper physicalization of the passions (*AA*, 134–35). He defined acting as "articulation, corporeal motion, and ocular expression" done in imitation of the "various mental and bodily emotions" incident to human nature. Tragedy held sway over "her empire of passions," defined in the *Essay* as "contractions and dilations of the heart," the correct interpretation of which could be judged in light of "reason, physics, and common observations." Here, Garrick's persona recommended that the actor make a particular study of the passions and humours of men in order to "discover the workings of spirit (or what other physical terms you please to call it) upon the different modifications of matter." His familiar mention of the idea that human nature was constructed by the operation of spirit on variously modified matter shows that Garrick had attained a working knowledge of interactive dualism with its mechanical overtones and, further, that he found it an appropriate issue to introduce into a short pamphlet on acting. In his analysis of the physiological manifestations of the emotion of fear in *Macbeth*, Garrick's persona marks out a position similar to that of Aaron Hill's taxonomic system. He hopes to address acting from a "scientific" point of view founded on "natural, metaphysical, and consequential deductions." When Macbeth kills Duncan, "his faculties are intensely riveted to the murder alone." This concentration of awed and terrified attention reacts on the entire body in a manner familiar to those versed in the mechanization of the passions. The sight of the daggers, the object or stimulus of the reaction, causes a kind of spasmodic paralysis of the limbs as the spirits rush to the head: "He should at that time, be a moving statue, or indeed a petrified man; his eyes must speak, and his tongue be metaphorically silent; his ears must be sensible of imaginary noises, and deaf to the present and audible voice of his wife; . . . every member, at that instant should seem separated from his body, and his body from his soul." When fear diverts the animal spirits away from the limbs, the spirit/soul cannot work upon the matter of the body, and the corporeal machine lurches to a paralytic halt. "Is it not in a purely mechanical way," La Mettrie asks rhetorically, having materialized the soul, "that the body shrinks back when it is struck with terror?" (*L'homme machine*, 131). To perfect Macbeth's ensemble Garrick even arranged to have his wig in disarray, although there is no evidence that he obtained Perkins's services at this time.

FIGURE 17. The mechanism of astonishment and dread. From Jelgerhuis, *Theoretische Lessen* (1827). (*Courtesy of Washington University Libraries.*)

Garrick knew about the application of the *homme machine* analogy to the actor. He spoke with evident scorn of those "automaton Players, who are literally such mere Machines that they require winding up almost every Time before they act, to put them in action and make them able to afford any pleasure to an audience."[40] It is hard to say at this distance what irritated Garrick more—the fact that these actors resembled automata or that they needed so much winding up. Garrick was noted for his extraordinary spontaneity, the suddenness of his transformations from passion to passion. Perhaps if his lesser brethren had recourse to Aaron Hill's inner Ideas or to the kind of outer, mechanical "working up a passion" described by Lessing, their offensive offstage rituals disturbed Garrick's equanimity as he waited in the wings and primed his wig. Yet at the same time, Garrick may have simply expressed the common-sense discontent with the limits of mechanism in defining what a great actor's body experiences as he performs. His colleague Noverre, whom he called the "Shakespeare of Dance," demonstrated a similar ambivalence. Although he cheerfully compared the *ballet d'action* to a machine in which the dancers are cogs, the solitary spectacle of purely mechanical technique left him cold: "When these parts [arms and legs] are managed without genius, . . . when [the artist] does not direct these different motions, and animate them by the fire of sentiment and expression; I feel neither emotion nor concern. The dexterity of the dancer obtains my applause: I admire the automaton, but I experience no further sensation."[41]

Garrick's jibe at automaton players and Noverre's preference for sensation born of "sentiment" and "fire" point toward an inescapable conclusion: mechanical philosophy contributed much to the eighteenth-century view of the actor, the actor's body, and the actor's expression, but it obviously failed to account for all the important facts. Its implications were not at all clear-cut: indeed, the same physiological principles could lead two commentators like Aaron Hill and Lessing to opposite positions on the process of embodying emotion. Moreover, mechanism taken alone could not explain enough of the available data to satisfy the best authorities. As a theory it was incomplete. A close reading of La Mettrie's *succès de scandale* discloses a similar inclination, despite his radical claims for man's bodily resemblance to musical instruments, Julien Leroy's repeater watches, or Vaucanson's flutist. Man may be a machine, but to La Mettrie he is not merely a machine, or at least not in the crude sense of a man-made automaton, however ingenious its inventor may have been. The *homme machine* does not exist as a dead mechanism, a spiritless statue pushed through space and time by invisible pressures. According to La Mettrie, man is a *machine vivante*, driven by self-sufficient motors.

The force that moves it lives inside it, is inseparable from it, and is indeed coextensive with it.[42] Some of the leading figures of eighteenth-century science struggled to isolate and define this force, which defied reduction to simple mechanical terms. From the push and shove of nerve against muscle, from the automatic reaction of matter to force, from the sudden contortions of the mechanical hairs on Garrick's head—something vital was missing.

3

Vitalism and the Crisis of Sensibility

It isn't as irritating to explain a phenomenon by means of some Mechanics and a big dose of the Incomprehensible, as to do so entirely by means of Mechanics.
—Georg Christoph Lichtenberg, *Aphorismen* (1775)

Pierre Polinière freely confessed his mystification. On one side of the dissection table he had placed the body of a frog that still showed signs of vitality. On the other side of the table he placed the frog's heart, which, even more perplexingly, continued to beat after it had been removed from the body. All the tubes connecting the heart to the brain had been severed. No animal spirits could exert pressure on the throbbing muscle. Nevertheless, as Polinière faithfully reports in the sixteenth experiment of his *Expériences de physique* of 1709, the heart's spasms persisted "for about an hour" following vivisection. Obviously, he could not explain this phenomenon by means of the paradigm of mechanical transmission available to him. He decided to withhold judgment for the time being in hopes that further experimentation would help him to penetrate "the admirable designs of the Supreme Being who acts in us, around us and far from us in the vastness of the universe."[1] Yet taking refuge in ancient panpsychism, against the rising tide of enlightened science, could not avert the coming crisis.

Even as Aaron Hill wrote his *Prompter* essays, experimental evidence mounted to prove inadequate the mechanistic model of tubes, spirits, and administrative glands. Outside the exalted system-building of philosophers, of course, naive vitalism never abdicated its reign over common sense: flesh just seemed to have a life of its own. This insight at

93

least offered a hypothesis capable of empirical inspection, which the non-extended ghost in the machine did not. As early as 1662, Francis Glisson, of the London College of Physicians, asked a heavily muscled man to flex his biceps while holding his arm immersed in a water-filled tube. This experiment proved that muscles do not increase in bulk when they contract, and Glisson therefore eliminated the infusion of animal spirits as a possible cause of such contractions. Also in the 1660s, Jan Swammerdam, the Dutch naturalist, showed through vivisection of small animals that the heart and other muscles retain their powers of motion and reaction even after they have been removed from the body and completely disconnected from the supposedly indispensable tubes. Swammerdam's *Biblia Naturae* did not appear until Hermann Boerhaave's posthumous edition of 1737–38, but popularizers of science like Polinière had replicated his results in public demonstrations and printed summaries: *Expériences de physique* had gone through five editions by 1741. The phenomena revealed in such widely known investigations obviously demanded explanation by more complex analogies than Descartes's comparison of a living body and its corpse to a ticking watch and a broken one (*Passions de l'âme*, Article 6). For men of science, the automata of St. Germain-en-Laye had neared the end of their metaphorical utility just as they entered the lexicon of drama critics. "The Similitude of a Machin put into Action and Motion by the force of Water convey'd in Pipes," concluded the physician and medical theorist George Cheyne tartly in 1733, "was the readiest Resemblance the *Lazy* could find to explain *Muscular Motion* by."[2] In pursuit of a less otiose solution, eighteenth-century science probed the anomalous space between dead mechanism and non-extended soul. The search was on for a model of body and mind that would account for an innate vitality, a capacity for sensation, motion, and response that was immanent rather than transcendent—in short, for a natural force that would supply physiologists and moral philosophers with an explanatory principle inhering to flesh as gravity inheres to matter.

How the results of that search impinged on theories of acting in the late eighteenth century is the question at hand. The pertinence of this scientific problem is obvious. If indeed each actor's flesh has an innate capacity for responsiveness, if his soul is simply a function of his physical organization, then the way a particular player embodies emotion would have to vary greatly from that suggested by the dualistic models proposed by adherents of the Cartesian system. To develop new explanations that could account for such responsiveness, theatrical theorists adopted the body of scientific and philosophical ideas now known as the doctrine of sensibility. Models based on hydraulic automata with their tubes and spirits gave way to models drawn from investigations into the behavior of electricity and acoustical vibrations. Such new analogies allowed the theorist to explain a demonstrable fact of theatrical life: the ability to act and to act well varies considerably from player to player. But the shift from mechanism to sensibility carried with it the seeds of yet another crisis, one that would not be solved by those who championed sensibility as a comprehensive and satisfying theory. That task would be left to Diderot, the theorist who, in Michel Foucault's terms, foresaw the main innovation of nineteenth-century science, the development of life as a mental category. For an understanding of the origins of the crisis of sensibility, however, we must turn once again to the example of David Garrick.

In his famous letter to Sturz on the acting of Mlle. Clairon, Garrick attempted to account for theatrical spontaneity without recourse to a transcendent soul. In the twenty-five years since *An Essay on Acting,* his vocabulary had changed significantly. In 1744 he had written of "the workings of spirit (or what other physical terms you please to call it) upon the different modifications of matter." In his critique of Clairon, penned in 1769, Garrick defines his own choice of "physical terms." He begins with an allusion to vivisection, the method then favored to explore the inner labyrinth of vital functions: "Your desection of her, is as accurate as if you had open'd her alive; She has every thing that Art and a good understanding, with great Natural Spirit can give her—But then I fear (and I only tell you my fears, and open my Soul to you) the Heart has none of those instantaneous feelings, that Life blood, that keen Sensibility, that bursts at once from Genius, and like Electrical fire shoots thro' the Veins, Marrow, Bones and all, of every Spectator." Some of Garrick's terminology shows the staying power of the ancient paradigm: "Life blood" refers to animal spirits; the flash of energy that leaps the gap between actor and spectator recalls the old Ciceronian fire. But the new paradigm is more forcefully in evidence. The reference to the "Electrical fire" that Clairon lacks clearly places Garrick's comments in the context provided by contemporary scientific investigations into the nature of electricity. Even more pertinently it foreshadows Luigi Galvani's theories of *animal electricity* (1780). Galvani discovered to his surprise that the contractions in the long muscle of a prepared frog could be triggered at a distance by sparks from a static electricity machine or even by flashes of lightning in the atmosphere. He concluded that nerves possess an innate fluid or current that can excite or be excited at a remove. According to Garrick, it was just such a power that Clairon could not command.

The heart of Garrick's criticism, however, resides in the word "Sensibility." He uses it to mean an inherent bodily capacity, differing markedly between individuals, that registers and communicates feeling. Spirit no longer merely works on matter, spirit emerges from a peculiar organization of matter. Such an organization possesses a non-reducible principle of vitality, the theoretical basis of *vitalism*. This is Garrick's first innovation in the letter to Sturz. The second is even less tentative and more revolutionary. In his view sensibility operates on a physical plane below conscious thought. Its existence, therefore, could not be explained in terms of the Cartesian dualism of cogitating ghost and insensate machine: "Mad^m *Clairon* is so conscious and certain of what she can do, that she never (I believe) had the feelings of the instant come upon her unexpectedly.—but I pronounce that the greatest strokes of Genius, have been unknown to the Actor himself, 'till Circumstances, and the warmth of the Scene has sprung the Mine as it were, as much to his own Surprize, as that of the Audience—" (*Letters* 2:635). To spring a mine means to ignite a massive explosive charge buried beneath the ground. In the military engineering of the period, mines were set off without warning in order to surprise the defenders under whose fortifications they had been surreptitiously placed. Garrick's colorful allusion marks an important development in the history of theatrical theory. Through it he introduces the concept of unconscious feelings as the cause of spontaneous expression. This distinctly modern deity may inspire with Delphic potency, but its sacred precincts are securely within the "Veins, Marrow, Bones and all."

Eighteenth-century theatrical theory makes sense only if we take into account the scientific paradigm of which Garrick's "Sensibility" is a part. This task is complicated by the burden of meaning that the word has acquired in conventional literary histories. Like *wit* before and *imagination* after, *sensibility* lent its name to the intellectual standpoint of an age. Scholarship has extensively explored and perhaps exhausted its moral implications—its well-known identification with those higher capacities of the tenderheartedness, refinement of sentiment, and expansiveness of imaginative sympathy associated with the man or woman "of feeling." This largely disembodied meaning stands behind our commonplace understanding of the drama or novel of sensibility, and we weep or laugh in its name when confronted by the minutely wrought states it has visited upon Clarissa Harlowe in deadly earnest or in jest upon Lydia Languish. Research on the relationship of science and literature in the eighteenth century, however, has uncovered important links between literary sensibility and its status as a neurological doctrine, the bailiwick of the physician rather than the philosophic divine.[3] As such, sensibility defined the terms of discourse in the neurophysiology and psychiatry of the Enlightenment, and it eventually revolutionized the language in which the actor's art was comprehended. As a property of the nervous system principally, it was called upon to express all the irreducible singularities of animate nature—its powers of reflection, its variegated responsiveness, its innate capacity for sensation and spontaneous action. In an *episteme* still dominated by physics, sensibility came to represent the vital principle.

On this subject it is most instructive to open Tom 15 of the Diderot-d'Alembert *Encyclopédie* to the rich sequence of entries, *Sens internes, Sensations, Sensibilité, Sentiment*. Significantly, this was among the volumes that Garrick, who boasted previous acquaintance with "all ye Authors of the *Encyclopédie*," urged his friend Suard to send him in 1766 (*Letters* 1:387; 2:524–25). The article headed "*Sensibilité, Sentiment (Médecine),*" signed by M. Fouquet, physician of Montpellier, takes up approximately twenty-seven columns to review contemporary knowledge of physical sensitivity. By way of contrast, "*Sensibilité (Morale),*" defined as the "tender disposition and delicacy of soul that renders one easily moved or touched," runs to only fifteen lines and those are airily vapid. Fouquet's article manages to intertwine hardheaded facts with rhapsodic enthusiasm. Sensibility is "the faculty of feeling, the sensitive principle . . . the foundation, cause, and preserving medium of life itself . . . the most beautiful and the most remarkable phenomenon in all nature." More concretely, he argued, sensibility grants organs the capacity to register an external impression and to move in response to the intensity of that impression. Fouquet's essay paralleled the contemporaneous work of Albrecht von Haller, the principal physiologist of the Enlightenment.[4] In *De partibus corporis humani sensibilibus et irritabilibus* (1752) and in his monumental *Elementa physiologiae* (1757–66), Haller distinguished between two intrinsic properties of tissue. *Irritability* he defined as the inherent contractibility of muscle fibres independent of the nerves. *Sensibility* he defined as the inherent responsiveness of tissues imbued with nerves. Other authorities fused both phenomena under the name of sensibility, but, terminology notwithstanding, the important point was that Haller had opened to experimental investigation a perceptible responsiveness intrinsic to animate creatures. Its relative strength could be measured in different parts of the body and in different kinds of tissue, in its variations from constitution to constitution, or in the same constitution under different conditions.

In one sense the implications of such an idea could lead easily to La Mettrie's atheistical conclusion. When Garrick evaluates Clairon in terms of "Electrical fire," he refers to a vital force inherent in the body itself. Soul in this scheme equals nothing more than its physical organization, its ability to respond to its surroundings. Mind consists of its brain and nervous system functioning under the influence of external and internal stimuli. But in another sense these ideas simply narrowed the terms of an increasingly uncontroversial medical proposition. As Jerome Gaub, Hermann Boerhaave's successor at Leiden and an international medical celebrity, put it in 1747: "The mind itself and the body, things generally held to be of entirely disparate nature, are so tightly and intimately knit when joined together in man that—if I may here speak as a chemist—they interpenetrate and dissolve in each other, so that while life flourishes, wherever there is mind there is body, and wherever body, mind. There is hardly to be found any smallest part of man in which something of mind and something of body, and in measure a mixture of both, is not to be observed."[5] In keeping with such principles, contemporary medical opinion resounded with new pronouncements on the interpenetration of flesh and spirit in the cause and cure of disease.

Mechanical physiology had itself initiated this movement in part by redefining hysteria as a nervous, rather than a visceral disorder. In his influential *Treatise on Madness* of 1758, William Battie (whence "bats" or "batty") developed the mind-body question into a clinical theory of insanity caused by "pressure [on] the medullary matter contained in the brain and nerves." Extreme pressure could be exerted by "tumultuous passions, *viz.* joy and anger," by "unwearied attention of the mind to one object," or by "the quieter passions of love, grief, or despair."[6] Battie addressed an audience already well acquainted with an extensive literature on the hysterical or hypochondriac diseases generally known as "the English malady" or "the Hyp." Every age has its fashionable diseases. In the view of brain and nerves prevalent in the eighteenth century, as students of Richardson and Sterne can attest, pathetic thoughts could be as deadly as the plague. The consequences of the fashion of psychosomatism, the devastation wrought on body by mind, were enshrined forever in the famous epitaph of the Dorchester lass: her "nerves were too delicately spun" to cope with the rude shocks of this world, and she therefore perished "a Martyr to Excessive Sensibility." In contrast to the uniformity and interchangeability of structure in the mechanical physiology of the passions, such a view of the body and nervous system implies that each constitution possesses a unique capacity or disposition to register feeling, some being inordinately sensitive, others hardly sensitive at all.

The terms *sensibilité* and *sentiment*, in their eighteenth-century meanings, were first incorporated into theatrical theory by Pierre Rémond de Sainte-Albine in *Le comédien* (1747). As author of a technical manual, *Mémoire sur le laminage du plomb* (1731), Sainte-Albine had demonstrated an early interest in applied science. In his treatise on acting, however, he was inclined to moralize *sensibilité* by equating it with "generosity of soul" and true "compassion."[7] *Le comédien* defends the extreme case for emotionality in acting. Although it maintains that the actor must possess a balance of attributes—understanding, feeling *(sentiment)*, fire, and figure—terms like *véhémence, extrême chaleur, feu,* and *enthusiasme* proliferate in his illustrations. Sainte-Albine interprets theatrical performance as an exhibition of the actor's personal moral fabric, his capacity not only for strong imaginative sympathy but for the truthful embodiment of high ideals. Without nobility of soul, the actor cannot play a hero. Without true buoyancy of heart, he cannot play comedy. This line of reasoning passes beyond the paradox of rhetorical *pathos,* in which the player should fictionalize yet embody his passion, and enters into the moral realm where sincerity attains the status of aesthetic beauty. Sainte-Albine hints that in order to play a love scene convincingly, the actor and actress should fall in love with one another or, at least, possess highly excitable natures and the power to fall in love with love.

The absurdity of these formulations has diverted Sainte-Albine's readers from the fact that he is really talking about an innate quality of the actor's body, his own characteristic ability to register feeling and sensation—*"designée communément sous le nom d'entrailles."* The actor must possess "the facility of making diverse passions succeed one another in the soul" (*Le comédien,* 32), and this is a faculty, a sensitivity, unique to the structure of his nerves. The actor's sensibility means his individual capacity for spontaneous responses to feeling.

Sainte-Albine's English translator, whose version appeared in 1750, put this issue into sharper focus. In searching for an equivalent to sentiment, he chose "sensibility," an individual's unique "disposition to be affected by the passions." He then claimed that this capacity inevitably "determines the force of the scene" and is therefore "of more consequence in playing than in any other profession" (*AA,* 126). English draws a fairly clear distinction between *sensibility* and *sentiment.* Sensibility is a capacity or inherent disposition: the readiness to respond to stimuli, the capacity for emotion as distinct from cognition or will, sensitivity to the pathetic in art and literature or to the feelings of others, and, interestingly, the sensitivity (reactivity) of plants or instruments of measure such as scales and magnetic needles. Sentiment means for the most part what Lord Kames took it to mean in 1774: a thought or feeling prompted by a passion *(O.E.D.).* Sensibility thus describes a capacity or disposition to respond to sensation, whereas sentiment describes the sensation itself. Sensibility is no more sentiment than a piano is music. The same discrimination is possible in French, though less insistently so: *sensibilité* means the quality whereby a subject is sensible to physical impressions—as in the sensitivity of optical fibers to light, of nerves to feeling, of a thermometer to heat; *sentiment* means first a faculty of feeling, of receiving impressions and, secondly, the passions, emotion, and affective phenomena in general *(D.A.F.).*

The translator's choice of "sensibility" for *sentiment* thus clarified a possible ambiguity of Sainte-Albine's usage. But it did far more than that. It brought theatrical theory in line with current science, in which vitalistic theories of bodily organization, assuming the innate capacity of matter to respond variously to stimuli, were complicating and transforming the mechanistic. This view challenged earlier theatrical theories of the passions by replacing the uniformity of the rhetorical significations or the general Cartesian templates with individual variations.

The identity of Sainte-Albine's translator explains the authority and precision with which he recast the original French. He was the remarkable Sir John Hill, M.D.—physician, actor, playwright, pharmacist, botanist, and prolific author on many scientific and medical topics. Popularly remembered to theater historians as "the second Hill" or as an irritating dilettante and quack herbalist, Sir John indulged in an early fling on the stage that poisoned his subsequent reputation. He selected his enemies with unusual carelessness, numbering Henry Fielding among them. He studied acting privately under Macklin and quarreled publicly with Garrick. When the several farces he submitted to the actor/manager failed to impress, Garrick replied with an epigram that has given historians an easy opportunity to dismiss Hill's theatrical and medical careers in a wicked couplet: "For Physick & Farces, his Equal there scarce is, / His Farces are Physick, his Physick a Farce is" (*Letters* 1:299).

Hill's reputation as a scientist, however, if not as a man of letters, has undergone a major rehabilitation. He was previously dismissed as a fraud and a quack: his *Sir* and *Dr.* were attributed to him in quotation marks— unjustly as it turns out, for both were authentic by the standards of the age. As "one of the best informed scientists of his day," Hill has now, however, been credited with priority in noting the link between tobacco use and cancer and with early applications of the compound microscope. In his *General Natural History* (3 vols., 1748–52), he introduced the Linnaean system of classification to England and coined the word *paramecium.* His monumental work in twenty-six volumes, *The Vegetable System, or a Series of Experiments and Observations Tending to Explain the Internal Structure, and the Life of Plants* (1759–75), won him international recognition and a knighthood from the King of Sweden. Hill extensively annotated the English translation of Boerhaave's edition of Swammerdam's *Book of Nature* (1758) and corresponded with Linnaeus, who recommended him to Albrecht von Haller. He also contributed to the Diderot-d'Alembert *Encyclopédie.*[8]

Although he left behind him wide-ranging commentary on geology, microscopy, optics, and pharmacy, John Hill's energies were principally absorbed in the study of what we would call the life sciences—botany, human physiology, and medicine. In this capacity he wrote *The Sleep of Plants and the Cause of Motion in the Sensitive Plant* (1757), which discussed the responsiveness of growing things to light and later gave Shelley the title for his poem. As a physician Hill brought forth *The Construction of the Nerves and Causes of Nervous Disorders* (1758) and *Hypochondriasis; A Practical Treatise on the Nature and Cure of that Disorder, commonly called the hyp* (1766), which showed his acquaintance with the medical literature on the neurology and pathology of sensibility, including works by Cheyne and Mandeville. All of this points to one obvious conclusion. Unusual authority and substance adhere to Hill's pronouncement in the introduction to *The Actor* of 1755: "Playing is a science, and is to be studied as a science" (12). His intention was clear: "to reduce to rules a science hitherto practiced almost entirely from fancy" and to do so for the benefit of both performers "in their attempts to attain perfection in it" and their audiences.[9] By the time he finished with the second version of *The Actor*, Hill had in effect written an adaptation that could stand as an original work.

The progress of scientific thought is rarely uninterrupted, however. Hill retained Sainte-Albine's four categories: understanding, sensibility, fire (spirit), and figure. When Sainte-Albine said that the actor should be transported beyond himself by the spirit of the passion he portrays, he looked back through Du Bos and seventeenth-century rhetorical theory to the *enargeia* of Quintilian and, beyond that, to the phantom of true inspiration, the possession of the rhapsode by the god. This was plainly the relic of a long-dead faith, and Hill uses this terminology even as he alters its implications. The actor of "true spirit" shudders with "the Promethean heat that animates": he "is no longer himself, when he assumes his character; he possesses himself that he is the king or hero he represents, and inspired by the sentiments of his author, and merely what his own mind conceives from the several circumstances and incidents, he lives, not acts the scene. He is the priestess of the Delphic God, who as soon as she ascended the sacred tripod, became possessed, and uttered with a voice and mien not her own, the sacred oracles" (*Actor*, 110–11). Apparently in the same spirit, Luigi Riccoboni, in his "Reflections upon Declamation" (Eng. trans., 1754), blithely advocated adoption of the ancient transcendence of self: "In order to succeed in [emotional expression] in some measure, we must first deliver the Soul from the Incumbrance of the Senses; an operation which, tho' violent, is by no means impracticable."[10] Riccoboni's baldly stated doctrine of "Enthusiasm" and

"Divine Madness," however, draws attention to the new twist that John Hill gives to the old idea: "All that the supposed celestial vapour, rising from the sacred ground, could do for this enthusiast [the priestess], the dignity of sentiment, and force of passion, execute for the player, who with his true perception, has in his nature this glorious heat" (*Actor*, 110–11). Spirit, like sensibility, is thus "in his nature"—something he possesses, not something that possesses him. On closer view, then, Hill's attribution of spirit to the flesh of the actor makes his point of view seem more at home in Haller's enlightened laboratory than in the precincts of Delphi.

Evolving from the rhetorical concept of *enargeia*, energy thus began to take on its modern meaning in the eighteenth century. As Geoffrey Carnall explains, mid-century aesthetic theory engaged in a "quest for energy" marked by the "prevailing interest in vivid impressions." The quest for ever more intense sensation gave the world Beckford's *Vathek* and pointed the way for the Marquis de Sade, but the pursuit of energy and vividness had its "most convincing application in the context of theatre and oratory rather than in the written word." Some feelings were thought to be too sublime for words, certainly for the printed word, and expressible only in vital gesture and countenance. The clear reason for this was the physical proximity of the spectator to the actor, whose innate mental energy, like Garrick's "Electrical fire," could shoot outward and inflame all hearts within the radius of his flashing eyes. As the terms of Garrick's letter to Sturz suggest, such a theory coincides approximately with the discovery of electricity as an unplumbed and all-pervading natural force, "still mysterious, but gradually becoming understood" through the work of Franklin and Priestley.[11] Like sensibility, this capacity for conducting energy was thought to be peculiar to each body, fluctuating under varying conditions.

John Hill combined several of these ideas, in somewhat more old-fashioned trappings, when he wrote of the power of a great actor's "fire" over the imaginative sympathies of his spectators. Speaking of the "sparkle" in the eyes of Spranger Barry's Othello, however, he flirts briefly with the ancient theory of "spirits" communicating from eye to eye, but settles on the metaphor of nervous vibrations as the method of physical transmission: "we not only see the character thus before our eyes, but we feel with him . . . the very frame and substance of our hearts is shaken . . . we swelled and trembled as he did; like strings which are so perfectly concordant, that one being struck, the other answers, tho' distant" (*Actor*, 10). Thus, communicating the physical force of his passion to his audience, the actor can both burn and vibrate with feeling. The same sort of eclecticism, though without the allusions to pagan mysteries and celestial vapors, marks John Hill's pivotal explanation of sensibility, the nervous capacity whereby the vibrations of the passions are registered on the mind and body and without which energy would be meaningless.

Sensibility dominates *The Actor.* Of the two hundred and eighty odd pages, nearly one hundred are devoted to sensibility or closely related topics. Hill defines it, in terminology familiar to the medical writers and physiologists of the period, as the "disposition to receive those impressions by which our own passions are affected." He states as obvious the fact that "some men possess this in greater, some in a lesser degree, and some scarce at all" (49). The variegated responsiveness of the nerves will naturally dispose an actor to play some characters and not others, depending on the predominating passion of the role. Quirks of native sensibility can thus limit the actor's range, even if that range is by twentieth-century standards almost unthinkably broad: "In those characters where rage prevails, Mr. Garrick, who is as naturally violent as Mrs. Cibber is melancholy, finds it very difficult to make the transition from anger to sorrow, as may be seen in several parts of Jaffeir: and in the same manner, Mr. Barry, whose natural tendency is to elegant distress, finds it as hard to pass from that to anger in some parts of the same character" (65). John Hill evidently thinks of the passions as states in transition from one to another, like notes in a scale, for which certain instruments have certain keys.

There exist, however, actors who possess what Hill calls a "general sensibility" (61). Obviously, the actor whose nervous system permits the experience of all varieties of sensations owns a decided advantage over the actor who can embody only a narrow range of particular feelings. The perfect player, Hill believes, "should be susceptible of all emotions, and of all equally; he should be able to express all, as well as to feel all in the same force; and so to make them succeed to one another ever so quickly; for there are characters which requires this" (59). Mrs. Pritchard was supposedly one of the happy few to enjoy this paradoxical "ductility of mind" (60–61), a distinctive personal capacity to obliterate her own personality.

True sensibility, general or particular, is therefore inborn; it is a trait and, in its highest reaches, a gift; but Hill believed that it can be improved like a garden. His method of cultivating sensible responses stands out as perfectly representative of the prevailing psychology of his age. Hill recommends stimulating and raising the nerves to an exquisite pitch of excitement by reading at random from a work of the literary sublime. The *Oedipus Rex* of Sophocles in the original would serve very nicely for this purpose, but for the actor without Greek, John Milton's *Paradise Lost* will do as well. The sensible Miltonist should steal away into "a perfect

retirement, and with a mind divested of all other thoughts" (96) read from
the poem *ex tempore;* then,

> Let him give himself up without restraint to the emotions he feels on
> this occasion, and without addition, or abridgment, throw everything
> into action. To observe every minute article of this, were as contempt-
> ible as to practice attitudes in a glass: But let him repeat and encourage
> the whole; and by a practice like this, he will fall into a way of giving a
> loose to himself upon the stage, on the like occasions. The action and
> expression will arise from the occasion, unstudied, unpremeditated,
> and as it were natural to him; and being natural as well as great, it will
> affect every body: And this is the character of true sensibility.(97)

Here is Dr. Gaub's view of mind and body, which "interpenetrate and
dissolve in each other," expressed with clarity and force by a like-minded
physician writing on acting. Here is a method whereby spontaneity, of
the sort Garrick vainly sought in Clairon, may be rehearsed. Hill presumes the readiness of the nerves to resonate when struck by Ideas, to
retain impressions of the original sensation, and to transform these mental impressions into muscular motions. The use of the association of ideas
to promote authentic emotion dates back at least to Quintilian, but John
Hill's revival of the old concept depends on contemporaneous theories
behind what he calls "the character of true sensibility."

The term *sensibility* with its suggestion of the properties of organism
sounds familiar to modern ears; in fact it reflects the scientific doctrines of
an age in which *life* did not yet exist. Nowhere is this point more evident
than in the widely held opinion that all sensation is caused by acoustical
vibrations in the nerves. The acoustical model provided all mental operations—memory, imagination, association—with a new, revised mechanical basis. John Hill used this model when he explained that the actor
and his audience are such "perfectly concordant" strings "that one being
struck, the other answers, tho' distant." Approximately twenty years
before, Aaron Hill had touched briefly on a similar idea when he drew an
analogy between an actor's body and a stringed instrument: "The passions are . . . what the keys are in a harpsichord. If they are aptly and
skillfully touched, they will vibrate their different notes to the heart and
awaken in it the music of humanity" (*Prompter,* no.64, 80). The acoustical metaphor of vibration, when applied to the nerves as strings, retains
the theory of the mechanical transmission of nervous impulses and could
therefore be invoked by even so steadfast a mechanist as Aaron Hill. By
implication, however, such a metaphor supplants the increasingly unten-
able concept of a hydraulic or pneumatic push of animal spirits through

hollow tubes. An English medical tract of 1730, Bernard Mandeville's *Treatise of the Hypochondriack and Hysterick Diseases*, put the matter to the test of simple observation: "The Nerves, through which [animal spirits] are supposed to flow, are not hollow, made like Pipes. . . . They are solid Bodies like Strings."[12] The theory of nervous vibrations also answered a crucial question of eighteenth-century science: as a modern historian of psychology has put it, "What sort of mechanism would make it the general rule that sensation would not disappear instantaneously upon the removal of its object?"[13] Obviously, a string continues to vibrate indefinitely after its plectrum has been struck.

The father of vibrations as a principle of nerve physiology was no less an authority than Isaac Newton, who, in an appendix to *Opticks*, suggested that vibrations in the aether, acting on the retina and brain, produce the sensation of light, just as vibrations in the air, acting on the inner ear, cause the sensation of sound. His model was not so crude as to present the nerves themselves vibrating like piano strings. Rather, he thought that the motion occurred at the subvisible level of ethereal particles oscillating within the nerve filament. Newton extended his idea of sensory vibrations to include motor functions as well,[14] and it was a short step from motor and sensory vibrations to the emotions. Everyone at one time or another has felt himself shaking with anger or trembling with fear, as if strong feeling literally vibrated through his frame, and Newton's followers could draw the obvious inferences from such commonplace experiences.

The use of an acoustical analogy to describe the physiology of the passions was not in itself new. Thomas Wright, in the *Passions of the Minde* (1604), evoked musical vibrations quivering through the air like ripples in a pond to explain how music first ravished the body and then the soul of the listener. He went on to compare the passions in the actor's soul to "the wind a trumpeter bloweth in at one end of the trumpet." The outward significations of the passions in the actor's body he likened to the resonance of the instrument itself (174). Although seventeenth-century authors favored images of bodily and vocal eloquence based on wind or brass instruments, those in the eighteenth century showed a decided preference for strings—violins or harpsichords. In his essay "Of the Passions," comprising Book 2 of *A Treatise on Human Nature* (1739), David Hume explains why this should be so: "Now if we consider the human mind, we shall find, that with regard to the passions, 'tis not of the nature of a wind-instrument of music, which in running over all the notes immediately loses sound after the breath ceases; but rather resembles a string-instrument, where after each stroke the vibrations still retain some sound, which gradually and insensibly decays."[15] Although

Wright's contemporaries rejoiced in trumpet-tongued eloquence and Hume lived at a time when the passions were more exquisitely bowed, the essential difference remains the contrast between mechanism and sensibility: vibrations in decay explain how feeling can recede gradually after its stimulus has been withdrawn—something that push or blow fails to do—because the inherent responsiveness of the nerves allows them to continue to register an external impression even after the stimulus is withdrawn. Newton recalls that he perceived a burning coal whirled through the air not as a point of light in motion but as a line. Surely, he reasoned, the subsiding vibration in his optic nerves caused his brain to retain an after-image of the coal as if curved along its trajectory, a delicate nervous tremor growing fainter by imperceptible degrees until it finally vanished from the threshold of consciousness like a dying note.

The physiology of vibrations proved remarkably durable in theatrical criticism. As late as the second edition of Henry Siddons's adaptation of Engel's *Ideen zu einer Mimik*, published in 1822, what Hume called the "fine vibrations of the passions" were cited as the most plausible physical bases of the actor's emotion.[16] The Victorian drama critic George Henry Lewes employed a similar idea to support his notion of "subsiding emotion," the litmus test for tragic passion to which he subjected Edmund and Charles Kean. More recently, Peter Brook has offered a version of the same analogy in language that would have been perfectly intelligible to Newton, Hume, or their theatrical contemporaries: "Acting begins with a tiny inner movement so slight that it is almost completely invisible. . . . Not only in actors—the movement occurs in anyone, but in most non-actors the movement is too slight to manifest itself in any way: the actor is a more sensitive instrument and in him the tremor is detected."[17] The pervasiveness of such vibrations, particularly in British theory, may be traced back to one principal root—the influential work of the eighteenth-century psychologist David Hartley.

Hartley's *Observations on Man, His Frame, His Duty and His Expectations* (1749) was perhaps the first book in English to use the word *psychology* in its modern sense. In it he wed Newton's vibrations to the doctrine of the Association of Ideas derived from John Locke's *Essay Concerning Human Understanding* (1690). In providing a contemporary and fundamental philosophical premise with a corporeal basis, Hartley could offer both mental and physical explanations of such phenomena as memory, imagination, habit, and emotion. Associationism posits that complex mental experiences are built up from simple Ideas derived from sensations. When associations between Ideas are reinforced by repetition and juxtaposition, complex networks of thinking and feeling develop. Hartley's innovation was to include muscular motion and emotion in this scheme—to transform empiricist epistemology into a version of psychophysiology. George Henry Lewes, in his *History of Philosophy,* identified Hartley's system "as the first attempt to explain psychological phenomena on physiological principles."[18] Hartley defined mind and body as separate but exactly parallel entities. Vibrations that have occurred frequently together tend to recall one another and the mental Ideas associated with them. When sensate vibrations subside, they leave behind impressions of themselves, a tendency to fainter vibrations, called "vibratiuncles." These impressions on the brain represent the origin of simple Ideas. They dispose the nervous system to miniature vibrations, echoes, of the same kind. Passions are aggregates of Ideas, traces of experienced pleasures or pains, reinforced by repetition and linked by association. Hartley's associations occur in what Thomas Hobbes was the first to call "traynes"—concatenated sequences of experiences, set in motion by an initiating vibration or Idea: "Any Vibrations, A, B, C, &c. being associated together a sufficient Number of Times, get such a Power over a, b, c, &c. the corresponding miniature Vibrations [vibratiuncles], that any of the Vibrations A, when impressed alone, shall be able to excite b, c, &c. the Miniatures of the rest."[19] Sensations and muscular activity can therefore excite memories, and memory can similarly set in motion a train of physical actions. A sensation, an Idea, or a muscular movement induces the sensation, Idea, or muscular movement with which it was formerly associated; then that brings along another.

Though he makes no specific use of Hartley's terminology, John Hill assumes the parallel association of physical and mental events.[20] If he did not know *Observations on Man* firsthand, he derived its essential concepts from the literature on nerve physiology with which he was certainly familiar, indeed some of which he was the author. In Swammerdam's *Book of Nature,* for instance, the opus that Hill supplied with annotations for English publication in 1758, the interrelationship of trains of images and sequences of spontaneous muscular actions is made explicit: "It is plain, that as our memory is local, and is assisted by the image of one thing in passing to that of another, and so on without end, the contractions of our muscles are in like manner natural; and the muscles themselves are urged by one cause of motion to another, and from this to a third, and so on without any interruption."[21] In this view imagination affects the body in an unconscious mode similar to psychosomatic disease. Mind creates physical symptoms with apparent spontaneity. According to Dr. Hill, when the actor gives way to sublime "sensations"— his use of this word is itself significant—he will "find his mind enlarge, and, as it were, dilate itself." Simultaneously, "he will find, as he gives way to the emotions these sentiments or several forms of sensibility require, his face, his features, and his person thrown into forms and attitudes of expression" (*Actor*, 98). Aaron Hill's mechanical imagination has here been reworked to conform to the behavior of a sensible instrument, a spontaneous physical vitality whose metaphors would seem to us derived more naturally from botany than from mechanics.

Furthermore, imagination in David Hartley's scheme consists of disordered memory. Flights of fancy interrupt the established associative sequences, and, as it were, mix up the cars of the train of thought, placing them in unprecedented, though still contiguous relationships. Memory and its decaying vibrations make the cars in this train run in the order in which they were originally experienced; imagination reorders them to form new combinations and sequences. This view portrayed a passion as a sequence of vibrations or Ideas—parallel lines of mental and physical experience—running through time, structured by memory and association, reordered and intensified by imagination. Hartley's associationism thus indirectly explains why John Hill, in his science of acting, would pack his actors off to the study to read Sophocles and Milton. Nerve-strings once plucked by the muse of poetry resonate long after the initial touch has been felt. Strong Ideas endure indefinitely as slowly vanishing but revivable traces, like those dark corridors that mark the passage of ships through the sea after their wakes have subsided. They can be of use to the actor, however, only when they have been forgotten and rendered unconscious. Then, the subvisible vibrations of the nerves, fading echoes of the sublime, amplified *impromptu* by the pressure of the moment, burst forth in an intensely palpable emotional discharge. To John Hill such outbursts of sensibility are exalted simply because they are "unstudied, unpremeditated" (*Actor*, 97). "Those instantaneous feelings . . . that keen Sensibility," as Garrick termed the source of such events, occur at or beyond the margins of conscious reflection or memory.

Hartley's model of the imagination thus allows for distant vibrations to awaken unbidden Ideas. A machine-soul dualist like Aaron Hill, whose "imagination" and "flexible fancy" consist of consciously willed mental events, could find little room in his theory to accommodate Garrick's testimony that the actor could surprise himself by his own psychic explosions. Read closely, John Hill's doctrine of sensible spontaneity offers a more satisfying explanation. Having once felt the enormous pressure of the Miltonic sublime against its nerves, the sensitive actor's mind

> will take in sensations which he was before unacquainted with, and for which there is no name. . . . These he is to encourage, and tho' in the immediate way of his profession he will never have occasion to use exactly any of these, because exactly the same circumstances will never

occur to the character, yet he will have formed and accustomed himself to expression in general, by the gesture and countenance; and without his studying the particular mode of it for any passage, some great, or at least proper attitudes and looks will always arise from the occasion; . . . [his expression] will be unconstrained, the effect of natural emotions, not artifice; and it will have another great perfection, it will be varied and appropriate; for it will rise out of the occasion, and be different under every circumstance. (*Actor*, 98–99)

Though Hill does not use the analogy drawn from warfare that Garrick found so expressive when writing to Sturz, his point is the same: unconscious and unconstrained emotions are the source of the most impressive theatrical explosions. In this matter Dr. Hill swam with the current of his age. In 1776 David Hume argued that outward behavior is directed by a "species of instinct . . . that acts in us unknown to ourselves." Similarly, the ubiquitous Lichtenberg was fascinated by the fabulous creations that his dreams could inspire, and he celebrated the way in which "unplanned wandering around, unplanned strokes of feeling often catch the wild animal which carefully planned philosophy can use in its careful husbandry."[22] Like Hill's reference to "natural emotions," Lichtenberg's interest in the "wild animal" typifies the strain of vitalism that became more prominent as the eighteenth century reached its last decades.

In the 1760s and 70s, the contest between artifice and untamed nature also epitomized the increasingly obvious anomalies inherent in the doctrine of sensibility. Like a present-day battle between land-developers and environmentalists, its opposition of aims and methods was so complete that rational discourse, much less compromise, sometimes seemed impossible. The model of acoustical vibrations might invite the aspiring actor to depend upon his constitutional powers to feel and therefore to represent feeling, but the fact was that such theories simply did not correspond to the ways in which other, admittedly accomplished actors went about their business. This anomaly was the source of Clairon's ongoing and widely celebrated rivalry with Marie-Françoise Dumesnil.

This conflict of style and temperament reached its apogee at the court performance of Racine's *Athalie* in 1770 when legitimate artistic differences provoked cabal and counter-cabal. As often happens in a lively theatrical debate of head versus heart, the superficial terms of the debate concealed a much more interesting substratum of assumptions about the creative process and the nature of consciousness itself. When the two rivals finally met face to face to air their differences, Dumesnil cried "Nature!" as often as Clairon could hiss "Fiction!" (*AA*, 177–78). Clairon's *Memoirs* seem to confirm Garrick's surmise about the conscious nature of her art. Her creations took shape in architectural stages

as her memory and imagination assembled the history, moral temperament, and physique of her character. She was proud to compare her
meticulous craftsmanship with the art of academic history painting, in
which the final overall effect depended on the building up of details in
careful steps. Clairon stated that in calculating his role, the actor must
"repeat a hundred and a hundred times the same thing, in order to sur-
mount the difficulties he meets with every step" (*AA,* 172). Conversely,
Dumesnil wanted it known that her passions entered her spasmodically,
instantaneously. She scorned the calculations of her rival as pedantry. She
set three goals for the actor: "To imbue oneself with great emotions, to
feel them immediately, and at will to forget oneself in the twinkling of an
eye" (*AA,* 175). Unsurprisingly perhaps, authorities granted her the eva-
nescent power of stunning effects, but concurred on the inequality of her
performances. Sensibility, so fervently touted by commentators like
Sainte-Albine and John Hill, was at root a theoretical problem, not a
solution.

In England the remarkable case of Susannah Cibber illustrated in one
actress the paradox of the Clairon-Dumesnil controversy. Contemporary
opinion was sharply divided on the role played by spontaneous sensibility in Mrs. Cibber's acting. She was primarily known to the theater-going
public for that "sensibility which despised all art." Theatrical puffs and
the sensational publicity surrounding her personal life certainly served to
cultivate this image.[23] To the inner circle of theater folk, however, Susannah Cibber's feelings seem to have been regarded as a tabula rasa on
which a series of tutors—including Colley Cibber, Georg Frederick
Handel, and that indefatigable automatophile, Aaron Hill—inscribed detailed lessons for her to memorize obediently. The great Handel willingly
pounded out notes for her because once she had the aria in her head, no
voice could jerk tears from an audience like Susannah Cibber's. To prepare her properly for performance, however, required mind-numbing
drill. Aaron Hill annotated the margins of her part in his play *Zara* with
an entire shorthand of the passions. As he later promised another potential disciple, "I will interleaf your part, if you send it to me, and make
room for the necessary notes upon the passions" (*Works* 1:156). Susannah Cibber evidently made plenty of room, and her patience for drudgery
was likewise capacious. Word by word, line by line, every movement,
pause, and intonation was coached and reiterated by Hill until the part
was her own to perform automatically.[24] Hill had greater success with this
pupil than with his nephew. The record shows that the general public left
the theater having accepted Mrs. Cibber as a *natural,* one whose sensibility flowed unprompted from a suffering heart. If Hill, in his role as the
Prompter, ever heard such comments as the pit emptied, his thoughts can

only be imagined. The gulf between theory and practice, between what the audience thought they saw and what the actress had done, demonstrates one of the several anomalies presented by the question of sensibility.

That question continued to vex eighteenth-century theatrical criticism with all factions claiming Garrick as exemplar and champion. John Hill, as one critic among many, singled out Garrick's spontaniety of transitions as a quality more actors should emulate if they could. Garrick possessed not only "the power of feeling" but the power of "instantaneously changing one [feeling] for another" (*Actor*, 68–69). On such "points" eighteenth- and nineteenth-century actors were applauded with show-stopping ovations of the sort now heard only in an opera house after a thrilling aria. Particular tumult accompanied a well-defined transformation from one passion to its opposite—love to rage, rage to joy, joy to grief. John Hill defined this capacity as a "ductility of heart" (64). Dumesnil herself could not have seized on a happier phrase to describe spasmodic sensibility—at its extreme a kind of peripeteia of local affects, bringing about an instantaneous change from one passion to its opposite. When the Ghost of Banquo suddenly rose before Garrick's Macbeth, reviewers were awed by the actor's instantaneous transition from the placid good cheer of the banquet to blood-curdling horror. During his visit to Paris in 1763–64, Garrick astonished the regulars at the *salon* of Baron d'Holbach by poking his head out from behind a screen to demonstrate the passions in rapid-fire succession. Baron Grimm thought these transitions in his features sprang from the depths of his feelings.[25] Diderot, who was also present, went on to develop quite different conclusions from the same exhibition.

As the ancient rhetorical paradigm continued to disintegrate, confusion increased. Robert Lloyd in *The Actor* (1760), attempting to apostrophize Garrick's sensibility, stumbled instead into a revealing contradiction:

> 'Tis thine to lead with more than magic Skill,
> The Train of captive Passions at thy Will;
> To bid the bursting Tear spontaneous flow
> In the sweet Sense of sympathetic Woe.

> (*PA*, 262)

Lloyd's selection of metaphors could not be less apt to express his aversion to prior calculation. His evocation of a train of captive passions led by skill and will hardly sustains the word *spontaneous* in the way he meant it. Searching for an underlying principle to resolve the contradictions in his account of the player's passion, Lloyd reverted to the most ancient explanation of all: "No Actor pleases that is not *possess'd*" (*PA*, 263).

But in Lloyd's poem, as earlier in Polinière's laboratory, animistic mysteries redolent of Delphi had simply exhausted their relevance. They were cultural atavisms, fossil relics extracted from an earlier historical stratum. Nor could superstitions about the soul continue to offer useful explanations. Once mind and body came to be viewed as intimately intertwined if not identical, medical or theatrical theorists could no longer use soul as a conveniently transcendent repository to which difficult questions could be referred and forgotten. They could not talk of it as something magical or otherworldly, as Riccoboni did when he suggested that the actor's soul should be liberated from his senses in order to induce divine madness. Nor could they detach it from the bodily machine, as Lessing and Aaron Hill had done. Mind was now part of the actor's physical instrument, subject to the same physical laws, limitations, and vital weaknesses as his body.

Viewed in terms now used by historians of science, theatrical theory in the mid-eighteenth century showed clear symptoms of a crisis. The positions of the leading theorists—Sainte-Albine, Aaron Hill, John Hill, Riccoboni—showed internal contradictions that ran counter to the very scientific premises from which they took their initial justification. For all their elaborate physiological descriptions, Aaron Hill and the mechanists, represented by dozens of treatises cataloguing the passions and their appropriate expressions, had ignored or suppressed an important passage in *Les passions de l'âme*, Article 46, entitled "The reason which prevents the soul from being able wholly to control its passion." Here Descartes described the slowness with which the strong passions, once stirred, relinguish their grip. This tends to make hash out of imaginative ductility. Garrick's portrayal of astonishment in *Hamlet*, his grand pause, fit the provisions of Article 46 nicely, but the sustained rapidity of his celebrated transitions in other roles did not fit them at all.

John Hill himself admitted that sensibility, once engaged, might easily "interrupt [the actor's] delivery, and his whole frame shall be so disturbed, that he shall not be able to pronounce the words articulately" (*Actor*, 54). Persons who vividly experience strong passions, argued David Hartley, are subjected to increased "vibrations" that are "associated in an unnatural manner. . . . Violent passions must therefore disorder the Understanding and Judgment, while they last." Moreover, as a matter of medical concern, "violent Fits of Passion" so "transport" those who suffer them that "they shall not be able to recover themselves" (*Observations on Man*, 398–99). Indeed, in his medical tract *Hypochondriasis, A Practical Treatise* of 1766, Dr. John Hill followed the prevailing

opinion that excessive indulgence in the sensible affections, far from reinforcing healthful ductility, tends to obstruct the organs. According to
both logic and popular belief, the most sensitive persons are the most
vulnerable. "The Hyp" glowers as a very real threat to sensible actors
who let their imaginations run riot with their feelings. In discussing "The
Causes of the Hypochondriasis," Dr. Hill gave an opinion that might
have legitimately alarmed an actor who has been closeted with his *Paradise Lost,* force-feeding sublimity into his nerves: "Real grief has often
brought [the Hyp] on; and even love, for sometimes that is real. Study
and fixed attention of the mind have been accused before. . . . This has
contributed too much to it; but of all other things night studies are the
most destructive. The steady stillness, and dusky habit of all nature in
those hours, enforce, encourage, and support that settled gloom, which
rises from fixt thought; and sinks the body to the grave; even while it
carries the mind to heaven."[26] Such a comment would seem particularly
chilling to the actor who was expected to enhance his powers of feeling
through solitary night studies. Dr. Hill seems to have had one kind of
advice for actors and another for the patients under his care—a disturbing
and perhaps literally fatal contradiction in his theory. The leading medical
authorities concurred with Hill on the pathology of heightened sensibility. At the same time theatrical theorists and actors joined Hill in promot-
ing it as a universal acting technique. The crisis provoked by this anomaly
was best summed up by Diderot. In a celebrated passage in his *Paradoxe
sur le comédien,* which he began in 1769 as a reply to the French translation of John Hill's *Actor,* Diderot enumerated the manifold symptoms of
nervous disorder. These he associated with acute sensibility complicated
by "vivacity of imagination." His etiology was worthy of Cheyne's *English Malady,* Battie's *Madness,* or Mandeville's *Hypochondriack and
Hysterick Diseases.* He singled out "delacy of [the] nerves" as the affliction that inclines the sensible soul "to fear, to being upset, to tears, to
faintings, to rescues, to flights, to exclamations, to loss of self-control, to
being contemptuous, disdainful, to having no clear notion of what is true,
good, and fine, to being unjust, to going mad" (*PC,* 43). This problem
was one sign of a more general crisis: given the nature of the body, true
emotion and artistic expression of emotion did not seem compatible.

According to Thomas Kuhn, a scientific revolution cannot occur in the
absence of two crucial preconditions. First, the existing paradigm must
show signs of failure to explain emerging data—significant signs and
failure widespread enough to precipitate a crisis in normal science. A
classic instance of such a crisis and its eventual resolution is the "scandal"
of Ptolemaic astronomy that was centuries old when Copernicus announced his revolutionary views.[27] Secondly, another paradigm must pre-

sent itself as a substitute, for the scientific imagination tends not to disregard a set of commonplace assumptions acquired over a lifetime, indeed sometimes the wisdom of centuries, without having a viable alternative, a clearly more satisfactory means of explanation, readily at hand. Thus, in theatrical theory ancient doctrines of inspiration, more old-fashioned than Ptolemaic epicycles, persisted into the 1700s and beyond. As the contradictory and incomplete theories of the mid-eighteenth century suggest, a satisfactory alternative explanation of the player's passion had yet to emerge, but the problem of spontaneity and sincerity as opposed to calculation and artifice had entered into a new and crucial stage of contention.

This historic moment was both precipitated and complicated by a proliferation of scientific data, an unknown quantity of which was pertinent to the actor's body and its emotions. Medical physiology seemed to suggest that the art of acting was potentially lethal, an assertion disputed, though not flatly contradicted, by the facts. Garrick's enormous reputation in Europe—swelled by his Parisian visit of 1764—intensified an air of crisis by challenging theorists to establish a definitive explanation of acting while the definitive actor lived. By the time John Hill's *The Actor* had been translated back into French by Antonio Fabio Sticotti as *Garrick, ou les acteurs anglois* (1769), a kind of information explosion, small by modern standards, but nonetheless substantial, had taken place in the sciences relevant to theatrical issues like sensibility. From 1747, when Sainte-Albine brought out *Le comédien*, to 1770, when Diderot reviewed Sticotti's *Garrick* for Grimm's *Correspondance littéraire*, a number of important works had been published or existed in manuscript in the right hands. In addition to the works of Hartley, Haller, and La Mettrie, these included Georges Buffon's *Histoire naturelle* (1749), Robert Whytt's *Essay on the Vital and Other Involuntary Motions of Animals* (1751), Condillac's *Traité des sensations* (1754), Charles Bonnet's *Essai analytique sur les facultés de l'âme* (1760), and various works by Diderot, particularly *Le rêve de d'Alembert* (1769), the *Eléments de physiologie* (1765–c. 1778), and the great reference work compiled under his supervision, the *Encyclopédie* (1751–72).

So a plethora of information emerged in the 1760s, complicating and deepening the bases on which an alternative theory of acting could be founded. But of this new learning what specifically was pertinent to the actor and what irrelevant? To sort things out required a thinker who knew the theater and knew actors but who also had easy access to current developments in science. To this end he would need a thorough grounding in art criticism because, as we have seen, the aesthetic issues there intertwined with the theatrical ones in several important ways. Further, he would have to possess not only an extraordinary breadth of learning, but a rare synthetic imagination, an ability to see the puzzles of one discipline in light of the solutions of another. Finally, this thinker would need an enlightened freedom from the historic bias against actors, a sense of the dignity and social necessity of acting as a profession, the goal of which was a truth far less trivial than sincerity. He would have to believe that actors were, above all, artists whose excellence was worth understanding in the light of science. The coexistence of all these attributes in one man seems highly improbable; that such a man would happen to come forth at this convenient juncture in time seems even more unlikely, but a genius like Diderot creates his opportunities as often as he capitalizes on them.

4

Diderot

I challenge anyone to explain anything without the body.
—Diderot, *Eléments de physiologie* (c. 1774)

Perusing at leisure the magnificent volumes of the *Encyclopédie, ou Dictionnaire raisonné des sciences, des arts, et des métiers,* the reader must come to revere at least two of Diderot's capacities as editor-in-chief. First, the intimidating range of ideas treated by the various contributors never overwhelmed him; rather, it seemed to exhilarate his philosophical sense of the continuity amid the diversity of knowledge. Second, he somehow managed to find out how almost everything worked—forges, clocks, tanneries, windmills, knitting machines, artillery, choreographic notation, dry docks, surgical instruments. In so doing, he revealed how the craftsmanship that makes civilization possible defined its processes, techniques, problems, materials, tools, and even its jealously guarded professional secrets. In any field of endeavor, things may be done poorly or they may be done well. The *Encyclopédie,* particularly in its twelve volumes of plates, sought to illumine what excellence meant to master craftsmen in every specialty; moreover, it demonstrated to laymen that such mastery did not arise mysteriously from a source in the magical occult, but from professional skills knowingly applied. As artisans strove for mastery over nature, the pursuit of underlying truth linked science to craft, as in the application of mechanical power to practical tasks, and it linked both craft and science to the fine arts, as in medical illustration or stage machinery. The latter instance provides a most piquant contrast: in the previous century certain ingenious theatrical designers attracted the attention of the Inquisition on suspicion of sorcery; now their "secrets"

116

stood fully exposed in precise technical drawings still unsurpassed in their clarity and explanatory value. After its demystification in the pages of the *Encyclopédie, le merveilleux* could be numbered among those useful arts whose professionalization benefited all mankind.

Diderot's seminal role in the development of acting theories stemmed directly from the attributes he displayed as an enlightened encyclopedist. An appreciation of professional craftsmanship, an understanding of processes and media, and an underlying vision of the ways in which science can illuminate art, all found expression in his famous pronouncement on acting, *Le paradoxe sur le comédien* (1773). This work has generated a substantial bibliography,[1] and it has done so in part by establishing itself as the paradigmatic text in its field, as Newton's *Principia* and Lavoisier's *Chemistry* did in theirs. Such a suggestion, which at first sight may seem grandiose, becomes increasingly plausible as investigation discloses the network of theoretical discussions prompted by Diderot's essay after its publication in 1830. To this day many acting theorists, knowingly or unknowingly, formulate their views in response to perspectives introduced in the *Paradoxe*. Foremost among them is its stand on the notorious question of emotionality. Like John Hill, the Riccobonis, Lessing, and Sainte-Albine, Diderot asked himself if the actor should sincerely feel the passions he portrays onstage. Unlike their answers, however, Diderot's firm negative had the power to revolutionize acting theory as surely as it scandalized actors. As he proposed in his blunt thesis, "extreme sensibility makes middling actors; . . . in complete absence of sensibility is the possibility of a sublime actor" (*PC*, 20). By construing the art of acting in light of his vitalistic materialism, Diderot synthesized the vitalistic and mechanistic explanations of the actor's body. He alternatively sustained and provoked both parties by using metaphors derived equally from machinery and organisms. The *Paradoxe* also left behind a sufficiency of open-ended questions or anomalies for subsequent investigators to explore. Among the concepts originating in or at least taking their modern form in Diderot's essay are emotion memory, imagination, creative unconsciousness, ensemble playing, double consciousness, concentration, public solitude, character body, the score of the role, and spontaneity. Above all, we owe to Diderot our concept of the actor's art as a definable process of creating a role. As the most fully informed philosopher ever to have addressed the art of acting, he knew that character emerges directly from the nervous system of the actor; it is not an Apollonian phantom entering the actor from without. Every theorist since Diderot has had not only to confront this issue but to do so on the *philosophe*'s terms.

How, then, did Diderot come to write such a pivotal work? To answer that question, we must understand how the *Paradoxe* evolved from his awareness of current developments in physiology and his own attempts to construct a psychology from those developments. In studying Diderot, however, one can never isolate a single strain of his thought as if he himself had conceived of the issues that fascinated him in terms of distinct and separable disciplines. As we shall see, the premises that became central to his scientific thinking emerge clearly in his art criticism. Furthermore, Diderot achieved what he did as a theorist by applying his scientific principles unflinchingly, by approaching acting as a craft rather than as a diabolic or sacred mystery, and by adhering strictly to the interconnectedness of truth as he saw it extending from one discipline to another. He pursued this truth even when it forced him to abandon some of his most deeply held convictions about the nature of the creative process. Previous theorists had used physiological models to illustrate the capaciousness of the actor's means of expression; Diderot became the first to explain, in light of the science of his day, how nature had placed certain limitations on those means through the internal structures of the body itself. As his autobiographical excursuses frequently make clear, his heightened awareness of his own physical constitution was the starting point of his inquiries.

More than most works of abstract theory, the *Paradoxe sur le comédien* provides a forum for the author to expose his anxieties, actual or assumed, about his own character. Impulsive, violently sentimental, prone to sudden outbursts of generosity or tears, Diderot, like Cyrano in his indebtedness to Cervantes, seemed to pattern his world on that of a novel and to imagine himself as a Richardsonian hero. He depicted himself as a frequent loser in a lifelong tilt at the windmill of his sensibility, that susceptibility to profound feeling he upheld as a sign of higher morality and lamented as a personal affliction. His biographers draw a compelling portrait of Diderot's sociability, his studied but fundamentally credible pose as the Good-Natured Man; his intellectual self-abandon extended from his lovers to his friends, even to innocent passersby, and often overflowed like a "gusher that has blown its top."[2] On these copious and volatile nerve endings, erotic excitability exerted an exquisite pressure. In the *Paradoxe* itself, the interlocutor "First," Diderot's spokesman, characterizes himself as the *homme sensible*, who is occasionally betrayed by a "weakness of the diaphragm" into behavior that passes beyond any kind of control. He presents himself as the sort of fellow who blurts out absurdities to the girl he desires, while his cold-blooded rival murmurs sweet hypocritical nothings and enjoys the prize. Characteristically, Diderot narrates these self-deprecatory anecdotes in the present tense, infusing them with the air of loquacious immediacy one expects from a letter or a confession. He repeatedly plays off the man of feeling, himself, against men of calculated self-control, his calmly victorious antagonists. We share in his confusion, when, after the triumph of Sedaine's *Philosophe sans le savoir,* he runs through the wintry Parisian night, tears stinging his face, to fling himself unashamedly upon the author, who responds to his exhilaration with cool self-possession and deflating irony. We share also in his exasperation when a sensible spasm chokes him in the midst of a vigorous literary debate with Marmontel, causing him to lose the point by default, only to inspire a perfect riposte when his equanimity returns—moments after leaving the *salon.* Diderot seems to remain convinced about the goodness of his heart, but emotional susceptibility has reduced his thought to the status of a hiccough or a blush. In such passages the word *sensibility* resonates through increasingly complex layers of meaning, ascending from the rudimentary responsiveness of the nervous system to the highest plane of human sympathy and moral imagination.

Like many other critics before and since, Diderot in his early career reflected the ideas he encountered in the hyperbolic mirror of his own artistic identity. As late as the 1760s, he championed sensibility as an integral constituent of the creative process. His belief centered on two interrelated propositions: that art exists to serve a higher moral purpose and that moral vision is inseparable from sensibility. Susceptibility to passion and goodness of heart coexist in his view as mutually sustaining virtues. "Yet it is only the passions, and the great passions," he wrote aphoristically in the *Pensées philosophiques* (1746), "that can raise the soul to great things" (*AT* 1:127). Art elevates the soul by intensifying feeling in both the creator and the beholder, but feeling in Diderot's lexicon implies physical sensations, excited impulses from which the bubble of eroticism inexorably arises. This complex intertwining of emotional stimulus, amorous sensation, and moral response underlies Diderot's art criticism. He reveals much when he fulminates against the uncomplicated pornography of Boucher's nude portraits of the royal mistresses and adulates Greuze for his sentimental picture showing a girl weeping for her dead bird. Diderot admires the emotional content of the latter for its moral earnestness, but he is also physically attracted to the sweetly modest virgin crying tenderly over the body of her pet. The attraction is so strong in fact that he imagines himself climbing through the picture frame and striking up an acquaintance with the girl as he solaces her loss. Moral sentiment and eroticism fuse as life penetrates art.

The fancied violation of "une jeune fille qui pleure son oiseau mort" is only one of many instances in which Diderot interpreted psychological drives in physical terms, which sexuality both symbolizes and embodies.

Before the change of heart that preceded the *Paradoxe,* he believed, like Sainte-Albine, that the physical experience of an emotion is an essential part of the creative activity of every artist—poet, painter, dancer, or actor. According to the suggestions he posed in the *Entretiens sur le fils naturel* (1757), emotion in artistic creation constitutes a physical necessity that can be defined only by explicit analogy to sexual response. In the "Second Entretien" the character Dorval itemizes the symptoms of rapture. When he fixes upon a striking object in nature, his "passion" begins to consume him

> by a shudder that starts from his chest and moves, deliciously and rapidly, to the extremities of his body. Soon it is no longer a shudder; it is a strong enduring heat that inflames him and makes him pant, consumes him, kills him, but which gives spirit, life, to everything he touches. If this heat were to increase further, spectres would multiply before him. His passion would rouse itself nearly to the state of madness. He would know relief only by pouring out a torrent of ideas which crowd, agitate, and chase one another. (*AT* 7:103)

Though he seems to reiterate ancient bromides about divine inspiration, Diderot in fact describes a physical experience of mental events far less impersonal than the penetration of the rhapsode by the god. His acute awareness of the body and its individual tremors, tensions, and reflexes predominates over the magic of any spirit from without. Passions are embodied, not inspired. Dorval's Muse seems to have taken up permanent residence between his solar plexus and his perineum.

Diderot's tendency to interpret the spirit by means of the flesh naturally reinforced his encyclopedic curiosity about new developments in the life sciences and medicine. Very early in his career his curiosity launched him on a course of scientific study that would eventually alter his views on aesthetic questions. He translated Robert James's three-volume *Medical Dictionary,* which advertised extensive articles on "Anatomy, Chymistry, and Botany, in all their branches relative to Medicine." To prepare himself properly for this task, he attended public courses in anatomy and physiology. A parallel interest in physics led him to produce *Mémoires sur différens sujets de mathématiques* (1748), which included well-informed essays on musical acoustics, the mechanics of vibrating chords, and the resistance of atmosphere to pendulums with reference to Newton's theory on that subject. His early acquaintance with Condillac's Lockean psychology, in which man is imagined as a lifeless statue awakened by the incremental addition of each of the senses, led him to write two wide-ranging scientific and psychological speculations based on the absence of specific senses, the *Lettre sur les aveugles* (1749) and the *Lettre sur les sourds et muets* (1751). In the wake of the scandal caused by the publication of La Mettrie's *Homme machine*, Diderot demonstrated his interest in eighteenth-century elaborations of Cartesianism, the application of mechanics to physiology: alluding to animal spirits and the pineal gland in his comic novel, *Bijoux indiscrets* (1748), Diderot claims playfully "that three-quarters of men and all women are merely automatons" (*AT* 4:247, 252). Provisionally at least, notes Aram Vartanian, "Diderot accepted at face value the key argument of La Mettrie's *Homme machine*."[3]

Diderot's mechanism, however, remained open to a broad range of influences, particularly the emerging testimony and experimental evidence in support of vitalism.[4] While imprisoned in 1749 at Vincennes for the irreligion of his opinions, Diderot annotated his copy of Buffon's recently published *Histoire naturelle*. He specifically underscored that prodigious author's concept of the *molécule organique*, a vitalistic atom anticipating the cell as the basic building block of higher forms. Diderot acquired a materialistic belief in the dynamism of nature, a conviction that matter has inherent properties of sensation and motion, which crystalized in his *Pensées sur l'interprétation de la nature* (1754). In this fundamental work he argued for "transformism," an evolutionary scheme of human origins that claims that over "millions of years" simple matter "has passed through an infinite number of successive organizations and developments; that it has acquired in turn movement, sensation, ideas, thought, reflection, conscience, sentiments, passions—signs, gestures, sounds, articulate speech, language—laws, science, and arts" (*AT* 2:57–58). Among the many captivating innovations in this passage, Diderot places the passions and arts on the highest rung of the evolutionary ladder, a refreshing reversal of the usual presumption that modern man has emotions in common with animals, art in common with troglodytes, and scientific reason all to himself. That Diderot would rate the passions above reflection and conscience in the refinement of evolutionary organization demonstrates the importance he attached to sensibility at this stage in the development of his thought. In his article "Bête" for the *Encyclopédie*, he rejected the Cartesian animal-machine as he subtly undermined the idea of a transcendent spirit: to say that animals have no soul, that they cannot think, and that they are mere machines is as insupportable as to say that men whose language we do not understand are automata. Man and beast have sensibility in common. It exists as a potential form of energy in all matter. Properly organized, it is spontaneously released into its kinetic form—vitality. At its highest level of organization, it constitutes the consciousness of geniuses. Sensibility has a moral dimension, which Diderot never denied, to be sure, but at this point he regarded it, in its most highly wrought and sensitized form, as truly indispensable in the physical organizations of creative artists. His position was an immensely sophisticated version of Sainte-Albine's. In the *Entretiens sur Le fils naturel,* published within four years of the *Interprétation de la nature,* he generalized Dorval's spasms into a universal principle: "Poets, actors, musicians, painters, first-rate singers, great dancers, tender lovers, truly religious men—all that enthusiastic and passionate troop, feels vividly and reflects little" (*AT* 7:108). Like Nature herself, they are vitally spontaneous.

During the 1760s Diderot changed his mind—not about nature, but about art. As the result of a deepening revelation rather than a mysterious self-contradiction, he substantially modified his opinion on the subject of sensibility. He came to believe that an actor should not attempt to experience onstage the emotions he enacts. Considerable speculation and controversy have attended Diderot's late substitution of head for heart as the mainspring of theatrical emotion. Theater historians have professed bafflement: "Why did Diderot reverse himself? Nobody knows."[5] In fact, a confluence of forces intensified his skepticism about his former views. Important among these was the growing sophistication of his art criticism, which, following years of close communication with artisans as he compiled the *Encylopédie,* prompted him to reassess the role of technique in the creative process. Certainly significant also was his contact with David Garrick, whose virtuosic demonstrations greatly stimulated his speculations into the inner nature of acting.[6] Finally—and decisively—there were his increasingly absorbing inquiries into physiology. In the actor, Diderot found a concrete instance of the keystone of his emerging philosophy of nature, the coupling of mind and matter, feeling and form. As with most other episodes in Diderot's intellectual life, these various strands intertwined around no one particular center, but they initially found their way into his seminal dialogue on genius and mediocrity, *Le neveu de Rameau* (1765).

Unlike the *Paradoxe,* in which a flattened personality lies down before Diderot's monolithic First, the two interlocutors in *Le neveu de Rameau* are seemingly endowed with the tangled psychological textures of life itself. Critics are challenged to do justice even to their salient qualities, which, like the rich themes of the dialogue, shift and double back upon themselves with protean agility.[7] LUI, nephew of the famous composer, himself a failed musician, frequenter of the drawing rooms of the not-so-great, immoralist, leech, and stupendously gifted mime, engages in conversation with MOI, the disapproving but utterly fascinated *philosophe,* perhaps Diderot's stand-in, perhaps LUI's double, perhaps an ego to his id. Their conversation ranges from morality to art, from language to education, from social performance to individual identity. LUI is subversive, vulpine, biding his chances; MOI is probing, relentless, the observant encyclopedist, reserving his judgments for the cross-references—a midwife to the free interchange of even the most disgusting ideas. The entire dialogue—which has been produced as a play—resembles an impromptu theatrical entertainment staged by LUI for the edification of MOI and for the incidental diversion of the chess players in the Regency Café, who now and then look up from their games to laugh at the sweaty antics of Rameau's nephew, who, in turn, welcomes the opportunity to take the ape's revenge on the visitors surrounding his cage.

Like the oracles of the Delphic Pythoness, LUI's antic disposition is subject to the inspiration of the moment. His gestures, thoughts, and sequences of pantomimed action burst forth in sudden flurries. They are spontaneous, furious, sublime. His entire nature is impromptu: "I say whatever comes into my head—if sensible, well and good; . . . I have never in my life thought before speaking, nor while speaking, nor after speaking."[8] Like the actress Dumesnil, LUI takes the stage uncertain of his part. In all endeavors from chess to theater, he frankly admires the inspired move. He claims to despise anything mechanical or calculated:

Myself. What of M. de Bissy?
He. Oh that one is to chess what Mlle. Clairon is to acting: they know about their prospective playing all that can be *learned.*
(11)

True to his own standards, LUI's sycophantic visitations to the homes of his patrons are minor masterpieces of instantaneous self-invention. He can burst like a thunderclap, whine like a lap dog, or whip up whatever buffoonery the lady of the house desires. He is used to being ruled by whim. MOI's chance presence in the Café inspires LUI to fabulous feats of spontaneous pantomime, including a sound-and-action rendition of an entire opera, featuring solos, recitative, accompaniment, instrumental ensembles with properly mimed playing, and choruses. The one thing he does not introduce into his whirling profusion of musical fragments is a score: he makes that up, as he goes along, out of the musical detritus of his age. As his improvisation gathers itself into a crescendo, LUI waves his arms, runs about the room, dances all the solo parts as well as the *corps de ballet,* and then, foaming at the mouth, he utterly abandons himself in a pantomimic ecstasy:

The heat was stifling and the sweat, which, mixed with the powder in his hair, ran down the creases of his face was dripping and marking the upper part of his coat. What did he not attempt to show me? He wept, laughed, sighed, looked placid or melting or enraged. He was a woman in a spasm of grief, a wretched man sunk in despair, a temple being erected, birds growing silent at sunset, waters murmuring through cool and solitary places or else cascading from a mountaintop, a storm, a hurricane, the anguish of those about to die, mingled with the whistling of the wind and the noise of thunder. He was night and its gloom, shade and silence—for silence itself is depictable in sound. He had completely lost his senses. (68).

Following his orgasmic exertions, LUI is semi-comatose. Like Dorval, he has found relief in the effusion of a torrent of ideas. He awakens by stages as if from a deep trance. His body twitches, and he speaks uncomprehendingly to the laughing faces grouped around him, asking them if anything is the matter—have they seen something odd? His mind retains no memory of the spectacle that his body has imagined. Eventually he adds, as if by way of explanation, "This, this merits the name of music. . . . We want the animal cry of the passions to dictate the melodic line" (68–69).

LUI's melodic line or score, if it can be called that, comes off the top of his head, or perhaps his lungs, for by tradition divine madness puffs up the thorax as the locus of the soul, inspiriting the *praecordia*, or diaphragm, with the delicious breath of the gods. Pricked by the more formal challenge of composition—the solitary, arduous, trial-and-error creation of a score—LUI's bubble of genius bursts: "When I take my pen by myself, intending to write, I bite my nails and belabor my brow but— no soap, the god is absent" (78). When the god is absent, the melodic line dies. This, then, is the essence of LUI's musical mediocrity: he can create brilliant fragments, sublime moments, but he cannot deliberately compose a score. He exudes himself without a plan. Like the "Changeling Proteus" of an earlier time or one of Dr. Hill's paramecia, he is imprisoned by his very fluidity in a shape without a structure. LUI detests his uncle, the true genius, whose self-possession has transcended the spasm and attained composition. In this dialogue, the two relatives stand in revealing opposition to each other, as Clairon and Dumesnil did on the stage. In the nephew's physical and psychological fabric, a flaw nullifies his considerable gifts. Some integral component of the genius is missing from him, the part that would allow him to transform impulse into process. The epitaph he writes upon his moral nature, which Diderot characteristically expresses in corporeal terms, also sums up his artistic mediocrity: "My fiber is loose, one can pluck it forever without its yielding a note" (71).

The similarity of spontaneously inspired passion to mental illness must have struck Diderot as he perused contemporary medical literature on sensibility and the intricacies of the mind-body relationship. When Dr. Jerome Gaub described a man under the influence of strong emotions (*De regimine mentis,* 1747), the principal symptoms he enumerates could be applied to the crisis of LUI's operatic pantomime and to its catatonic aftershock: "How unlike itself is every part of his body, how devoid of control is his mind! Countenance, color, and deportment are changed, the bodily motions are altered, there are unbidden movements of the muscles, involuntary movements and uncontrollable tremors."[9] As Diderot's deism matured into atheism, the last threads binding his thought to the ancient doctrines of inspiration dissolved. Divine madness without the gods is just plain crazy. But as he pondered the predicament of Rameau's nephew, Apollo's musical pawn, he was also at work framing a materialistic solution to the problem of the creative process in his wide-ranging *Salons.*

Beginning in 1759 his contact with painters and sculptors challenged him repeatedly to reflect on the role of technical and mechanical processes in shaping creative energies to attain premeditated effects. As he visited the studios of the artists whose works he reviewed, his respect redoubled for the orderly procedure of bringing a work of fine art to fruition from preliminary life drawing to finished artifact. He wrote of the many beauties never seen by the museum-goer—the beauties attendant upon process, not product—that emerge and recede momentarily as the artist labors over his materials. In contemplating this process, Diderot frequently returned to the question of mimesis—how does the artist imitate nature, how does the beholder partake of that imitation? He concluded that true art does not really create an imitation of reality at all, but rather an illusion of reality. Each artist casts this illusion by skillfully selecting details from observation or memory, recombining them in his imagination, and then finally expressing them in the materials of his chosen medium. Diderot called the product of the intermediate stage, after the inspiration but prior to the final execution, the *modèle idéal.* This phrase has usually been literally translated as "ideal model" or "type," correctly conveying a sense of Diderot's allegiance to the neoclassical commonplace of art improving on nature. That certainly gets at part of his meaning, but only the least interesting part. *Modèle idéal* may be more suggestively rendered as "inner model," implying not only a refinement of nature, but the creation or collection of diverse images to form a picture in the mind of the artist. Diderot himself elsewhere employed the

term *modèle intérieur* to distinguish it from the painter's exterior model
(*AT* 12:128). According to this view, when the artist executes his project
in stone or on canvas, he merely copies the magnificent model he sees in
his mind's eye. The illusion must first be created or collected with all the
detail of an architectural blueprint before it can be materialized, brought
out into the open, to be viewed by the beholder. The executive phase
requires immense technical skill and meticulous craftsmanship—as does,
say, putting up a building—but the true act of artistic creation exists in
imagining the original model.

Diderot explained the process clearly in his pedagogical remarks to an
imaginary audience of art students in his *Essais sur la peinture* (1765), a
kind of mock-academic recapitulation of what he learned in writing the
journalistic *Salons*. In the chapter entitled "My Eccentric Thoughts on
Drawing," he proposes an unusual technique for rendering the nude
figure. After offering the conventional advice that the draughtsman strive
for an illusion of dimensionality and vitality, he breaks with tradition
when he suggests that this illusion should be founded on the artist's
imaginative experience of the mechanical operations of the body he depicts. Diderot would direct the mind's eye to the inner springs of potential motion rather than the superficial pose:

> Try to imagine, my friends, that the whole figure is transparent, and to
> place your eye in the middle; from there you will note all the outward
> play of the machine, you will see how some parts expand, while others
> contract, how some swell as others collapse, and, continually engaged
> with a complete whole, you will succeed in showing in the part of the
> object that your drawing shows, all the due correspondence with the
> unseen part, and, showing me only one side, you will nonetheless force
> my imagination to see the opposite side also,—and then it is that I will
> cry out that you are an astonishing draughtsman. (*AT* 10:466–67)

Here Diderot defines the nature of illusion. He views the task of the artist
as perfecting a double illusion—first in his own experience, then in the
beholder's. The artist imagines himself into the center of a body that does
not belong to him or to any one living person; he creates a body by
studiously combining his observations of the outward actions of others
and by remembering the inner feelings and external effects caused by his
own muscular efforts. In science or in art, Diderot believed, the investigation of natural phenomena requires both subjective and objective
methods, an alternation of concentration from information registering on
the senses to inner reflection; in short, a combination of observation and
introspection. "Creative persons," he wrote elsewhere, generalizing
across all disciplines, "have this distinctive character trait. . . . They

discover [ideas] now by plunging into the depth of their own selves, now by looking outward onto the external world and casting a more attentive and penetrating glance at the natural objects surrounding them" (*AT* 14:436–37). Writing about the epistemology of draughtsmanship in his "Eccentric Thoughts on Drawing," Diderot carried over into aesthetics his physiological premise that the body is a machine endowed with vital properties of motion and consciousness. In advice ostensibly intended for young painters, but really more meaningful for actors, he stressed the study of the body in action in time and space rather than the body in repose in space alone: "Every attitude is false and little; every action is beautiful and true" (*AT* 10:466).

The obvious applicability of the inner model to the actor's bodily art links the *Salons* to Diderot's changing ideas on theatrical emotion; in fact, in the *Salon de 1767* he goes so far as to attribute to David Garrick a concise summation of the theory of the *modèle idéal.* Garrick had appeared on the Parisian scene during the winter of 1764, dazzling the *salons philosophiques* with his performances of monologues from Shakespeare, including the dagger scene from Macbeth, and his methods of expressing the rapidly fluctuating physiognomy of the passions. Garrick established himself as a principal specimen of artistic genius among the luminaries of Diderot's circle, including Holbach, Helvétius, Grimm, Suard, d'Alembert, Morellet, and Marmontel.[10] He became the central exhibit in their taxonomy of genius, a natural phenomenon to be studied for clues to the general workings of nature. Whether the views put in Garrick's mouth by the *philosophe* actually belonged to him remains a matter of conjecture, but Diderot's skill in utterly transforming the chance remarks of his contemporaries and acquaintances into masterfully elaborated dialogues on aesthetics and science had already produced *Le neveu de Rameau* and would shortly bring forth *Le rêve de d'Alembert.* His penchant for imaginary conversations may have done some disservice to biography, as d'Alembert and Mlle. de Lespinasse hotly contended in urging him to destroy the manuscript of the dialogue in which they appeared, but it certainly did enliven his theoretical exposition. Two years before he wrote the preliminary draft of the *Paradoxe,* Diderot had "Garrick," appearing as himself in the *Salon de 1767,* buttonhole the hapless Chevalier de Chastellux to press home the following advice:

Garrick. However sensitive Nature may have made you, if you act only after yourself, or after the most exact real nature that you know, you will be nothing but mediocre.
Chastellux. Mediocre! Why so?
Garrick. Because for you, for me, for the spectator, there is a cer-

tain possible ideal man who, in the given circumstances, would be affected very differently from you. This is the imaginary being whom you must take for your model. The stronger your conception of him, the greater, the more rare, marvellous, sublime you will be.

Chastellux.   Then you never are yourself?

Garrick.   I take good care not to be. Not myself, Chevalier, nor anything that I exactly know around me. When I rend my heart, when I utter inhuman cries, it is not my heart, they are not my cries, but those of another whom I have imagined and who does not exist.

(*AT* 11:16–17)

Perhaps it is not too fanciful to hear in this exchange between an overwhelming Garrick and a conveniently pusillanimous Chastellux an anticipation of the protagonistic "First" and choric "Second" in the *Paradoxe sur le comédien*. More certainly, "Garrick's" idea that the actor should not play himself, a trivial personage, but rather a model character he has invented out of his imagination grew into Diderot's dominating thesis on the art of acting, effectively supplanting the spontaneity of Dorval's intimately personal spasms with the craftsmanly reenactment of premeditated illusions. In the example of Garrick, Diderot saw the possibility of translating LUI's inspired pantomime into a form and structure that would allow the artist to repeat his creation exactly. At this point Diderot might have been content, as many others have before and since, to establish a more compromising theory of stage performance, one that could accommodate a balance of spontaneous emotionality and calculated craftsmanship, of heart and head; but in order to do that he would have been compelled to suppress the latest theories on the relationship between the body, the mind, and the natural force called sensibility. That was not the sort of thing the encyclopedist could easily bring himself to do.

Beginning in 1765 Diderot began collecting materials for a massive project that he never completed, but to which he gave the working title *Eléments de physiologie*. In its modern edition it runs to nearly four hundred pages divided into three parts: "Living Beings," "Elements of the Human Body," and "Mental Phenomena." The third section includes chapters on "Sensation," "Understanding," "Memory," "Imagination," "Will," "The Passions," "Organs," and "Illnesses." His purpose seems to have been to write a summation of the current knowledge of the body with particular emphasis on the physical nature of mental phenomena.[11] To that end he made notes on his wide reading and organized them into chapter headings, while adding his own running commentary. Although his efforts to bring forth a physiology of the mind may indeed have been "historically premature," the *Eléments* represents a practical, handbook-like counterpart to the great speculative dialogue on nature, evolution, and reproduction, *Le rêve de d'Alembert*, which he completed in 1769.[12] The *Eléments* continued to grow by accretion throughout the next decade, overlapping the several revisions of the *Paradoxe sur le comédien*, which was begun as a book review in 1770, greatly expanded and put in dialogue form in 1773, and finally completed in perhaps 1778. In fact, the three works—the *Eléments*, *Le rêve de d'Alembert*, and *Le paradoxe sur le comédien*—conceived so closely together in time, may be usefully interpreted as a triptych, each taking the human body as a central theme, but probing its mysteries from the different perspectives of practical physiology, speculative biology, and the aesthetics of theatrical creation and expression.

In the first of these endeavors, Albrecht von Haller played the part of Diderot's principal informant on technical matters, his steady point of reference in a complex and rapidly evolving field of inquiry. Early on, the *philosophe* knew Haller's *Primae linaeae physiologiae* (1747; translated in 1752 by Pierre Tarin as *Eléments de physiologie*), and the title of the last section of his own *Eléments* also echoes that of the last volumes of Haller's *Elementa physiologiae corporis humani* (1757–66). The twin Hallerian concepts of irritability (contractibility) and sensibility pervaded Diderot's thinking on body and mind, but, unlike Haller, Diderot did not distinguish sharply between them. In his view they coexist as the life force, an inherent property of living tissue, a property so fundamental that it survives in the individual parts of the body for some time after the death of the whole. At its most primitive, sensibility represents the central fact of vital organization, of animal motion, of matter in ferment, and of the spontaneous flux of evolving forms. It mediates between the creature and his environment and is crucial to both his survival and his behavior (*Eléments de physiologie*, 21).

On theological questions Diderot parted company with the devout if perplexed Christianity of Haller, for the *philosophe*, following La Mettrie, brought his atheistical materialism directly to bear on his study of the body, which he continued to regard as a mechanism, albeit one with a vital organization. Not only did he define the human body as a machine, but as a machine whose ghostly operator he tried to deny or shrink by ridicule to the point of meaninglessness. Duality of body and soul struck him as a superstitious chimera: "What difference is there between a sensible living watch, and a gold watch, or a watch of iron, silver or brass? . . . If the union of a soul with a machine is impossible, show me. If it is possible, tell me what the effects of this union would be. The peasant who sees a ticking watch, and who, unable to understand its inner mechanism, invests its hands with a soul, is neither more nor less foolish than our spiritualists" (*Eléments*, 60). However deep and thoroughgoing his attribution of vitality to matter, he thus continued to explain the functions of the organism, animal and human, in mechanical terms and urged his view of the *homme machine* in the same breath with which he invoked sensibility as a vital principle. This apparent contradiction between mechanistic and vitalistic modes of thought diminishes when viewed in the context of Diderot's determinism, which defined human will as the mere aggregate of bodily functions and impulses. An act of will without a physical cause does not exist. "Sensibility," he noted, "is more powerful than will" (21). In fact, pain, pleasure, passions, imagination, instinct, the functioning of the organs, and especially habit—for *l'habitude* was very significant in his physiology—"all give orders to the machine," which obeys them automatically (262).

Diderot's image of the human body as a virtually soulless machine possessing vital drives but not will had inescapable implications for his views on questions of emotion, expression, and the creative process. Having done away with the nonextended rational soul of Descartes, Diderot could see no virtue in retaining its principal agents, the tubes and animal spirits, and he cast them aside in favor of more modern-sounding nerve *fibres* (*Eléments*, 87–99). In the poetic terminology of *Le rêve de d'Alembert*, he defines consciousness by comparing the mind in the body to a spider in its web, sensitive to the slightest tug of the smallest filament. Such subtle vibrations convey impulses along the nerves.[13] After the ghostly operator had been exorcised from the interlacing fibres of La Mettrie's machine, however, what remained behind offered Diderot a much less tidy model than Descartes's. He conceived of a complex vital mechanism pulsating with great generating power, but offering no assurances of its manageability. Diderot's concepts of mind, reflection, habit, and particularly will were far less potent than the rational soul as agents controlling the nervous system. "The nerves are the slaves, frequently the ministers, and sometimes the despots of the mind," he wrote in carrying to an agnostical conclusion Article 46 of Descartes's *Passions de l'âme* on the incomplete mastery of the soul over the passions: "Everything goes well when the mind commands the nerves; everything goes wrong when the rebellious nerves command the mind" (*Eléments*, 90). Passions are not created by design in a well-ordered system; they emerge under the pressures of the evolutionary transformation of matter endowed with vitality.

Emotion, according to Diderot, is therefore a state of increased excitement caused by a general rebellion of the nerves. In fact, he comes close to defining passion as nervous activity that has passed beyond the threshold of control to reach a state of general chaos and destructiveness:

grief "agitates the strands of nerves in a violent and destructive manner" (*Eléments*, 267); "violent outbursts of passions can corrupt the bodily fluids"; extreme episodes may also result in fainting, rashes, diarrhea, or catatonia (270). Rationality and self-possession inevitably yield before the inexorable pressure of strong feelings: "Whenever the sensation is violent . . . we feel, we scarcely think at all, and still less are we able to reason. . . . It is thus when we are in awe, in sympathy, in anger, in fear, in pain, or in bliss" (239). These involuntary perturbations resemble the shudders of an untended, runaway machine. Once set in motion, passions build up a head of steam; they must run their course, and no voluntary interventions will influence physical events that must obey their own predetermined laws. These laws operate throughout the entire body, but Diderot found them most emphatically demonstrated by what he had reason to believe was the physical center—the diaphragm.

Albrecht von Haller devoted his earliest physiological research to the structure of the human diaphragm, and his views on the importance of this organ as a plexus of sensibility found a most sympathetic and responsive audience in Diderot. The *philosophe* also found that his personal intimations were independently and objectively sustained by Buffon, who, in his comparative anatomy of carnivorous animals, attributed to the diaphragm a decisive role in sensibility.[14] "The diaphragm is the center of all our pains and all our pleasures," Diderot concluded, ratifying the locus of pagan inspiration but not its cause, through "its liaison, its sympathy with the brain." The brain and the diaphragm "are the two great springs of the human machine" (138), one propelling the mechanism of thought, the other of feeling. The conspicuous, psychophysiological sympathy between the diaphragm and the mind may be felt vividly and inexorably: "If his diaphragm contracts violently, a man suffers and is saddened; if a man suffers and is saddened, his diaphragm contracts violently" (289–90). Pleasure and pain are in fact merely two different movements of the diaphragm (37); joyous feeling makes it expand, while dolor makes it contract. In the average person these fluctuations cannot be readily suppressed. In extreme circumstances this mind-body mechanism operates so powerfully that it can even cause fatal complications, or so Diderot believed.

Applying the concept of diaphragmatic sensibility to ethics and aesthetics yielded divergent conclusions. The "mobility" of the diaphragm tends to make men "compassionate" (*Eléments*, 138) and to extend the range of their sensible affections and moral sympathies. On the other hand, it sharply limits their powers of self-control and judgment and therefore dooms them to a life of "mediocrity," to a crippling paralysis of their means of creative thought and expression. This mediocrity besets

LUI in *Le neveu de Rameau,* though he also lacks the consoling benefits of goodness of heart, and in the *Salon de 1767* the pseudo-Garrick warns against it with special reference to the actor. The spastic diaphragm confines the strivings of those affected to the perimeters of their own trivial bodies, to their merely personal emotions, and it narrows the imaginative aperture through which they might otherwise behold far grander if colder visions of the world. Diderot returns to the same theme in a vigorous exchange from *Le rêve de d'Alembert.* Dr. Bordeu, the tough-minded physician and physiologist of Montpellier, shocks the sensitive Mlle. de Lespinasse by claiming that "extreme mobility [of certain fibres in the nervous system]—that is the dominant attribute of mediocre people." He brusquely sets aside her arguments on behalf of heightened sensibility. The man of feeling, the *homme sensible,* is helplessly "moved in all things by the behavior of his diaphragm." If he merely hears a touching word or sees a touching spectacle, his self-possession dissolves into shudders, tears, and choking sighs. His judgment vanishes along with his resourcefulness. The truly great man, by contrast, will have mastered any tendency to this disposition, if indeed he is disposed to diaphragmatic sensibility at all; he will have thus taken control of his own movements and hence his own destiny. He is a great rarity, a genius, and perhaps a freak of nature: "At the age of forty-five he will be a great king, a great statesman, a great political leader, especially a great actor" (*Rêve de d'Alembert,* 155).

Therefore, when Antonio Fabio Sticotti produced his translation of John Hill's *The Actor* under the title *Garrick, ou Les acteurs anglois* in 1769, Diderot naturally thought he had something worthwhile to say in rebuttal, particularly since its extensive discussion of the actor's emotion turned on the word *sensibility.* Sticotti retailed the notion, which Hill had already appropriated from Sainte-Albine, that love scenes play best when they are performed by actresses and actors who are themselves in love. This proposition stood or fell as a corollary to their general thesis that actors' private dispositions to passion should inspire and direct their performance of roles on the public stage. Sticotti dutifully categorized these assertions under *sensibilité,* a word he simply took over from the English text.[15] Thus the rubric that Hill chose to translate for Sainte-Albine's various references to affective experiences and organs seems to have entered into Sticotti's lexicon without his being fully aware of its history, its variations in meaning in French and English, or its current scientific implications.

Diderot's refutation of Sticotti appeared in Grimm's *Correspondance* for October–November 1770 as "Observations sur une brochure intitulée

Garrick . . . ," a polemic disguised as a review, actually a prolegomenon to the *Paradoxe sur le comédien:* "All [the great actor's] talent consists, not in leaving everything to his sensibility as you suppose, but in imitating the exterior signs of emotion so perfectly that you can't tell the difference: his cries of anguish are marked in his memory; his gestures of despair have been prepared in advance; he knows the precise cue to start his tears flowing" (*AT* 8:348). Diderot took Sticotti to task for the imprecision of his definitions. Indeed, the flaccid terminology of his contemporaries in the 1760s epitomized the general crisis in theatrical criticism. The "Observations sur *Garrick*" served to narrow the issues and to identify the terms requiring further explication in the *Paradoxe,* including *sensibilité, modèle idéal, acteurs médiocres,* and *grands acteurs.* In drubbing Sticotti, Diderot posed the vital questions he went on to argue in detail in a larger arena: Why should the actor's art differ from that of the sculptor, the painter, the orator, and the musician? Why should the great actor not command materials, processes, and techniques from which issue, in orderly stages, illusions of surpassing beauty and grandeur (*AT* 8:347)?

Le paradoxe sur le comédien is a one-sided dialogue about how geniuses go about creating artistic illusions. Specifically, it treats great actors who can make the image of a person other than themselves materialize in time and space before the eyes of ordinary people. This power, which the more mystically inclined before and after Diderot have dismissed as miraculous, is defined in the *Paradoxe* by repeated references to its principal medium and its principal material impediment: "because the development of a machine so complex as the human body cannot be regular," the actor has special problems as well as possibilities for creating illusions (*PC,* 40). When the flesh comprising the actor's bodily mechanism is carefully controlled, expressive possibilities unfold; when it is weak and abandoned to the momentary fluctuations of its sensible fibres, the opportunity to create artistic illusions recedes accordingly. A great actor will first create within himself the *modèle idéal* of the character he is portraying. Only after he has "considered, combined, learnt and arranged the whole thing in his head," even down to the last "twentieth part of a quarter of a tone," is he ready to present his grand illusion of being not himself—a Regulus, Ninias, or Macbeth—free from threat of random intrusions by merely personal emotions. The inner model acts as a kind of linear matrix and template: it structures sequences of passions, not still expressions, and directs all subsequent embodiments of the illusion, so that the great actor who plays from "reflection" and "memory" will "be one and the same at all performances" (*PC,* 15–19). Diderot's ideal actor thus performs *mechanically* in one of the basic meanings of that word—capable of exact duplication, replicable by rule and measure. The creation of the inner model is an art; performing it is a métier.

Diderot came to this problem equipped with a common-sense awareness of the relative smallness of the actor's instrument measured against the size of the theatrical space he was asked to fill in the late eighteenth century. While the encyclopedist granted that the voice, gesture, and attitudes of a purely sensible actress playing *d'âme* might well be affecting "in a drawing room," he insisted that the same performance would be trivialized if it were to be transferred to the stage where "a different impersonation was needed, since all the surroundings were enlarged" (*PC*, 57). He understood why the problem of scale visits itself upon the various arts—why a figurine is not a statue, and why a nude model, shivering among the colossal marbles in Pigalle's studio, though beautifully proportioned and very fine, had once reminded him of a "kind of frog" (*PC*, 63). Obviously, expanded surroundings require amplified gestures and heightened expressions, a requirement demanding calculated technique from the actor as it did from the sculptor. An exact duplication of life would not appear to have the right proportions—the illusion would be spoiled. The momentary spasms of individual sensibility can express only the actor's own inconsequential personality, in which no spectator has any interest; and, worse still, they fail to aggrandize into correct proportion the giant heroes of Shakespeare and Corneille.

Actors, like athletes or ancient gladiators, can be classified according to merit on a physical scale: the greater the measurable influence of nervous sensibility during his performances, the narrower an actor's range of characterization and expression over the course of his career. Great spasmodic bursts of sensible emotion, Diderot conceded, can occasionally account for inspired moments (*PC*, 14–15), as they do for Rameau's nephew, but these are thoroughly unreliable, varying wildly from performance to performance and even within a single performance: they are therefore useless to the professional, who naturally seeks to achieve consistent results through reliable technique. Only "in complete absence of sensibility is the possibility of a sublime actor" (*PC*, 20). Now sensibility exists as an inherent property of vital tissue, as Diderot knew better than most authorities, and no human body can exist without it except as a corpse. Diderot believed, however, that the actor begins to approach perfection according to the degree to which he can train himself to overcome the influence of sensibility onstage, to discipline his gestures and expressions to the threshold at which their sensible content ceases to register on his consciousness, in short, to strive for the regularity of a mechanism. As a near absolute, such a freakish capacity characterizes only a great actor such as Garrick. Great sensibility, then, is the opposite of great genius. Diderot brought to bear in the *Paradoxe* all the evidence he had gathered from medical doctrine and contemporary physiology for the *Eléments de physiologie* and the *Rêve de d'Alembert* to discredit diaphragmatic sensibility as a medium of theatrical expression and emphasize its inherent affinity to mediocrity. In the passage in which he identifies sensibility with "organic weakness," he states explicitly that such a disposition "follows on easy affection of the diaphragm" as well as on "vivacity of imagination" and "delicacy of nerves" (*PC*, 43). In the *Eléments de physiologie* Diderot took additional note of the fact that the diaphragm serves as a "muscular membrane" dividing the chest cavity from the entrails, as a "kind of vault" supporting the breath and speaking voice (137). It is therefore of crucial importance to the actor—if he cannot control his diaphragm, he cannot control his speaking voice, which must carry the sound of his illusion over considerable distance.

Diderot devotes much of the *Paradoxe* to examples illustrating the power of actors who play from mechanical "reflection" and "memory" and the contrasting feebleness of those who practice diaphragmatic inspiration. Garrick and Clairon consistently exalt the stage. Dumesnil and Madame Riccoboni usually disappoint. Diderot relished backstage anecdotes depicting the coldness and self-possession of actors under the stress of performance, those delectable ironies measured by the mental distance the artist placed between himself and the illusions he created, a distance that Diderot sometimes emphasized by hyphenating the actor's name with that of his role. There was Lekain-Ninias in *Sémiramis*, entering in convulsions after cutting his mother's throat, trembling limbs still reeking with her gore, kicking offstage an earring dropped by a careless actress in a previous scene, no doubt on an inconvenient spot down-center. Then, as a rejoinder to those who insisted that an actress must be romantically inclined toward the actor with whom she plays a love scene, there was Arnauld-Télaire, gently pillowed on the breast of Pillot-Pollux in *Castor et Pollux,* nearly suffocated by his overwhelming body odor; between gasps of "Ah, Pillot, que tu pues!" she sweetly chirped her part in the love duet with no apparent lack of conviction (*PC*, 69). Diderot recognized that this remarkable ability to divorce outward gestures and expressions from their ordinary affective content, this freedom from the presumed continuity of inner impulse and outer action which society calls sincerity, must derive from unusual moral (i.e., psychological) and physiological conditions. Theatrical geniuses have this quality in full measure; lesser luminaries have it to lesser degrees. The *Encyclopédie* shows how each

profession requires special instruments peculiar to its brand of handi-
work; the *Paradoxe* details how acting necessitates a specialized variety of
physical and moral fabric.

Diderot variously saw the actor as a blank slate, an automatic instrument waiting to sound the notes composed by other men's feelings on the
strings of its own neutral memory. Unlike the harpsichord and the cello,
which have particular tone colors of their own, he is capable of any and
every coloration, timbre, or pitch (*PC*, 46). He saw the actor as an empty
vessel filled by observation and emptied by performance or as a machine
for the fabrication and demonstration of inner models. Diderot's actor
seems to stand in relation to moral character as the hermaphrodite does to
sex: the best actors "are fit to play all characters because they have none"
(*PC*, 48). At a moment in theatrical history not too long after the time
when the most highly exalted international stars, the Italian *castrati*, had
mutilated themselves in the cause of virtuosity, Diderot defined actors'
characters in terms of absences—of unfrivolous private affections, of
warm friendships, of family ties, even of identities (*PC*, 47). His version
of their moral neutrality might be likened to the function of the faceless
characters who populate pornographic novels or films, depersonalized
bodies serving as blank screens on which multiple fantasies may be projected. Having decanted out the substantial essences, Diderot allows the
actor only the most rarified Newtonian ether as a basis for his psychology: "A great actor's soul is formed of the subtle element with which a
certain philosopher filled space, an element neither cold nor hot, heavy
nor light, which affects no definite shape, and, capable of assuming all,
keeps none" (*PC*, 46). This definition recalls the ancient ideal of the
Protean actor, but here physics, not spirit, is the source of his trans-
formative powers.

Henry Irving, who represents only one link in an unbroken chain of
actors to have been insulted by the *Paradoxe*, accused Diderot, not without some justice, of voicing his general philosophical complaints about
human nature while using the actor as sole exhibit and scapegoat. To be
sure, the *philosophe*'s opinions necessarily involve a moral ambiguity.
Extreme sensibility may be the mark of a mediocre artist, say Mlle.
Dumesnil, but it also characterizes an exceptionally compassionate man,
for example Diderot himself: while the "head makes men wise, the diaphragm makes them compassionate and moral" (*Eléments*, 138). Conversely, the man who utterly lacks sensibility, except on the brute
neurophysical level, may possess genius and therefore attain artistic
greatness, but he cannot possess truly spasmodic fellow-feeling and
goodness of heart—the sort that would send him running through the
streets to rejoice in the success of another artist. Though Diderot applied

this measure to men in general, it has particular relevance in the case of actors, for he rooted his moral uneasiness about their natures in the social history of the profession itself.

Turning theater historian and social apologist for a moment, Diderot traced the psychology of the actor to its source in historic persecution and ostracism, the ill-consequence of corrupting nurture if not nature: like heretics, actors were routinely excommunicated by a church that readily forgave rapists and fratricides. The heretic may recant, the murderer repent, but actors have nothing to renounce but their livelihood. Like prostitutes, they are despised by a public that cannot do without their services. "Think you that the marks of so continual a degradation," asks the *philosophe*, "can fail to have effect?" (*PC*, 52). He also seems to recognize, though he does not say so precisely, that society has a self-defensive need to degrade the actor whose transformations it desires to witness. From the time of Solon's persecution of Thespis, the unsettling symbolism of the actor contemplating his mask, the very etymology of the word *personality* (or of *hypocrisy*) has chilled and fascinated those moralists who value sincerity as the surpassing virtue. The greater the actor, the more pointedly he reminds the public of what powerful instruments nature has placed in the hands of the deceitful. He has always had to confront the paradox that the more professionally proficient he becomes, the more he invites moral disapprobation. On similar suspicions Plato banished the pantomimic tribe from his Republic, and Rousseau hastily threw up a *cordon sanitaire* of rhetoric to keep the theater out of Geneva.

In contrast to these utopian absolutists, Diderot reveals an enlightened tolerance of actors' principal idiosyncracy, their professionalization of two-facedness, perhaps because he felt a greater sympathy for the idea that the individual self in society consists of the amateur act that each person puts on for the benefit of other amateurs. As he notes, "The man of sensibility obeys the impulse of Nature, and gives nothing more or less than the cry of his very heart; the moment he moderates or strengthens this cry he is no longer himself, he is an actor" (*PC*, 37).[16] Duplicity is the price we pay for civilization, and for Diderot, by and large, though not for Rousseau, it was worth it. As a practical gesture of enlightenment, in his article "Comédiens" for the *Encyclopédie*, Diderot spoke up eloquently for the social utility and dignity of the profession of acting. Less publicly, for the *Paradoxe sur le comédien* was not published until 1830, he showed an ungrudging admiration for the Protean cunning, the existential sleight of hand whereby an insignificant magician could magnify his trifling body into a sublime illusion. Like many self-styled innocents, Diderot seems to have hugely enjoyed watching the inner workings of the machinery that seduced and deceived him. The true innocent values the tears shed onstage as an infallible proof of the actor's emotional authenticity. At this assertion the false innocent betrays himself by an arched brow and a knowing smile.

Early in the *Paradoxe*—right after stating its famous thesis—First compares the actor's tears to those of an atheistical priest preaching the Passion, to those of a roué trying hard to bed the girl he does not love, to those of a beggar who insults his mark as soon as he despairs of making a touch, and predictably after what has gone before, to those of a whore who feels nothing for the man she is with, but who lets herself go in his arms anyway as a demonstration of her professional competence (*PC*, 20). Here in everyday life around town, Diderot sought examples of histrionic dissimulation of emotion used to create controlled illusions. The beggar, the seducer, the prostitute, and the unbelieving priest act as professional illusionists, selling not their bodies but their images. To this end, true feeling, like true character, may be more or less convincingly feigned by calculated manipulation of physiognomy, gesture, posture, and voice. That in its modest way is their métier. Diderot's examples reintroduce, in a somewhat startling context, the encyclopedist's enthusiasm for technical craftmanship, and they recall at the same time his account of the *salon* exhibition in which Garrick put his head between two screens and in a few seconds ran his face back and forth through nine distinct passions like a pianist playing arpeggios: "Can his soul have experienced all these feelings, and played this scale in concert with his face? I don't believe it; nor do you" (*PC*, 33). Garrick, a true genius, professionalized feigned emotion into the realm of fine art, but the encyclopedist's classification of arts and trades was never arbitrary. Historically viewed as professions, begging, seduction, prostitution, and apostasy, like acting, have been practiced at or beyond the margins of society's tolerance. In order to survive, practitioners have been compelled to live by their wits, without permanent roots or identities, without "those holy and tender ties which associate us in the pains and pleasures of another, who in turn shares our own" (*PC*, 47). Like Rameau's nephew, but without even the security of a post as music master, actors have been obliged to create themselves anew moment by moment as their fortunes pass in a hat through the fickle crowd of strangers. Swiftly dissimulated emotion, therefore, lively and varied enough to fill a square, eloquent enough to tug at purse strings or corset strings, evolved by necessity as both professional method and professional merchandise.

Although the actor may intensify qualities found generally in human nature, in low life or in high, he is clearly portrayed in the *Paradoxe* as a creature apart from the common run of men. Because of his very moral and emotional neutrality, at his greatest he ranks as the intellectual equal or superior to the most distinguished geniuses in other fields. Great actors are "rarer" even than great poets (*PC*, 46), for instance, because they must dispassionately embody "the outward symptoms of the soul [they] borrow" (*PC*, 53). This constitutes a physical as well as a mental challenge. Acts of mental agility, however, must precede the physical. Any great genius, whether an actor, a musician, a statesman, or a natural philosopher, may be distinguished in society by his capacity to engage in detached observation and coolly creative reflection before he acts. The word *réflexion* recurs in the *Paradoxe* to describe the great actor's characteristic attribute, but it had wider implications in the development of Diderot's philosophy of science. Reflection meant to him the power of beholding and imagining the world as it is, objectively, free from the stigmatism of personal feelings. Whereas self-absorption blurs the vision of mediocrities, by contrast "all great copyists of Nature," who are the "least sensitive of all creatures," can penetrate into nature's truths through observation, imagination, and interpretation: "It is we who feel; it is they who watch, study, and give us the result" (*PC*, 17–18). The method of watching, studying, and exhibiting followed by the theatrical genius as he appears in the *Paradoxe* closely resembles Diderot's formal explication of scientific method in his *Pensées sur l'interprétation de la nature* (1754). "We have three principal means," he wrote, "observation of nature, reflection, and experiment. Observation gathers the facts, reflection combines them, experiment verifies the result of the combination. It is essential that the observation of nature be assiduous, that reflection be profound, and that experimentation be exact. Rarely does one see these abilities in combination. And so, creative geniuses are not common" (*AT*, 2:18).

This three-staged process reappears in Diderot's accounts of the artistic creation of the inner model. He describes one aspect of the first creative stage, observation of the passions, in the *Eléments de physiologie*. In the chapter entitled "Passions," he sets forth a methodological approach that simultaneously looks back to Della Porta and Le Brun's comparative anatomy and ahead to Charles Darwin's *Expression of the Emotions in Man and Animals* (1872): "The correspondence of the passions with the movement of the bodily members is observable in men and animals. It is the foundation of the studies of those who would imitate nature" (*Eléments*, 267–68).[17] In harmony with the doctrines of neoclassical generality, Diderot regarded the "Passions"—fear, rage, awe, joy, and the rest—as readily definable categories of experience consistent throughout the higher species. In his view they function as a universal system of causes registering their effects analogously from one individual to another. The

FIGURE 18. Five universal passions as depicted in Buffon's *Histoire naturelle* (1749): 1) Sadness, 2) Terror, 3) Scorn, 4) Envy, 5) Happiness. *(Courtesy of Alderman Library, University of Virginia.)*

passions are thus as eminently knowable through observation and as classifiable through comparison of their external signs as, say, the visible spectrum of light or the phases of the moon.

In his "Réponse à la lettre de Mme Riccoboni" (1758), Diderot gave an example of detached observation of the passions and its usefulness to the actor. He recounted a version of the now famous anecdote of Garrick's preparation for the role of King Lear (*AT* 7 : 402). It seems that a madman was kept locked in a room near the actor's lodgings. Years before this unfortunate fellow had been holding his little girl in his arms near an open window in an upper story of his house. When a commotion in the street below distracted him for a moment, the child somehow tumbled out of the window and was killed. The demented antics of the father took the form of a horrible pantomime in which he would reenact the entire scene with all its horror and anguish. The madman's keeper allowed Garrick to study at leisure these screams and desperate gestures. The applicability of the father's grief to Lear's situation need not be elaborated, but Garrick also worked up the detached scene as one of his parlor entertainments, which he would conclude with the explanation: "Thus it was I learned to imitate madness." The coolness of such a summation suggests exactly the emotional distance that Diderot would have the actor place between the models he studies and his own heart.

In the second stage of the process, reflection, the observed facts of emotional behavior, expressive physiognomy, gestures, and vocal colorings, which have been stored in the actor's memory, are recombined in the imagination as a sequence of passions appropriate to the character or "type" he enacts. Reflection, drawing upon both conscious and unconscious sources, gathers these selected sense impressions together in a "collection" (*PC*, 16–17). The third stage, experimentation, overlaps reflection. The precise tones and gestures appropriate to the type are arrived at only through an exhaustive series of tests: "to hit the right mark once, they have been practiced a hundred times; and despite all this practice, they are yet found wanting" (*PC*, 19). "Inspiration," if it comes at all, will come at this stage of exhaustive labor "when the man of genius is hovering between nature and his sketch of it, and keeping a watchful eye on both" (*PC*, 17). Before the actor hits on a solution, he has repeatedly measured each vocal quality and each movement against the inner model as it has emerged from his imagination. The great artist continues to experiment, using a mirror if necessary, until "he has considered, combined, learnt and arranged the whole thing in his head" (*PC*, 15).

After exhausting the range of choices open to him, the actor will have created the inner model, which serves as the matrix for all his subsequent performances of that role. This explains to Diderot's satisfaction the several reasons why great actors perform consistently from day to day: nothing is left to the inspiration of the moment; the blueprint remains before their mind's eye, guiding each step and each utterance onstage; it promotes a uniformity of muscular motions, carefully built up bit by bit during rehearsal, comparable to the fusing of reflex and habit in the creation of a gymnastic routine; it disengages the organs of sensibility by suppressing their spontaneous impulses into habit. In the *Paradoxe* Mlle. Clairon consistently embodies this principle, the mark of the true professional, the difference between Garrick's acting and LUI's mime:

> Doubtless she has imagined a type, and to conform to this type has been her first thought. . . . This type, however, which she has borrowed from history, or created as who should create some vast spectre in her own mind, is not herself. Were it indeed bounded by her own dimensions, how paltry, how feeble would be her playing! When, by dint of hard work, she has got as near as she can to this idea, the thing is done; to preserve the same nearness is a mere matter of memory and practice. . . . As it will happen in dreams, her head touches the clouds, her hands stretch to grasp the horizon on both sides; she is the informing soul of a huge figure, which is her outward casing, and in which her efforts have enclosed her. As she lies careless and still on a sofa with folded arms and closed eyes she can, following her memory's dream, hear herself, see herself, judge herself, and judge also the effects she will produce. In such a vision she has a double personality; that of the little Clairon and of the great Agrippina. (*PC*, 16)

The recurring terminology of psychophysical locality—inner, outer, mind, body, "double personality," "memory's dream"—alerts the reader of the *Paradoxe* to the fact that the application of the three-staged process to the actor's art may not be as straightforward as it seems at first. Diderot's conception of the body involves more than simple mechanical analogies. Characteristically, he advances clear-cut precepts only to complicate them by counter examples, a tendency that makes the open-ended dialogue a perfect vehicle for his thought. The *Paradoxe* offers fewer perplexities of this sort than his other, more balanced dialectics, but it quickly sets in motion its own counter marches and fifth columns. Although one may quite properly associate Diderot with external and mechanical acting methods, the deeper meaning of the *Paradoxe*, interpreted in light of the *Rêve de d'Alembert* and the *Eléments de physiologie*, is far more subtle than those terms would suggest. The actor's professional material, his instrument, consists of his body, as opposed to, say, the sculptor's marble, no matter how mechanically structured that body is, and that fact invited Diderot to probe more deeply into the recesses of its inner workings. According to his psychophysiology, the body is a vital entity, capable of unbidden sensations as well as mechanical repetitions. There is more to vitality than consciousness.

The bodily process of creating a theatrical illusion requires at the outset the participation of two interlocking functions: memory and imagination. The actor who diligently draws upon these inner resources "will always be at his best mark" (*PC*, 15)—or so the *Paradoxe* confidently assures the reader. Memory retains the image; imagination revives it, vivifies it, and combines it with other images to form the living mosaic of the inner model. Though he wrote under the enduring spell of the sensationalism of Locke and Condillac, which held that nothing can exist within the mind except what sense experience puts there and links by association to prior sense experiences, Diderot allowed the imagination a power of recombination that falls only just short of a creative, originating force. He did not hesitate to define it as a dynamic physical process carried on within the corporeal machine, a process especially appropriate to a machine engaged in making art. In the closely linked chapters on "Memory" and "Imagination" in the *Eléments de physiologie,* he speaks of both functions in metaphoric language encompassing the fine and performing arts: "Imagination is a colorist, memory is a faithful draughtsman. Imagination excites both the orator and the auditor more than memory" (257). Alluding to the ancient rhetorical principle of *enargeia,* he defines imagination as the faculty of portraying absent entities as if they were present to the senses or, alternately, of attaching a vibrant body of colorful association to a coldly abstract word. Diderot goes so far as to say that memory amplified by imagination resonates with such intensity through the body that revived sensations can duplicate actual experiences: "If I believe I hear a sound, I hear it; if I believe I see an object, I see it" (252). Whatever the plausibility of such a testimonial to vividness—"believing is seeing" so to speak—an advocacy for revivability of sensation akin to Diderot's has withstood the test of time to reappear in today's acting textbooks as an invitation to make-believe.[18]

Every experience, in the form of sensation, Diderot believed, leaves some impression on the nervous system. He followed Charles Bonnet's *Essai analytique sur les facultés de l'âme* (1760) in describing the "nervous fibres" as apt to "reproduce sensation" (*Eléments,* 241 n). The nervous fibres fitted to reproduce sensation permeate the entire organism (89), mere images and words can produce waves of ecstasy or nausea that engulf the system (292), and the power of suggestion can operate so overwhelmingly on this delicate web that Diderot felt obliged to credit

Seneca's account of the unfortunate Gallus Vibius, the actor who went mad while attempting to imitate the movements of a madman (85). Here Diderot may once again have written the autobiography of his diaphragm in the guise of science, and the cycle of his thought on creative imagination seems to have returned yet again to Dorval's spasms. The key to Diderot's ultimate psychophysiology of acting, however, is that vividness of memory and imagination—"inspiration" in the ancient language— should overpower the actor, if at all, only in preparing for a performance, not in the performance itself. LUI's café exhibition might be an acceptable acting exercise, but like the warm-up rituals that actors engage in, it is hardly part of the show itself. Acting before an audience is a dispassionate imitation of what the actor has already created in rehearsal. Any number of physical and mental experiences may contribute to that creation, but cool reflection directs the work onstage. All honor rebounds to the performer who can "feel" sublimity "with his passion and his genius, and [then] reproduce it with complete self-possession" (*PC*, 24). No doubt the feigned tears of professional beggars, prostitutes, and unbelieving priests derive in some way from the original sense experiences associated with true deprivation, true love, and true faith: that is how they must first learn the mechanics of the emotion they enact. But as they gain mastery over the mechanisms of their physiognomical expressions and vocal tones, an inner resonance of sincere emotion can only hinder, not help their performances. Since the stage exists at a remove from daily life and requires a multiplicity of illusions, the actor, with the same basic means of expression at his disposal, faces a more complicated task than the average hypocrite. In the course of his career, the actor must master not only one persona, or several, but many, perhaps hundreds; each of these characters is different, and each one is at least the partial product of another creative intelligence—the playwright's.

Recent criticism has suggested that the real paradox of the *Paradoxe* resides in the contrast between the actor as puppet of the dramatist and as original artist in his own right.[19] That probably puts the matter too strongly, but certainly the original contribution of the actor to the creation of characters, if there is to be an original contribution at all, must somehow grow out of his remembered experience, observations, and imagination as they pertain to fictive personae in the texts. He must literally embody the text before the eyes of the spectator. Consistently in Diderot's dramatic theory, words offer the theater no more than stark symbols, the barest indication of thought and feeling; the actor must provide the flesh-and-blood reality, the real presence, through action, gesture, tone, and expression. Only then can he infuse these abstract symbols with "a whole context of circumstance" in order "to give them their full significance" (*PC*, 13). Diderot's fascination for the process of physicalizing emotion may be traced back through his thought to the *Lettre sur les sourds et muets* (1751), in which he recounts how he used to sit in the theater with his fingers stuck in his ears, muffling all sound, so that he could follow the fluctuating passions as expressed by the actors' faces and bodies alone without the interposition of their spoken words (*AT* 1:359). The same concern marks his later accounts in the *Paradoxe* and the *Salons* of Garrick's wordless pantomime and helps to explain Diderot's special enthusiasm for the eloquence of muscles faultlessly shaped into passions by imagination and memory. Over such virtuosity the playwright could have no dominion, except implicitly in the stage directions. Diderot celebrated Lady Macbeth's silent hand-washing as one of those sublime moments of bodily eloquence in which gesture triumphs over discourse (*AT* 1:354–55). At such a moment spoken language collapses in upon itself, and its meaning can only escape the soul as a gesture: "The great passions," Diderot notes in the *Eléments de physiologie*, "are silent" (268).

Spoken or unspoken, the actor's precise muscular control over expression emerges slowly over time and many repetitions, "a matter for hard work, for long experience, for an uncommon tenacity of memory" (*PC*, 64). Diderot's meaning obtains today when a pianist speaks of practicing "to get the music into my hands." The *Paradoxe* accords the same dignity of corporeal memory to the actor playing a role on the instrument of his body. But even more sweepingly it restates Diderot's general contention, maintained in the *Rêve de d'Alembert* and the *Eléments,* that the individual is a succession of experiences bound together, given coherence, by the thread of memory. Memory has two implications in Diderot's theatrical scheme: first, in terms of performance, it means the training of muscles into patterns of facial and bodily movement as in mime or ballet; second, in terms of the creation of the inner model, it means wealth of stored sense impressions and associations known generally to the eighteenth century as decaying sensations or vibratiuncles, but which later theorists, retracing ground first covered by Diderot, categorized as "affective memories."[20] Emotional events, sharply experienced by the body, become intelligible—and hence useful to the actor—only in retrospect; they are anything but intelligible as they occur, palpitating the diaphragm and shocking the mind. The passage of time permits reflection to order violent experiences into coherence, while imagination serves to revive at least some of their original piquancy: "It is when the storm of sorrow is over, when the extreme of sensibility is dulled, when the event is far behind us, when the soul is calm, that one remembers one's eclipsed happiness, that one is capable of appreciating one's loss, that memory and imagination unite, one to retrace, the other to accentuate" (*PC*, 36).

This version of emotion memory had substantial support from Diderot's physiology. In still another of those anecdotal asides that personalize his scientific prose, he described the interdependence of his own memory of sensation and of emotion: "The sound of a voice, the presence of an object, a certain place, and behold, an object recalled—more than that, a whole stretch of my past—and I am plunged again into pleasure, regret, affliction" (*Eléments*, 248). Such sentiments have been described as direct precursors of Wordsworth's "emotions recollected in tranquillity"[21] and even Proust's "privileged moments" (*Eléments*, 248n). But it is possible to define Diderot's position at once more generally and more precisely: he took a bold step towards the modern psychological concepts of *subconsciousness* and *unconsciousness* so notably neglected by the Cartesian dualism of pure thought and pure mechanism. His modernity on this point seems particularly tangible in a remarkable passage from the chapter "Memory" in the *Eléments de physiologie*. It describes an apparently bottomless reservoir secreted deep within the mind and teeming with all the images and sensations the body has ever known; far from the conscious architecture of Renaissance memory arts, it is the chaotic residue of sense impressions, subliminally experienced and unconsciously retained:

> I am inclined to believe that everything we have ever seen, known, heard, or glimpsed, even to the trees of a deep forest, even to the arrangement of the branches, to the shape of the leaves, and to the variety of their colors, their tints and shades of green; even to the appearance of the grains of sand at the seashore, to the irregularities of the wave crests as they are furled in a light breeze or foamed and billowed by the winds of a tempest; even to the multitudes of human voices, of the cries of animals, and all the sounds in nature, to the melody and harmony of every tune, of every musical composition, of every concert we have ever heard—all of that exists within us without our knowing it is there. (241)

This eloquently poetic evocation of the buried life did not diminish Diderot's belief that subconscious memories really exist as physical impressions made by physical objects on the body. To explain the "mechanism" of memory, he said that one must regard the "soft substance of the brain as a mass of sensitive and living wax," capable of receiving new impressions while retaining and reviving the old (243).

Diderot's metaphors describing the linked faculties of memory and

imagination hover restlessly and suggestively between British associationism, already mature, and the modern psychophysiology of reflex
arcs, as yet unborn, but to which his kind of thinking proved an important forebear. Although Diderot does not cite Hartley's *Observations on
Man*, the metaphor of mechanical vibrations as the physical basis for
memory and imagination figures prominently in his description of the
physiology of mental operations in the *Rêve de d'Alembert:*

> Besides these vibrating strings have still another property—they can
> make other strings hum—so that in this way one idea can call forth
> another, the second can call forth a third, and so on. . . . The instru-
> ment has astonishing range, for a newly awakened idea can sometimes
> provoke a sympathetic response in a harmonic that is almost inconceiv-
> ably remote. (100)

Diderot employs this physiological function to explain the immense recombinant power of the imagination, which can collect diverse parts from
living nature, once observed always remembered, to create such phan-
tasms as sphinxes, winged horses, and hippogriffs (*PC*, 21).

The same mechanization of artistic imagination underlies the *Paradoxe*.
In the creative effort of forming the inner model based on recombinant
observations and experiences, mind and body function as one:

The First.	[Great artists] keep a keen watch on what is going on, both in the physical and moral world.
The Second.	The two are the same.
The First.	They dart on everything which strikes their imagination; they make, as it were, a *collection* of such things. And from these collections, *made all unconsciously* [*en eux, à leur insu*], issue the grandest achievements of their work.

(PC, 17, emphasis added)

Diderot's insistence on the mind-body continuum, a presupposition of
the "Mental Phenomena" chapters of the *Eléments* and of the logical
psychology stemming from his vitalist materialism, leads him to the point
of apparent contradiction: If the actor's mind and body constitute a single
entity, then how can his mind coldly direct his body through sequences of
passion without mentally experiencing the same emotions? In his answer
to this question, Diderot became the first theorist to describe in detail
what William Archer, in his extended commentary on the psychology of
acting, *Masks or Faces?* (1888), termed "the paradox of dual consciousness" (*MF*, 184).

The great actor's extreme rarity stems from his highly unusual, even freakish capacity to detach himself from his bodily machine, to divide himself into two personalities in performance, and so to direct the outward motions of his passions by an inward mental force, itself unmoved, undistorted by the physiological effects it oversees. Thus little Clairon could coolly manipulate the strings that moved the great puppet Agrippina across the stage, and her ability to disentangle her own diaphragm from the empassioned gestures of her character defined her as a genius. As evidenced by the case of Dumesnil, mediocrity cannot extricate soul from mechanism so readily: as the *homme sensible* embodies the passions he enacts, his ghost becomes enmeshed in the workings of his machine. One of the several subsidiary paradoxes of the *Paradoxe* resides in the apparent retreat from monism implied by "double personality." Diderot seems to suggest a kind of dualism of spirit and matter in the true genius: Clairon's detachment from herself appears almost supernatural, god-like, akin to what today's popular psychology would term an "out-of-body experience."

Before resolving this paradox, it is helpful to note that Diderot's formulation of dual consciousness demonstrates the inappropriateness of attempts to identify his psychology of the actor with William James's theory of emotion.[22] James, it will be recalled, rejected the separation of the mental experience of an emotion from its physiological symptoms, while advancing the related proposition "that any voluntary arousal of the so-called manifestations of a special emotion ought to give us the emotion itself." By contrast, Diderot identified the separation of manifestation from the mental experience as the measure of an actor's art: "The broken voice, the half-uttered words, the stifled or prolonged notes of agony, the trembling limbs, the faintings, the bursts of fury—all of this is pure mimicry . . . which leaves him, luckily for the poet, the spectator, and himself, a full freedom of mind" (*PC*, 19). This freedom of mind, a calm at the center that persists despite whatever paroxysms the body suffers outwardly, constitutes, in the argument of the *Paradoxe*, the *sine qua non* of great acting. But how is it physically possible?

In explicating the physiological mechanism of dual consciousness in the *Rêve de d'Alembert*, Diderot shows that his apparent retreat from mind-body monism in the *Paradoxe sur le comédien* was merely a tactical feint. He held an opinion he probably encountered first in La Mettrie (*L'homme machine*, 112), though it was common elsewhere at the time: the mind-body can do two things at once because its components resemble those of a stringed instrument. As he explained, "It is a vibration of this sort, it is this kind of necessary resonance, that keeps an object present to our minds while our understandings deal with whichever of its qualities we please to study" (*Rêve*, 100). Such separable vibrations provide the physical basis of dual consciousness as their harmonies describe association and imagination. The stronger the mind, presumably, the more exact the separation, so that the mind of a genius resembles a kind of one-man band, capable of performing independent operations simultaneously under the precise direction of a single intelligence. Diderot returned to the subject of dual consciousness with particular reference to the performer in the *Eléments de physiologie*. In the chapter "Organs," he speaks of a musician playing a concert on his harpsichord, but striking up an interesting conversation with his neighbor. Though he completely forgets that he is performing, his fingers continue to play the keys unhesitatingly without missing a note. Diderot describes this automatic performance of the muscles as the "animal" part of the musician's nature. It is only when the conversation stops and his eyes return to his score that the "man" loses his place and falls into confusion. "If the distraction of the man had continued for a few more minutes," Diderot claims, "the animal would have finished the concert to the end, without the man having guessed otherwise" (286–87).[23] Such a lapse hardly recommends itself as normal performance technique, but it is easy to see how the same inherent capacity for divided consciousness could be harnessed to more productive uses by a theatrical genius. The "animal" of carefully conditioned muscle and sinew performs while the "man" observes, reflects, and corrects by reference to the inner model. Thus the performer can be both the organist and the organ, a comparison of the mind and body to the musician and his instrument that underlies Diderot's most profound psychophysiology: "The philosopher-instrument has sensations, so he is simultaneously the performer and the instrument. Because he is conscious, he has a momentary awareness of the sound he produces; because he is an animal, he remembers the sound. This organic faculty, by linking together the sounds inside his mind, both produces and preserves the melody. Imagine a clavichord endowed with sensation and memory, and then tell me whether it will not learn and be able to repeat by itself the tunes you play on its key-board" (*Rêve*, 101).

Diderot based his claims for the particular physique of theatrical genius on his scientific opinion that bodily organs, though "interconnected, sympathetic [and] concordant," can function independently "without the participation of the entire animal" (*Eléments*, 287). In fact, each organ exists, he believed, as a separate animal with its own special functions preserved apart from, though habitually cooperating with, the body as a whole. In the *Rêve de d'Alembert* he compares this multiple independence amid a unified entirety to a swarm of bees, each organism or "animal" having at once an individual existence and an existence as part of the mass (112–14). Such a notion may seem peculiarly quaint until it is recalled that a similar theory currently provides surgeons with the justification they need in order to perform organ transplants or, differently defined, outlines the bases of cellular biology. Although the diaphragm, the principal organ of sensibility, has close ties to the mind of an average man, it can be isolated in the bodily system of the genius so that the impulses to action flow to the muscles without misadventure. By implication such a diaphragmatic bypass may be achieved by constant repetition of physical actions until they are rendered automatic. Here Diderot tentatively groped toward a theory of bodily memory that modern psychophysiology has continued to advance under various names including conditioned reflexes. He noted a phenomenon he called "memory of habits, of movements linked by reiterated acts or of repeated sensations." Such movements introduced into bodily organs will set in motion sequences of related movements and sensations pre-established by habit (*Eléments*, 244).

A specific reference to the actor in the *Eléments de physiologie* proves that Diderot's physiological account of *l'habitude* was cross-referenced in his mind to his description of bodily and physiognomical control in the *Paradoxe:* "If by repeating the same actions, you have acquired a facility in performing them, you will have become habituated. The first action leads to the second and the second to the third because one wants to do easily what one does often—in both mind and body. . . . One commands the bodily organs by habit. The actor has acquired the habit of commanding his eyes, his lips, and his face. It is not the effect of sudden feeling of what he is saying, but the result of lengthy preparation; it is habituation" (293). Habit commands the features and the limbs, and it immobilizes the diaphragm, which would otherwise inevitably participate in a spontaneous burst of emotion. That is why preserving the nearness to the inner model constitutes a "matter of memory and practice" (*PC,* 16). In Diderot's view a theatrical performance consists of sequences of muscular events, meticulously organized by the actor, empty of their prior emotional content: "Like other gymnastics, it taxes only his bodily strength" (*PC,* 19). Acting, then, is a kind of nonaffective athleticism, in which the consciousness of certain actions is suppressed to enhance the actor's control over others.

Diderot was aware of the definition of *spontaneous* shared by some of the most advanced physiologists of his day. He followed with great interest the work of the Englishman Robert Whytt, a pioneer of what he termed *reflex consciousness,* a faculty that operates automatically in response to internal and external stimulus. In his *Essay on the Vital and Other Involuntary Motions of Animals* (1751), Whytt grouped "under the general denomination of SPONTANEOUS" only those "involuntary motions" that are "performed by several organs as it were of their own accord, and without any attention of the mind, or consciousness of an exertion of its active power; . . . which have been also distinguished by the name of AUTOMATIC." At the present time, some dictionaries cite *automatic* and even *mechanical* among the synonyms of *spontaneous,* but most of us usually think of them as opposites. Whytt listed the beating of the heart, respiration, and the digestive functions as spontaneous actions—automatisms—which he hesitated to reduce to the motions "of a mere inanimate machine," but which did inevitably suggest that analogy to him. Even more pertinently, eighteenth-century psychology distinguished another kind of spontaneous automatism that, unlike vital functions such as heartbeat, is acquired through association, memory, and habit. Anticipating Pavlov by more than a century, Whytt observed that the mere "Idea" of food could cause a marked flow of saliva into the mouth of a hungry person.[24] This phenomenon implies an associative process of automatization, a progressive fusing of mental image and physiological manifestation into a mechanism of response, which can be triggered by imaginary stimuli. David Hartley recognized the same mechanism in his *Observations on Man* and labeled it "secondary automatic motions." These automatisms, inculcated through habit, permit the harpsichordist to play a complex piece "spontaneously." After lengthy practice sessions, in which each note is first played by "an express Act of Volition," the musician is actually able to perform as he carries on "a quite different Train of Thoughts in his Mind" (108–09). The notes flow from the unconscious half of a divided consciousness.

A similar concept of the dramatic role as a score, memorized as a sequence of psychophysical events and performed by habit, reappears in twentieth-century acting theory.[25] In this as in so many other things, Diderot's thoughts proved seminal. In the *Rêve de d'Alembert* he argued that without the thread of memory life would be merely an "interrupted series of sensations without anything to bind them together" (99). In the *Paradoxe,* alluding to a famous phrase in Aristotle's *Poetics,* he described how the great actor, by beginning with smaller segments, shapes remembered sensations into an overriding sequence of actions: "His passion has a definite course—it has bursts, and it has reactions; it has a beginning, a middle, and an end" (*PC,* 15). In the *Eléments de physiologie,* applying associationist and sensationalist theories to the body, he outlined a physical basis for such a structured sequence as "a faithful linking [*enchainement*] of sensations, which are revived successively [in the order that] they were received" (246). One sensation will call up the next, with which it has been previously associated, and that second sensation will call up a third and so on—*enchainement* reinforced by "reiterated acts" and "habits" (244–45). In Diderot's view mind and body are inextricably interwoven in the same web of nervous fibres that can be shaped into patterns of response by repetition. When highly organized in the body of a genius, such physiological structures and functions are perfectly suited to the enactment of those "distinct passions separated by spectacular transitions" that are said to have characterized the particular excellence of David Garrick.[26] When Diderot recounted the English Roscius's *salon* exhibition of the fluctuating passions, he described a physiognomical musculature rapidly shifted through a pre-established sequence with the unerring rhythm of mechanism:

> Garrick will put his head between two folding-doors, and in the course of five or six seconds his expression will change successively from wild delight to temperate pleasure, from this to tranquillity, from tranquillity to surprise, from surprise to blank astonishment, from that to sorrow, from sorrow to the air of one overwhelmed, from that to fright, from fright to horror, from horror to despair, and thence he will go up again to the point from which he started. Can his soul have experienced all these feelings, and played this kind of scale in concert with his face? I don't believe it; nor do you. (*PC*, 32–33)

In short, Diderot thought he had discovered a perfect acting machine.

Restating the paradox of acting in terms of Diderot's dialectic of vitalistic and mechanistic modes of physiological explanation suggests that the real paradox turns on the two meanings of *spontaneous*. In Diderot's scheme the actor rehearses his actions until his emotions appear to be spontaneous in our conventional, organic sense of that word— proceeding from natural feeling, produced without being planted or without labor—but in fact they are really spontaneous in Robert Whytt or David Hartley's mechanical sense of acquired automatisms. The audience finally sees an illusion of reflexive vitality, responding to outer stimuli as if for the first time; but the actor's real experience is of a sequence of reflexive mechanisms, responding to an inner plan that has been carefully worked out in advance. Allowing the actor affective inspirations in the form of memories and imaginative discoveries during rehearsals, Diderot maintains that by the time the rehearsal process ends, it is meaningless to call the automatized results sensible emotions or spontaneously vital expressions.

Diderot regarded rehearsals as the "decisive fact" in the actor's creative process (*PC*, 57). First, ample rehearsals "strike a balance" between the actors, encouraging ensemble playing (*PC*, 26). Second, an acting company producing a play under the meticulous direction of the dramatist really begins to approach perfection when its members "are worn out from constant rehearsals, are what we call 'used up.' From this moment their progress is surprising; each identifies himself with his part; and it is at the end of this hard work that the performances begin" (*PC*, 57–58). Diderot describes an ideal situation in Naples where the sovereign takes his diversions seriously and insists on unusually long rehearsal periods approximating those of later theatrical utopias such as the Duchy of Saxe-Meiningen or the Moscow Art Theatre. Diderot's attitude toward the importance of extensive rehearsals stands out as revolutionary at a time when Garrick, who was more sensitive than most managers in such matters, could harangue Mrs. Abington ruthlessly for begging twenty-four hours notice before playing Charlotte Rusport in *The West Indian* and then, when she refused, substitute Jenny Barsanti, borrowed from the rival house, with virtually no rehearsal at all (*Letters* 3:990–91). In such an emergency the singular gifts of Rameau's nephew would no doubt have proved invaluable, but they would have also made a long evening's work of it for the other actors, wondering as they must at every turn what was coming next. For Diderot the process of theatrical creation was at once more simple and more complex than improvisation. In its simplicity the French word for rehearsal, *répétition*, came to the aid of his meaning, a word and a tradition still resounding in the admittedly polemical outburst of Laurence Olivier, who on many other grounds as well would qualify as a *grand acteur* in Diderot's pantheon: "I'd rather have run the scene eight times than have wasted that time in chattering away about abstractions. An actor gets the right thing by doing it over and over. Arguing about motivations and so forth is a lot of rot."[27] In its complexity, however, Diderot's view of the actor's creative process was no less intricate than the inner watchworks of the mind-body itself.

In the final analysis all these diverse concepts converge in one central nexus in Diderot's aesthetic theory—the theatricalization of the *modèle idéal.* For the painter or sculptor, the inner model composes the passions as forms in space, whereas for the poet the inner model arranges them as images in time. As early as 1751 in the *Lettre sur les sourds et muets,* Diderot clearly differentiated between the arts-in-space and the arts-in-time, and his perspicacity in this regard was not lost on Lessing, who reviewed the *Lettre* enthusiastically before he wrote the *Laöcoon* (1766). Diderot revived the distinction in the *Salon de 1767,* and we have already seen how carefully he negotiated his boundaries, when, in the *Essais sur la peinture,* he invited the art students to imagine themselves into the moving center of a bodily machine in order to draw gesture rather than pose. The fact that First refers Second to his *Salons* (*PC*, 41) reminds us that while Lessing promised a sequel to the *Laöcoon* showing how theater spanned the gulf separating the arts, Diderot quietly accomplished the same task between the lines of the *Paradoxe.* He did so by explaining that the actor's inner model must compose and arrange the passions in both space and time. It must show the mechanics of motion and the transformation of expressions in perpetual flux; it is not the blueprint for a still form, but the flow chart for a dynamic machine. After discussing the power of the plastic imagination to compose ideal images from composite models (*PC,* 40–41), Diderot returns to Clairon's distinctively theatrical ability not only to put an inner model together but to put it in motion: "Where, then, lay her talent? In imagining a mighty shape, and in copying it with genius. She imitated the movement, the action, the gesture, the whole embodiment of a being far greater than herself" (*PC,* 43).

This process of embodiment resembles a dream in which the form the actress imagines for herself, the shape that modern theorists have come to call the *character body,* seems to expand to noble proportions. The artist first forms an illusion in her own mind. Then because these inward vibrations transform the scale and dimension of her outward expressions—gesture, posture, voice—the audience comes to share in the illusion she has generated, "following her memory's dream" (*PC,* 16). Mlle. Lespinasse describes just this sort of phenomenon in the *Rêve de d'Alembert:* at night when she lies awake in the dark, her mind's eye sees her body expanding so "that my arms and legs are stretching out to infinity, and that the rest of my body is growing at the same rate." She concentrates solely on her mental effort, totally absorbed: "the universe is annihilated as far as I am concerned" (*Rêve,* 139). Similarly, Clairon conjures "a huge figure, which is her outward casing, and in which her efforts have enclosed her" (*PC,* 16).[28] These efforts require an exceptional power of mental concentration and an intense introspection. They suggest a consciousness heightened to the point at which activities outside the perimeter of attention are rendered unconscious, automatic, absorbed.

In the great *Salons* of the 1760s, Diderot conducted a profound inquiry into what has been termed *absorption* in French painting of the period. Recent art-historical scholarship has drawn attention to the prominence of figures depicted as totally absorbed in their actions. Their unselfconsciousness is literal; they are withdrawn into the picture with an intensity sufficient to deny the presence of the beholder. As an important study of his criticism shows, Diderot's formulation of the idea of a theatrical fourth wall in the *Discours sur la poésie dramatique* (1758) carried over into his *Salons* as a dominant aesthetic principle.[29] In his most celebrated theatrical innovation, he advised the dramatist to write the play as if the curtain had not risen, as if the spectators did not exist. What has never been adequately understood, however, is that Diderot's dramaturgical revolution—his interposition of the imaginary fourth wall between stage and auditorium—was made possible only by his final break with the ancient rhetorical theory of acting and its inspiring *pneuma*. The rhetoric of the passions literally incorporated the audience into the performance event. The fiery spirits, emanating from the eyes of the inspired actor, flowed across the intervening space and penetrated the eyes of the spectator, linking their emotions physically. Diderot's scientific internalization of the actor's potencies revolutionized this archaic paradigm, dissolving the occult ties between the rhapsode and the rhapsodized. Such absorption draws our attention to the unconscious side of acting, the side that can "spring a mine" as much to Garrick's surprise as to the beholder's or launch Dumesnil into Nirvana in "the twinkling of an eye." Yet the professedly conscious preparation of Clairon—repeating her actions hundreds of times, immersing herself in her character by gradual states until her illusion is perfected—ultimately has a striking similarity to the self-abandonment of her rival. The concept of absorption therefore explains the central contradiction in the doctrine of sensibility, the contradiction between theory and practice that typified the crisis of the mid-eighteenth century. Furthermore, it represents the birth of the modern theater of illusion in which the spectator pays to be annihilated. Diderot thus looks ahead through the *tranche de vie* of the Naturalists to what Stanislavski took to be the ideal state for the actor to attain, "public solitude." No magical spirits ripple through the air of this theater of illusions and moving pictures.

Clairon, as the chief instance of this process, embodies her inner model in the world defined by the stage action, a world completely severed from the auditorium. She is absorbed in a double sense—in her mental effort and in the frame of the stage picture. Physical passions are represented by physical means. Clairon's mind-body is an instrument, self-activating within its own fibres, vibrating in time and tune with the preconceived score. LUI would call this score the "melodic line"; Stanislavski, the "score of the role." The dramatist assisted Clairon by setting down on paper images depicting the temporal succession of the passions, but only Clairon, or another performer of comparable technique, can consistently and repeatedly vivify that sequence before the eyes and ears of an audience that pretends it does not exist. Only a theatrical genius, whose medium was carefully crafted flesh and blood, could embody a chain of linked word-symbols as a chain of linked sensations and enlarge them into an illusion of terrifying veracity. "The poet had engendered the monster," Diderot concluded epigrammatically, but "Clairon made it roar" (*PC*, 43).

FIGURE 19. *Absorption* (detail) in the preparation of a role. From *Strolling Actresses Dressing in a Barn* by William Hogarth (1738). *(Courtesy of Washington University Libraries.)*

In a broadly philosophical sense, then, Diderot regarded the actor as highly specialized matter in expressive motion, "the subtle element with which a certain philosopher filled space" (*PC*, 46), an ordering intelligence amid the constant flux of nature; to him the theatrical genius was an intelligence who most efficiently organized that motion in duration, shape, and purpose. Such a body can reach beyond the normal limits imposed by its inherent sensibility to attain near absolute precision and flexibility, "the art of mimicking everything, or, which comes to the same thing, the aptitude for every sort of character and part" (*PC*, 14). This phase of Diderot's aesthetic based on scientific materialism, his mechanized ideal of the actor's impersonal craft, persists in theatrical theory down to the present day—through Bertolt Brecht, Futurism, Biomechanics, and the *übermarionetten*. At the same time, however, the more vitalistic strain in Diderot's materialism yielded an equally rich harvest for the modern acting theorists working the other side of the vineyard. His allowance for the role of unconsciousness in the creative process, his emphasis on the organism's capacity to remember and imagine sensation and emotion, his prophetic insistence that mind and body are inextricably interwoven in the same web of nervous fibres, which can be shaped into patterns of response by repetition, recur in some of the most influential writings of modern theorists and in the acting textbooks that dominate formal study in the field.

Diderot knowingly wrote for posterity and wisely so. Save for the *Encyclopédie*, for which he had to take into account the threats of censorious bigots, his greatest works appeared posthumously. The *Paradoxe* itself was not published in its complete form until 1830. Though that text circulated in manuscript, the *Paradoxe* was best known through the early version that was privately disseminated in Grimm's *Correspondance littéraire* in 1770 and then popularly reprinted in 1812–13. *Le rêve de d'Alembert* first appeared in 1830. *Le neveu de Rameau* originally saw light in 1805 in Goethe's German translation of an incomplete manuscript. Although a truncated version of the *Eléments de physiologie* was published in the complete works of 1875, the full text was only made available in 1964. In these and other prophetic works, Diderot foresaw such extraordinary nineteenth-century developments as evolutionary biology, nerve physiology, and the emergence of psychology as an independent science. He did not create these trends, but he did anticipate them.

In theatrical criticism and theory, Diderot played the more substantial role of instigator and catalyst, but here his contribution has been consistently slighted or misunderstood. Only Constant Coquelin in *L'art et le comédien* (1880) ratified Diderot's principles openly and unreservedly: "I hold [Diderot's] paradox to be literal truth" (*PA, 26*). Coquelin met head on the logic that most others evaded: once the crucial phenomenon of double consciousness is admitted, the rest of Diderot's position naturally follows. "The actor is within his creation, that is all," Coquelin concluded: "It is from within that he moves the strings which make his character express the whole gamut of human consciousness; and all these strings, which are his nerves, he must hold in his hand, and play upon as best he can" (*PA, 27*). Claude Bernard, the leading medical physiologist of the nineteenth century, arrived independently at the same conclusion, doubting the actor's capacity to maintain the necessary mental equilibrium under the physical pressure of an unmediated emotion.[30] But among actors it was different. Epitomized by Henry Irving's contention with Coquelin over sincerity, public denunciations of varying intensity have marked the critical history of Diderot's *Paradoxe*. His antagonists have included most of William Archer's English-speaking interviewees in *Masks or Faces?* and such French actors as Jacques Copeau, Louis Jouvet, and Charles Dullin.

There is, however, an overriding clue to the real success of Diderot's essay and the extent of the revolution it created. Whenever Diderot's self-declared foes attack his views, they tend to adopt—sometimes openly, but more often not—his concepts, arguments, and terminology.[31] One instance among many may be taken as typical. Although Alfred Binet, author of the intelligence test that bears his name, ostensibly sided with Diderot's opponents, the modern psychological principles he introduces to undermine the *Paradoxe* derive from those that most clearly support it, including *actions réflexes* and *adaptation inconsciente*.[32] Whatever their point of departure, theorists keep coming back to the *Paradoxe*. They find it a source of answers, but, more importantly, they find it the source of the pertinent questions to ask—questions about memory, emotion, imagination, characterization, unconsciousness, process, illusion, and double consciousness. Diderot's successors can scarcely avoid doing so because the *philosophe* foresaw the main directions of the future development of the life sciences and, along with them, the course that the evolution of acting theory would take in the nineteenth and twentieth centuries, the period we term modern, and the theoretical issues we are still defining in our acting schools and by our performance practices. At this juncture it should be recalled that Thomas Kuhn has defined two essential characteristics of a paradigmatic text. First, it must attract (or "deflect") a group of practitioners away from prevailing or competing views and assumptions. Second, it must at the same time be "sufficiently open-ended to leave all sorts of problems for the redefined group of practitioners to resolve."[33] In this respect, the questions that Diderot proposed or variations on them have become the preoccupations of an ongoing revolution in theatrical theory, a revolution that has followed the contours of an emerging science of life.

Diderot would probably not have been surprised to learn that the *Paradoxe* became one of the most frequently attacked as well as one of the most frequently quoted works on acting in theatrical history. In researching the various crafts and trades for explication in the *Encyclopédie*, he encountered occasional resistance from practitioners on the grounds that he was divulging professional secrets, as indeed he was. The *Paradoxe* alludes to the same reluctance on the part of actors to acknowledge that a professional mystery as ancient as the expression of emotion was comprehensible in the light of recent physiological discovery. "You may prove this to demonstration," admits First with the air of a *philosophe* who has entered the arena on the side of modern science and lost, "and a great actor will decline to acknowledge it; it is his own secret" (*PC*, 18). Then as now superstition exerted its not inconsiderable charms on spectator and performer alike, raising the veil of mystification and magic over the inner source of stage effects. The encyclopedist, however, wanted to explain, according to the best evidence then available, the physical basis of a useful art, a craft that, like any other, requires an instrument and is determined by the nature of that instrument.

5

Second Nature:
Mechanism and Organicism from Goethe to Lewes

Habit creates second nature, which is a second reality.
—Stanislavski, *Creating a Role* (1961)

In "The Actor and the *Übermarionette*" of 1908, Edward Gordon Craig insisted that the normal human body had utterly failed as the instrument of theatrical art. "The whole nature of man," he wrote, "tends toward freedom; he therefore carries the proof in his own person, that as *material* for the theatre he is useless." Spontaneous bodily sensation can only enslave the actor's mind. Random impulse trivializes his movements into accidents, and accidents negate art. Because of the human organism's unpredictable disposition and its corresponding indisposition to technical control, Craig banishes both the actor's ordinary vital tissue and its inspiring breath of emotion from the stage. As a stand-in he offers the "super-puppet," an automaton whose idiosyncracies have been annihilated by technique. In Craig's utopian vision a new ensemble of *Übermarionetten* is to repopulate the theater after all the mortal actors have taken Eleonora Duse's advice and died of the plague. Drawing on the widest range of authority to support his modest proposal for a truly modern art, Craig approvingly quotes Gustave Flaubert on the duties of authorship: "Art should be raised above personal affection and nervous susceptibility. It is time to give it the perfection of the physical sciences by means of a pitiless method."[1] Like the *mot juste*, super-puppet offers an ideal of machine-tooled precision.

The highly charged overstatement of Craig's essay has blinded readers to its proper place in an ongoing controversy. Hailed as a revolutionary anticipation of the "abstract man" and the "mechanical man" in twentieth-century art, "The Actor and the *Übermarionette*" in fact perpetuates a pattern of radical statements on the actor's art made in light of nineteenth-century science. In 1801–02 the word *biology* appeared simultaneously in the works of Lamarck and Treviranus. If we follow Michel Foucault and see in this event a sign of the emergence of the modern concept of life, we can understand the reasons for the celebrity of Diderot's *Paradoxe sur le comédien* at its publication in 1830 and its secure place at the center of theatrical controversy thereafter. As Diderot specifically anticipated, the lines of modern theatrical argument paralleled and overlapped the historic contention between biological vitalists and mechanists, a collision and at times a confusion of viewpoints that had more complicated implications than those increasingly obsolete terms could depict. At root the question came down to this: Is the actor's bodily instrument to be interpreted as a spontaneously vital organism whose innate powers of feeling must somehow naturally predominate? Or is it best understood as a biological machine, structured by and reducible to so many physical and chemical processes, whose receptivity to reflex conditioning determines its behavior?

On the ancient grounds of spontaneity, therefore, a new battle was inexorably joined, and from this struggle modern concepts of acting emerged. At one extreme adherents of mechanism threatened to abandon the human body as the material of theatrical expression or, at least, to transform it so utterly as to eliminate its behavioral unpredictability. Beginning with the Romantics, theorists from Heinrich von Kleist to L. Moholy-Nagy were driven to mechanism by the invention of life. If organisms are inherently spontaneous, infinitely variable, and as mobile as Diderot's diaphragm, then Craig has grounds for saying that unless stern measures are taken, whatever happens live onstage is in danger of happening by accident. At the opposite extreme—according to a viewpoint that did not fully emerge until the 1960s—radical vitalists rejected first the dramatic text and finally the preconceived structure of the theatrical event in order to minimize the need to constrain the performer's spontaneous impulses. In the following chapters we will see how the principal modern opinions on acting, beginning with Goethe, continuing through Stanislavski, and still accumulating in our journals and theatrical laboratories today, follow Diderot in mediating between the two camps, wary of both, yet borrowing from each in turn.

But within this general framework there are more specific concerns that must be addresssed. Diderot's theory of sensibility anticipated three issues in nineteenth-century biology of immediate relevance to acting. The first is the emergence of evolutionary theory, which defined the emotions as involuntary phenomena in both man and animals alike. This leads us from d'Alembert's dream to Goethe, and, through the work of Sir Charles Bell, directly to Charles Darwin's *Expression of the Emotions in Man and Animals* (1872). Darwin's treatise in turn heavily influenced William Archer's *Masks or Faces?* (1888), which posed Diderot's question to a generation of actors and ultimately accepted Diderot's answer on their behalf. Archer's attempt to refute the *Paradoxe* ends with his appropriation in the name of Victorian science of most of its contents, especially the idea of double consciousness. Second, and perhaps more significant, was the growing conviction that mind and body are organically inseparable and comprise not a duality, but a continuum. Monism became a major premise of nineteenth-century psychophysiology and of twentieth-century acting theory. This trail leads us from the *homme machine* to the dual-aspect monism of George Henry Lewes, the subsequent formulation of the James-Lange theory, and, later on, the development of Russian Reflexology as an objective science of behavior. It culminates—as succeeding chapters will show—in the works of Meyerhold, Grotowski, and contemporary actor-training theories based on *self-use* systems. The third and final issue is the role played by unconsciousness in feeling and action. The discovery of the unconscious revolutionized theories of the imagination, but it also incorporated the emerging concept of conditioned reflexes into the doctrine of spontaneity that Stanislavski called "second nature." The theory of the creative unconscious leads directly from Diderot to the preface that François-Joseph Talma provided for Lekain's memoirs, the *locus classicus* of a deflected text, which was read and admired by Lewes and Stanislavski among others.

All three issues—evolution, monism, and the unconscious—flourished in a scientific context transformed by the idea of organicism, but paradoxically devoted to the investigations of the mechanisms whereby living creatures respond and endure. Modern concepts of what acting ought to be resulted from the interaction of Diderot's paradox with these basic elements of nineteenth-century scientific thought. The theoretical context in which such thinking developed was provided by an aesthetic founded on ideals of organism and vitality.

It is a commonplace that the late eighteenth-century revolt of *Naturphilosophie* against the mechanization of nature transformed the theory of creativity. In Romantic poetics, models of organism clearly predominated over those of mechanism in the depiction of the artistic imagination. Poets and critics extolled the poem as plant, spreading its tendrils organically as directed by imponderable inward yearnings. The botanical definitions of *spontaneity*—coming freely without premeditation or effort, growing naturally without cultivation or labor—seemed the most appropriate terminology to apply to the work of art. The distance Coleridge finally placed between his mature formulation of the "secondary imagination" and his early enthusiasm for David Hartley is but one instance of the general success of vitalistic interpretations of imaginative life. Organic processes attained the stature of fundamental explanatory principles, which were then projected onto the forms and forces of inanimate nature, reversing the mechanical metaphor of Cartesian physiology and biologizing the world picture. Variety, spontaneity, and fluctuating responsiveness now characterized the natural order in a way that gave *life* and *organism* something approaching their current meanings. This new science of life seemed to stand firmly behind Wordsworth's famous definition of creativity in the Preface to *Lyrical Ballads* (1802): "all good poetry is the spontaneous overflow of powerful feelings."[2]

As Wordsworth digs more deeply into the question of spontaneity, however, another network of assumptions begins to emerge. His preface contains an oft-neglected series of qualifications and complications that turn the word *spontaneous* inside out and stand it on its head. "For our continued influxes of feeling," he explains, "are modified and directed by our thoughts, which are indeed the representative of all our past feelings; . . . so by repetition and continuance . . . such habits of mind will be produced, that, by obeying blindly and mechanically the impulse of those habits, we shall describe objects, and utter sentiments of such a nature, and such connection with each other," that the audience will be both enlightened and moved (*Prose Works* 1:127). Far from the musings of a self-obsessed poet waiting for the winds of divine inspiration to sweep through his soul, Wordsworth's turn of phrase—repetition, habit, blind obedience, modified feelings, directed thoughts, mechanical impulses— would seem more at home in the lexicon of eighteenth-century psychophysiology. It could take its place along side Robert Whytt's "reflex consciousness" or David Hartley's "secondary automatic motions." It also shows an affinity to the mental gymnastics performed by Diderot's Clairon, summoning up a phantasmic body stirred by imaginary passions. Like Wordsworth's poet, the actress draws upon the "collection" of decaying sensations retained unconsciously by her memory and rematerialized by repetition. For both Diderot and Wordsworth, *spontaneous* and *automatic* describe the same set of phenomena, a coincidence of meaning that evokes not the free overflow of emotions but their progressive canalization into habit. For both, the mind "in tranquillity" recollects the body's past feelings. Reflection shapes memory into an expressive illusion—an illusion of feelings spontaneously overflowing as if for the first time. This is not Nature, then; it is second nature.

As Wordsworth's dilemma shows, the paradox of organism and mecha-

nism presented nineteenth-century theorists with a range of options inexorably narrowing around the concepts of unconsciousness and the reflex.
Craig's version of second nature leaves a deliberate ambiguity as to
whether his *übermarionette* will be an actual automaton or a new kind of
human body reborn into behavioral regularity by some unspecified technique. Both his disenchantment with the corporeal status quo among
actors and the vagueness of his alternatives have deep roots in the Romantic period. By the 1820s literary critics had anticipated his defeatism in
most details. Craig himself quotes Charles Lamb on the futility of acting
Lear and alludes to William Hazlitt's similar doubts about *Hamlet*—
Shakespeare's ideas are simply too great to be enacted by the only bodies
available, human ones. More sweepingly, Craig's essential arguments as
well as his provocative metaphor were pre-empted by Heinrich von
Kleist in "Über das Marionetten Theatre" published in 1810. Kleist's
remarkable essay takes the form of a dialogue between the author and an
anonymous dancer-choreographer-philosopher whose fondness for pup-
pets extends beyond Punch and Judy into the realms of physics and
psychology. Like Mary Shelley's scientist, Kleist's choreographer proposed to construct an original and magnificent "monster": "He smiled
and replied that he dared to venture that a marionette constructed by a
craftsman according to his requirements could perform a dance that
neither he nor any other outstanding dancer of his time, not even Vestris
himself, could equal." Like the mad physics professor, Spalanzani, and
his robot daughter, Olimpia, from E. T. A. Hoffmann's *Der Sandmann*,
the choreographer favors the certainties of mechanism over the frailties of
flesh. Some Romantics despised actors because their creations were lim-
ited by their bodies; others, forgetting that there was no difference, found
fault with their minds. But puppetry gives the disembodied imagination
ascendency over matter. The marionette defies both gravity and fatigue:
as it is without sensation, so it is without indisposition. The marionette's
body retains its innocence and therefore its expressive plasticity: as it is
without identity, so it is without inhibition. By rendering expressive
automatisms perfectly unconscious, Kleist's marionette recalls Diderot's
specifications for the *grand acteur:* only in "the complete absence of
sensibility" does the possibility of sublime acting exist. Garrick seemed to
ratify the mechanical basis for both Kleist and Diderot's brand of sublimity when he framed his face between two screens and ran up and down a
scale of passions. "Grace," Kleist's interlocutor concludes, "appears to
best advantage in that human bodily structure that has no consciousness
at all—or has infinite consciousness—that is, in the mechanical puppet,
or in the God."[3]

Kleist's dancer-philosopher spoke from a certain authority about trends in virtuosity. Romantic performance embodied a paradox, if not the *Paradoxe*. As poets and theorists stressed the primacy of organism and spontaneous vitality in artistic creation, theatrical practice entered an age of unprecedented worship of technical virtuosity. By their very nature, virtuosic displays tend toward the premeditated and the mechanical. In the representative triumphs of early nineteenth-century performance, allied to acting and establishing a context in which Romantic acting may be understood, artists made their reputations by probing the outer limits of physical technique: on the concert stage, Paganini; in opera, *bel canto* singing; in the dance—most particularly in the dance—the high *jetés* of Marie Taglioni. Of the latter's fantastic elevation, her spectral hovering *sur les pointes*, it was said that the body defied gravity and attained geometry. Its fabulous technique literally and figuratively seemed to lift it above the sublunary sphere inhabited by ordinary flesh. Her audiences, indulging titillating fantasies of her Paganinian diabolism, professed to find in her floating body intimations of the preternatural. Everyone really knows, however, that such flights through the aether begin and end everyday at precisely three feet and six inches, the height of the *barre* off the rehearsal-room floor. Viewed in broad historical perspective, the Romantic ballet extended into modernity the eighteenth-century aesthetic of the operatic *castrato*. The ballerina's body, like the singer's larynx of yesteryear, is tortured into shapes and launched into physical trajectories that are not in nature. In the absence of suitable automata or in spite of them, repetition of exercises must fix the positions and motions of the dance so indelibly on the artist's muscles that she becomes capable of transcending artistically extraneous impulses such as pain. The art of the dance is motion recollected in tranquillity.

By the early years of the nineteenth century, it had become obvious that the theater, despite the earnest efforts of eighteenth-century mechanical theorists from Aaron Hill to Jelgerhuis, lagged far behind the other arts in developing the universal notation systems, training methods, and established techniques that promise to show the ways whereby the resistance of the body to itself and to art may be reliably mastered. Actors lacked a *Code of Terpsichore*, a handbook for the mastery of the wayward organism in the cause of expression. This sense of a lack of a fundamental technique, or a science of theatrical art, stirred a defensive reaction of which Craig's polemic was but one belated manifestation. The earlier recognition of the need for a kind of manual, a specific method to attain second nature, can be seen in the work of Goethe, who was perhaps the last figure in history to survey the realms of science and art with an authority equivalent to Diderot's.

The extent of Diderot's direct influence on Goethe is a matter of scholarly contention, but their intellectual affinities, particularly in matters of biology and theater, are beyond question.[4] Goethe's insights into the morphology of plants prompted George Henry Lewes, his best-informed biographer, to remark on a phenomenon that could apply equally to the author of the *Rêve de d'Alembert:* "Biology has peculiar fascinations for the poetical mind, and has seduced several poets to become physiologists." The long chapter on Goethe's contributions to science reveals his biographer's personal enthusiasm for the poet's "clear announcement of biological laws." Lewes especially celebrates his subject's revolutionary understanding of organism. Every living being is a "reunion of beings living and existing in themselves"; its parts have evolved from an original type, but they are differentiated in structure and function according to the economy of the whole; they are subordinated, that is, to the autonomous organization of which they are specialized components in a perpetual process of being rearranged. The key to understanding "organic bodies," therefore, is "development." In order to comprehend the grown, science must study growth.[5] Here relationships founded on adaptation, change, and evolutionary differentiation have replaced the matrix of fixed forms that characterized eighteenth-century taxonomy, even that of Goethe's beloved Linnaeus. Although this formulation of *life* was the achievement of Goethe's generation, not Diderot's, d'Alembert's dream had evoked remarkably prescient images of the impending biosphere: "In this immense ocean of matter there is not one molecule that is just like another, not one exactly like itself from one instant to the next. . . . Everything changes, everything passes away—only the whole endures" (*Rêve,* 117). One can see why such an intoxicating vision of constantly evolving wholeness would appeal to the Romantic artist.

Among the other fascinations of biology to the poetical mind is the concept of the unconscious impulses underlying mental creation in all its forms, impulses that Goethe viewed as microcosmic analogues to the growth and responsive adaptability of organic nature at large. Both Diderot and Goethe saw art and science as compatible disciplines linked by common imaginative processes. In each case these processes refine the raw material of intuition into demonstrable truth and ideal beauty. To attain this refinement, they believed, a certain detachment is required. The dialectic of artistic inspiration and collectedness in Goethe's mature thought emerges from the pages of Madame de Staël's account in a form and with an emphasis remarkably similar to her countryman's thesis in the *Paradoxe:* "The artist," Goethe is reported to have said, "should conserve his *sang-froid* in order to excite more forcefully the imagination of his audience."[6] Art is organic process, but the process of organic growth above all follows orderly rules.

In more practical terms Goethe's *Rules for Actors* (1803) and his tyrannical directorial reign at Weimar essentially harmonized with Diderot's view of the mechanical nature of the actor's bodily art. If anything, the Intendant's prescriptions, owing a greater debt to the rhetorical and painterly tradition, seem more reductive than the *philosophe's*. Diderot left to the actor much of the creative freedom that Goethe usurped by directorial fiat. He argues that rules of diction, gesture, and posture should be incorporated into habitual actions until they become "second nature." When Diderot wrote of Clairon manipulating the great "puppet" of her character, he attributed the work of art to the actress. In rehearsal she fashioned the doll from the materials supplied by her imagination and the poet's. In performance she exerted virtuosic control over its every expressive turn. She moved inside her creation, willing its shapes and movements with the economy of a master puppeteer. Goethe, on the other hand, placed the strings of the marionette in the director's hands. He prophesied the coming of Edward Gordon Craig's "Artist of the Theatre" and, beyond him, the cinema director. At Weimar the actor danced to the *regisseur*'s tune, no longer imitating a model of his own devising, but pressing his body into kinesthetic templates fashioned for him by the director. Under strict coaching Goethe's actor worked to perfect details such as the angle at which his elbow bends and the precise position of the fingers, which should be calculated separately for each expressive pose. The two middle fingers, however, should be held together at all times; the little finger should always remain slightly bent. More generally, sequences of gestures and expressions should be rehearsed in front of a mirror until the actor can depict the entire action of the role with his body alone while he repeats the text silently to himself. Goethe enthused about what Diderot had termed the inner model: "At the same time it must be assumed that the actor has previously made completely his own the character and the entire circumstance of what is to be presented and that his imagination has correctly worked through his material; for without this preparation he will be correct neither in declamation nor in gesture."

Goethe further thought that the stage should be regarded as an empty space into which carefully choreographed figures project beautiful shapes. For the actor's clarity of reference, the stage floor should be divided into a grid, resembling a chessboard, so that he "can determine into which squares he will enter, can note this pattern on paper, and can then be sure that in emotional passages he will not rush here and there inartistically."[7] This brand of stagecraft necessitated meticulous rehearsal during which the director beat time with a baton and after which he imposed fines to penalize haphazard execution. Goethe's rules for the actor represent for the most part an ethics of rehearsal. In order to offset the adverse theatrical consequences of organism, they outline a conscious process of responsible creation.

Audiences and critics have always resisted this view of the theater, particularly so in the Romantic age. They resisted it even when some of their favorite performers upheld it explicitly. Daemon "inspiration" reigned in the popular conception of theatrical genius, not to be put off by demurs of craftsmanship. Nowhere can this rift between the artist and the critical public be better seen than in the career of Edmund Kean, by acclamation the definitive Romantic actor of the English stage. Lurid accounts of the spectators who fainted dead away during his passion-swept and supposedly improvised tirades make for some of the liveliest reading in theatrical biography. His audiences craved to find in him something of the supernatural, some forces at work in him beyond the ordinary confines of flesh and blood. But to understand Kean's acting on the basis of these testimonials is like trying to read Coleridge by flashes of lightning. Of course, the average spectator tends to explain an actor's methods in terms of the effects he sees before his eyes. This represents faulty procedure in analyzing the efforts of the artist whose business is illusion, but it is a perfectly natural mistake for the casual theatergoer to make. The false penumbra of pathetic sensibility that surrounded performances by Susannah Cibber is one example of such benign misinformation. Nothing seems to have irritated Kean more, however, than for critics, who should have known better, to praise him for the "impulsiveness" of his acting. Like Diderot, he expected those who wrote professionally about the theater at least to understand that acting constitutes a process. He expected them to respect the fact that the actor of integrity tries his best, within the limits of his daily mental and physical disposition (and for Kean this did vary), to execute at each performance the model or conception he has created in rehearsal. When Kean blocked a cross, he counted the steps. Why should he devote to his art less care than Taglioni gave hers? In tones of a craftsman whose intelligent mastery of his material has been frivolously dismissed as inspiration, he complained bitterly to Garrick's widow: "These people don't understand their business; they give me credit where I don't deserve it, and pass over passages on which I have bestowed the utmost care and attention. Because my style is easy and natural they think I don't study, and talk about the 'sudden impulse of genius.' There is no such thing as impulsive acting; all is premeditated and studied beforehand. A man may act better or worse on a particular night, from particular circumstances; but although the execution may not be so brilliant, the conception is the same" (*AA*, 327–28). Kean's outburst demonstrates a practical application of Diderot's inner model, exposing the naïve understanding of spontaneity by those who would confound the promptings of second nature with those of the first. Falling away from the conception reflects not genius, but a lapsed craftsmanship attributable to physical indisposition.

Kean would no doubt have taken comfort in an anecdote related by his French colleague François-Joseph Talma. Playing the pathetic death scene in *Tancrède* one night in Marseilles in 1814, Talma experienced a spontaneous rush of inspiration, palpitating his nerves at the prospect of his character's imminent demise. "Never have I played like this," he was thinking ecstatically to himself, when suddenly at the climactic moment, his final agonized collapse to the stage floor, a blood-curdling shriek resounded through the auditorium, followed by commotion and uproar. He instantly deduced that a young woman had fainted at the sight of his death, a prospect he found so thrilling that he himself swooned as the curtain fell. When he revived backstage, he set aside all the doubts about sensibility that his reading and rereading of Diderot's *Paradoxe* had caused. From this moment forth he would play from inspiration rather than calculation, letting the spontaneous promptings of his soul carry him whither they might. Later he recounted his triumph at a soirée. A certain lady, listening intently to his conclusions with an odd mixture of amusement and embarrassment, invited him to her house the following day. There she confessed that she was the one who had cried out so piercingly, but not because of anything she had seen on the stage. She screamed because her estranged husband had stabbed her during a fit of jealous rage. The pain had been excruciating, but fortunately the weapon punctured nothing vital—except for Talma's new theory.

As one might surmise from this story, Diderot's ironic muse haunted Talma onstage and off. For a time he evidently had access to a manuscript of the complete text of the *Paradoxe sur le comédien*, and he owned the reprinted version of Grimm's *Correspondance littéraire* (1812–13) in which the "Observations sur *Garrick*" had first appeared in 1770. If imitation is the sincerest form of flattery, then Talma's several straightforward plagiarisms from Diderot tell us a good deal about how his views of acting evolved. In a letter written shortly after *l'affaire Tancrède*, Talma attempted to pass off the passage on the inner model from the *Paradoxe* as his own sentiments on the art of acting, making only minor changes in phrasing and deleting nothing.[8] As time went by, Talma readjusted his views, ostensibly to insist on a greater role for sensibility. His final revised statement on acting came in an essay he wrote for publication at the head of Lekain's memoirs, *Quelques réflexions sur Lekain et sur l'art théâtral* (1825). Its subsequent influence far exceeds the actual originality of its arguments. It was translated into English at Henry Irving's urging and printed in *The Theatre* for 1877. Irving hailed it as a "vade mecum" of the profession, all the more persuasive and useful to actors because it had been "written by one of themselves" (*PA*, 42). William Charles Macready's *Reminiscences* shows its influence in detail. G. H. Lewes cites Talma in several key passages in his important collection of essays *On Actors and the Art of Acting* (1875), and *Lekain* was among the books that Stanislavski used as a springboard into the System. In assessing the connections that these facts suggest, however, it is vital to recognize the primary influence behind such a "deflected" text: *Lekain* was central to later theories of acting because of its unacknowledged indebtedness to the *Paradoxe*.

Like many actors who have since written on Diderot, Talma expressed his distaste for the coldness and insincerity he found imputed to actors by the *Paradoxe sur le comédien*. He repeatedly argued for two qualities in the great actor—sensibility and intelligence—and he pointedly championed Dumesnil over Clairon. At the same time, however, he relentlessly pillaged Diderot's thought for the very substance and, sometimes, for the very language of his theory. Above all, Talma depicted acting as a psychophysical process. The larger process, the actor's career, begins with a "nervous system" of particular mobility and responsiveness (*PA*, 49) and ends with a repertoire of roles that have been honed and polished to perfection over at least a twenty-year period, the minimum time an actor requires to master his instrument and his line of business (*PA*, 51). At the end of this extended period of apprenticeship, Talma believed, Lekain for one had achieved an impeccable technique founded on repetition, habit, intelligence, and memory. His instrument had at last fallen into perfect tune:

> It was then that his acting was fixed on such bases, and was so subservient to his will, that the same combinations and the same effects presented themselves without study. Accent, inflections, action, attitudes, looks, all were reproduced at every representation with the same exactness, the same vigour; and if there was any difference between one representation and another, it was always in favour of the last. (*PA*, 51)

Talma filched the final sentence here verbatim from the *Paradoxe*, as he had done before, but the most significant borrowing consists of the paradoxical concept itself. Lekain has attained apparent spontaneity by conditioning his nervous system into certain regular patterns of action and response. His actions have become so thoroughly studied that they require no study. His body has been worked and reworked until the merely accidental impulse cannot turn his actions aside from their prede-termined course. Lekain has become an acting machine in much the same way that Taglioni was a dancing machine. As one commentator observed of *Lekain*, you cannot be spontaneous a second time (*PA*, 62). This problem developed into one of the central issues in nineteenth-century acting theory, giving rise to William Gillette's well-known essay "The Illusion of the First Time in Acting" and to a revealing remark made by Henry Irving in his introduction to *Lekain*, which conceded much more to Diderot's position than Irving seems to have realized: "The essence of acting is its *apparent* spontaneity. Perfect *illusion* is attained when every effect seems to be an accident" (*PA*, 42–43, emphasis added). Here spon-taneity has become part of a prefabricated illusion, and the term loses any semblance of its original meaning.

Talma's particular virtue was that he outlined a method whereby re-hearsal can purify impulse into art and yet leave room for a periodic refreshment or an overhaul of the role. The method obscures almost as much as it reveals, but in its obvious debt to the *Paradoxe* and in its equally obvious influence on Stanislavski, it represents a crucial passage among revolutionary "deflected" texts:

> In order that [the actor's] inspirations may not be lost, his memory, in the silence of repose, recalls the accent of his voice, the expression of his features, his action—in a word, the spontaneous workings of his mind, which he had suffered to have free course, and, in effect, every-thing which in the moment of his exaltation contributed to the effect he had produced. His intelligence then passes all these means in review, connecting them and fixing them in his memory, to re-employ them at pleasure in succeeding representations. . . . By this kind of labour the intelligence accumulates and preserves all the creations of sensibility. (*PA*, 50–51)

The method outlined here echoes the process of creating the inner model that Diderot attributed to Mlle. Clairon in her *rêverie*. The actor is encouraged to collect the sum total of appropriate gestures and tones and to shape them into a design for the role. Measured against the actor's career, this design represents the building of an individual character, the smaller process. In Talma's view, much of this construction of a character happens unconsciously. Its materials derive from outward observation of nature and from the introspective contemplation of emotion through memory. Creative intelligence collects these elements into a truthful fiction. Speaking directly to the point of affective memory, Talma apologizes for secretly observing himself at moments of personal sorrow with the intent of later incorporating his findings into his work (*PA*, 58).

The theory of the actor's use of his own personal associations in the construction of a role coincided conveniently with the Romantic heritage of complexity and idiosyncrasy in the development of dramatic character.[9] Character dominated Romantic criticism of Shakespeare, and it helped to promote the concept of a character biography. This interesting idea, which lent itself readily to Antoine's type of naturalism and ultimately to Stanislavski's, presumes that each dramatic persona has a life anterior and (if he survives the disease of the fifth act) posterior to the text. It thus becomes the actor's task, as it had been the task of Romantic criticism in such works as *The Girlhood of Shakespeare's Heroines,* to fill in the offstage life of the character through his analysis of the role and his own creative imagination. The question of "How many children had Lady Macbeth?" is one that the modern actress taking the role might reasonably be expected to answer. The life sciences encouraged her to view character as the behavior of an organism with a history, raising difficulties of the sort that would not have troubled her predecessors. Taxonomic review of generalized passions as featured in eighteenth-century acting texts lent itself much more readily to the supposed neoclassical universality of types than it did to this kind of individuality. The obsolescence of the generic "Passions" opened the way for revised approaches to characterization based on more complex and up-to-date psychologies, particularly the emerging psychology of the unconscious. At this point the theorist needed to explain how the interior life of the character and the interior life of the actor could somehow be brought together, subtly fusing imagination and memory, character biography and autobiography.

On the subject of characterization, Talma stands between two worlds. His definition of the process of creating the inner model at once nods to neoclassical generality as it looks forward to the masochistic particularity of naturalism. He distinguished between memory and imagination in a way reminiscent of Diderot's *Eléments de physiologie,* which he could not have known, and the *Paradoxe,* which he once again paraphrases *in extenso.* Talma says that the actor's

> imagination which, creative, active, and powerful, consists in collecting in one single fictitious object the qualities of several real objects, which associates the actor with the inspirations of the poet, transports him back to the past, and enables him to look on at the lives of historical personages or the impassioned figures created by genius—which reveals to him, as though by magic, their physiognomy, their heroic stature, their language, their habits, all the shades of their character, all the movements of their soul, and even their singularities. (*PA,* 49)

As a resource for vivifying the *modèle idéal,* Talma proposes the storehouse of the actor's own inner experience, "the impressions his soul has felt" and their impact on his outward behavior, voice, and physiognomy: "He meditates on these, and clothes the fictitious passions with these real forms" (*PA,* 57–58). Imagination and memory of emotion, therefore, once again emerge as the theoretical bridge between sincerity and art, between inner feelings and outer form.

The issue of the singularities of characterization drew attention once again to the individual resources of the actor's instrument. The question was as old as Quintilian's *Institutio,* but the answer supplied by science had been revolutionized by the development of the concept of organism. Talma specified the kind of nervous system required for acting, but the increasing interest in individual bodily and psychic fabrics rendered the trend toward specificity entirely more personal. The individual organism came to be scrutinized as a network of endowments and limitations, themselves the complex product of heredity and environment. If the actor's art requires him to lend his peculiarities to his imaginative creation, then an inventory of those quirks would seem to be necessary as a preliminary step. This inventory of the actor's means could take many forms, but none perhaps more remarkable than that sketched by Sir Charles Bell in *The Anatomy and Philosophy of Expression as Connected with the Fine Arts,* first published in 1806 and again in many subsequent editions to 1880. Bell shares priority in establishing the Bell-Magendie law of nerve physiology, which differentiates between motor and sensory channels entering and exiting the spinal cord, an important contribution to the understanding of reflex action. His principal interest was anatomy, but like his brother, G. J. Bell, who left richly detailed notes on Mrs. Siddons's Lady Macbeth (*PA,* 79–109), Sir Charles became a close student of actors and the art of acting.

Bell's *Anatomy and Philosophy of Expression* anticipated Darwin's *Expression of Emotion in Man and Animals* (1872) by proposing a comparative method for demonstrating the continuities of emotional expression among the higher animals including man. At the outset he claims "special provision" for human expression, but his most stimulating observations concern the expressive machinery that man has in common with savage and domesticated creatures. He divided the muscles of the face in higher animals into three classes: those that raise the lip from the teeth, those that surround the eyelids, and those that move the nostrils. The first category he divided into two divergent subtypes: *ringentes,* the "snarling muscles" of carnivorous animals; and *depascentes,* the feeding muscles of "graminivorous" animals. Bell inventories both types, carnivores and graminivores, in currently popular actors and actresses. Though he regarded the horse as the possessor of the noblest of animal physiognomies, one wonders if Mrs. Siddons could actually bring herself to accept the compliment in the spirit Bell intended:

> In the countenance of Mrs. Siddons, or Mr. John Kemble, there was presented the highest character of beauty which belongs to the true English face. In that family the upper lip and nostrils were very expressive: the class of muscles which operate on the nostrils was especially powerful, and both these great tragedians had a remarkable capacity for the expression of the nobler passions. In their cast of features there was never seen that blood-thirsty look which Cooke could throw into his face. In him the *ringentes* prevailed: and what determined hate could he express, when, combined with the oblique cast of his eyes, he drew up the outer part of the upper lip, and disclosed a sharp angular tooth![10]

Bell's assessment of the anatomical and physiological limits imposed on expressiveness ushers in a new concept of the particularity of emotion. His view derives from the emerging doctrine that expressive behavior is inherited, that the motors driving emotion are held in common by certain evolutionarily related species, but that singular characteristics may emerge under the determining influence of unique inheritance and individual experience. To view the actor's expression of emotion as part of the continuity of nature, as Sir Charles Bell did, opens up new avenues leading from physiognomy inward to psychology and to the anatomy of emotions at their source. To view the player's passion as a manifestation of his animal nature, comical as Bell's example may appear, invites theatrical theorists to examine emotion in light of the findings of the most important revolution in nineteenth-century science, the developmental hypothesis or Darwinism.

Underlying the *Paradoxe sur le comédien* there resides Diderot's presupposition that the authentic emotions, by their very nature, resist voluntary control. Behind this assumption, in turn, exists his concept of negative *will* as he explored it in the *Eléments de physiologie*, namely, that will has no real existence apart from a congregation of biological drives dictated by the animal origins of the human machine. By will Diderot means instinct. Throughout the *Rêve de d'Alembert*, he upholds the continuity of the forms of nature and their evolutionary mutability: "Who knows whether our species is not simply a hatchery for another generation of beings who will supplant our species after the lapse of countless centuries, during which successive modifications will occur?" (*Rêve*, 116). Sensibility exists from the lowest to the highest levels. Give way to your sensibility, Diderot says in effect, and you experience the spasms of a nonrational force you have in common with the rest of

FIGURE 20. Mrs. Siddons. *(Courtesy of Washington University Libraries.)*

FIGURE 21. *Depascentes.* "In the graminivorous they are directed so as to raise the lips from the incisor teeth." From Charles Bell, *Anatomy and Philosophy of Expression* (1806). *(Courtesy of Washington University Libraries.)*

FIGURE 22. George Frederick Cooke. *(Courtesy of Arnold Hare.)*

FIGURE 23. *Ringentes.* "A Mass of Muscular Fibres, always the strongest in this class of animals, and which with those concealed under them, I call Ringentes [K]. They raise the upper lip and expose the [canine] teeth." From Charles Bell, *Anatomy and Philosophy of Expression* (1806). *(Courtesy of Washington University Libraries.)*

evolving nature. It operates from below, trembling the filaments of your web, beyond your conscious control. Charles Darwin's own account of emotion and expression, illuminated by his explanation of the mechanism of natural selection, makes Diderot's point specifically: "That the chief expressive actions, exhibited by man and by lower animals, are now innate or inherited,—that is, have not been learnt by the individual,—is admitted by everyone. So little has learning or imitation to do with several of them that they are from the earliest days and throughout life quite beyond our control."[11] Ethology, the modern science Darwin founded with *The Expression of the Emotions in Man and Animals,* explores the continuities of emotional behavior in nature, and it has influenced contemporary theatrical theory on questions of communication and social interactions.[12] In the nineteenth century, however, Darwin's authority was brought to bear directly on the question of the actor's feeling. In *Masks or Faces?* William Archer quotes *The Expression of the Emotions* to prove, among other things, that perspiration during performance indicates the presence of powerful emotions in the actor and that, once excited by the imagination, these emotions continue to produce manifestations involuntarily (*MF,* 166–67). To illustrate his point Archer turns to the involuntary phenomenon of the pallor of terror and the flushed complexion of rage in a chapter called "Nature's Cosmetics."

Darwinism portrays the body as organized principally to meet the exigencies of the exterior milieu. The senses turn outward on the objective world to meet any threats to the well-being of the organism, not inward to monitor the vague impulses that will burst forth as emotion. Expressive movements more naturally spring from the reflexes of the species than the conscious will of the individual. Intriguingly, Darwin suggests in passing that a certain family of great actors—the Kembles, no doubt, though he does not name them—may have possessed voluntary control over specific groups of facial muscles to an abnormal degree (*Emotions,* 183–84). Diderot raised the same issue when he described Garrick's astonishing physiognomical virtuosity, but pinpoint control over the inward physiology of emotion was another, more complex question. Though not impossible in the broad spectrum of mutations, the natural emergence of this quality would be a rarity indeed. As Archer observed: "Physiological records may furnish cases of a power to blush and blanch at will; but even if these exist (they have not come to my knowledge) we can only regard such a faculty as a freak of nature, much more abnormal than (for example) the power of moving their ears which some people possess" (*MF,* 159). Diderot suggests that this sort of control, if not conspicuously present in the organization to begin with, may be developed by the exceptional organism-machine through practice or

FIGURE 24. *Terror* as represented by an actor *(above)* and induced by the electrical stimulation of the facial muscles *(below)*. From Darwin's *Expression of the Emotions in Man and Animals* (1872). *(Courtesy of Washington University Libraries.)*

habit by the artful cultivation of a second nature (*Rêve*, 149–56). Diderot would have agreed with Darwin and Archer on the scarcity of this attribute in the wild. By 1769 he already held the modern view that in nature's plan the conscious mind looks outward on the light of the world; behind it there prevails an inner darkness, harboring not only the unspeakable, but the unthinkable: "If your little savage were left to himself and to his native blindness," observes MOI in *Le neveu de Rameau* of LUI's son, "he would in time join the infant's reasoning to the grown man's passion—he would strangle his father and sleep with his mother" (76).

Nineteenth-century theories of mind-body relationships increasingly adopted the view that nonrational and instinctive forces in man reside in a mysterious and capacious place called the unconscious. By the 1870s the word *unconscious* and its physiological counterpart *subconscious* achieved a popularity pervasive enough to constitute a fashion. This trend provided a meeting ground for Darwin and Freud.[13] Physiological biology sought to locate the "higher" mental processes in the cerebrum and the emotions in the brain stem, which had evolved at a more primitive stage in the descent of man. Speculative psychology, on the other hand, divided the mind into two interdependent but unlocalized spheres of influence—consciousness and everything else. The rise to prominence of these concepts may be gauged by the phenomenal success of Eduard von Hartmann's *Philosophy of the Unconscious* (1868), which straddled both the biological and speculative views. This deeply thoughtful, well-informed, and extremely boring book went through nine German editions by 1882. Translations appeared in French (1877) and English (1884). Chroniclers of intellectual taste reported that during the decade of the 1870s two topics dominated the discussions of the Berlin intelligensia: "Wagner and von Hartmann, the music and the philosophy of the unconscious, Tristan and instinct."[14]

William Archer approached von Hartmann with deference as "the Philosopher of the Unconscious" (*MF*, 172). To describe the actor's recourse to his unconsciousness, he adopted von Hartmann's term *autosuggestion. Masks or Faces?* cites several examples of actors whose powers of concentration allowed them to maintain an intense absorption in their roles, beginning with Burbage putting on his part in the Globe tiring house. A number of actors who responded to Archer's questionnaire reported spending introspective moments in their dressing rooms or backstage before their entrances. Their purpose seems to have been to prepare the kind of mental perimeter that Stanislavski would later call "the magic circle." Like Stanislavski, Archer emphasized the fugitive nature of the actor's subconscious mind, all too easily driven to hide itself in inaccessible places. It would not be forced. Through autosuggestion,

Archer maintains, such an actor works on his feelings indirectly; he does not will them into existence consciously, but creates a psychological environment into which they can penetrate more easily. Ibsen's translator seems to have been aware of current developments in medicine. Hypnosis as a therapeutic device, after suffering a serious reverse with the discrediting of Mesmer and *animal magnetism,* had made a strong comeback by the 1880s in the psychiatric practices of Jean-Martin Charcot, Hippolyte Bernheim, and the young Sigmund Freud. Its status at this juncture was complex and controversial, but enthusiasts viewed it as a hidden pathway to the unconscious mind. The use of hypnosis by actors to attain a trance-like concentration on the role was shortly thereafter proposed by Max Martersteig in *Der Schauspieler: ein kunstlerisches Problem* (1900). Martersteig's *transfiguration theory* made specific use of the premise that hypnotic suggestion can release creative energies "without voluntary participation." The hypnotic instrument is the play itself, which begins to work its magic on the actor's "cerebral system" from the very first reading.[15]

Drawing on *The Expression of the Emotions in Man and Animals* yet again, Archer introduced the term *innervation* as a physiological counter-

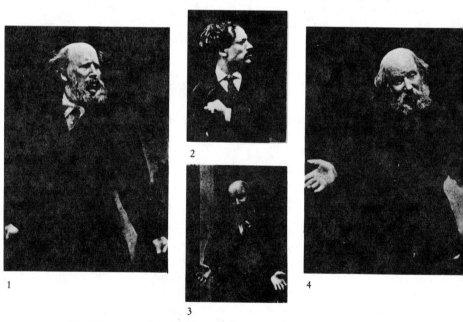

FIGURE 25. Nos. 1 and 2: *Pride and Contempt.* Nos. 3 and 4: *Helplessness, Impotence, Shrugging the Shoulders.* From Darwin's *Expression of the Emotions in Man and Animals* (1872). *(Courtesy of Washington University Libraries.)*

part to von Hartmann's psychological *autosuggestion.* By *innervation* Darwin meant the physical preparation of the animal's muscular system for violent exertion, combat, or display. Archer begins his discussion on this question with the following anecdotes: "G. H. Lewes relates how Macready, as Shylock, used to shake a ladder violently before going on for the scene with Tubal, in order to get up 'the proper state of white heat'" (*MF,* 171). He goes on to cite the passage in the *Hamburg Dramaturgy* where Lessing argues that an actor can work up an emotion by performing the physical actions associated with the emotion. As Darwin put it in another passage that Archer quotes: "He who gives way to violent gestures will increase his rage; he who does not control the signs of fear will experience fear in a greater degree; . . . These results follow partly from the intimate relation which exists between almost all the emotions and their outward manifestations; and partly from the direct influence of exertion on the heart, and consequently on the brain" (*Emotions,* 366). Archer's vague duality alternates between working from the inside out through mental concentration and from the outside in through physical actions (he himself seems to confuse the processes). In such an idea Aaron Hill might have recognized his "plastic imagination" and Lessing his contrasting "involuntary mechanism." The immediate source of Archer's bipolar division of theatrical emotion was, as his reference to the anecdote about Macready suggests, much closer at hand. He was George Henry Lewes, Victorian scientist and drama critic, whose expert inquiry into the psychophysiology of acting confronted the complex issues raised by the concept of organism.

Archer credited Lewes with the introduction of the word *psychology* into the vocabulary of dramatic criticism and proposed him as "the most highly trained thinker who ever applied himself to the study of theatrical art in England." Other testimony supports Archer's view. In *La psychologie anglaise contemporaine* of 1870, Théodule-Armand Ribot described Lewes as "a physiologist" and Comptean "philosopher of science" whose efforts were part of a movement to establish psychology as an independent branch of scientific inquiry. Histories of psychology link him with Herbert Spencer as a thinker who grasped the implications of evolutionary biology for the study of behavior.[16] After exploring incidental topics in the history of science in his *Biographical History of Philosophy* (1845) and *The Life of Goethe* (1855), Lewes turned to research in marine biology and animal physiology. His studies led to an extremely popular publication, *The Physiology of Common Life* (1859). His culminating work was a five-volume study of psychology, *Problems of Life and Mind* (1874–79). As drama critic and essayist on theatrical subjects for such journals as the *Leader, Blackwood's,* and the *Pall Mall Gazette,*

Lewes thus brought expert knowledge to bear on his interest in what he called the "psychological conditions on which [theatrical] effects depend."[17] Late in life he temporarily set aside the middle volume of his *Problems, The Physical Basis of Mind*, in order to assemble his scattered dramatic reviews and essays into a single collection, *On Actors and the Art of Acting.* Reflecting on Lewes's attainments, Archer wished that Diderot's paradox could be reargued, not by a "dogmatic 'First' and docile 'Second,' " but by an actor and a "trained psychologist" (*MF,* 76). Lewes was able to speak in both of these capacities. He had acted in amateur and professional productions, and he employed his extensive knowledge of physiology to pursue the anomaly of spontaneity, the paradox of organical and mechanical modes of behavior.

As a psychologist, G. H. Lewes was an associationist in the direct line of descent leading from David Hartley's *Observations on Man*, a book he admired as an early attempt to adduce a physiology of mental processes. He retained Hartley's term *vibrations* even though he confessed it lacked literal meaning when applied to nervous tissue.[18] Abandoning Hartley's parallelism for monism, however, Lewes believed that mind and body constitute one entity, not two. Every experience presents a double aspect—objective and subjective. The body is merely the objective aspect of a subjective process called mind. Every mental change has a corresponding physical change, and every mental act is carried on by the entire organism. In the mind-body continuum the nervous system represents a single entity. The primary mechanism of experience is the *neural tremor* or sense datum. The secondary mechanism is *sensation* or grouping of neural tremors; the tertiary mechanism, the reproduction of sensation to form an *image.* When an image loses its immediacy in sensation, it becomes an idea or *symbol.* The most intimate reciprocity exists between higher and lower forms of nervous activity. The idea or mental symbol may recall the primary tremor; an external stimulus may recall the image, the idea, and the feeling. Mind equals *Organisation*, which Lewes defined in *The Physiology of Common Life* as "the whole sum of necessary conditions" to sustain life, the connection and coordination of parts for vital functions or processes.[19]

The emerging concept of *reflex* also played an important part in Lewes's thinking about the body, and it led him to some of his most productive experimentation. Vivisectionists had previously discovered that the spine could respond with surprising versatility even in the absence of a brain. In 1853 Eduard Pflüger, in an experiment later repeated by Lewes, reported on the "wash reflex" of the spinal frog. After removing its brain, Pflüger poured acid on the animal's right side. It responded by washing its back with its right hind leg. Then Pflüger amputated the

right leg and restimulated the right side with acid. Thereupon the de-
capitated frog washed its right side with its left leg—a reflex adapted to
special circumstances with the expedience of thought. Startled by this
apparently purposive act carried out by the spinal frog, Pflüger was
moved to locate a part of the soul in the spinal cord. Less abstractly put,
he concluded that the spine thinks. Once the reflexive nature of higher
nervous activity was established, physiologists could attribute sentience
to the organism as a whole. Lewes did not hesitate to include man in the
generalizations derived from animal experimentation: "*It is the man and
not the brain that thinks;* it is the organism as a whole, and not one organ
that feels and acts" (*PLM, Physical Basis of Mind,* 441). On the basis of his
replication of Pflüger's work and of further experiments along similar
lines, Lewes concluded that: 1) all action is based on a "reflex arc" and
that "the cerebrum and spinal cord constitute an axis of reflection";
2) reflex actions—all action—are due to a complex of physiological mechanisms, but are not merely mechanical in Descartes's sense of automatism
because they are sentient ("felt") even in the absence of a brain.[20] The
cerebrum is an indispensable center for the coordination of the higher
reflexes, but it is not the exclusive seat of sensation. When the brain is
removed, reflex coordination is reduced sufficiently to give the appearance of mere mechanism, but the organism is still sensible. "All actions
are the actions of a reflex mechanism," he wrote in a sentence that distills
the vitalist-mechanist controversy à la Diderot; "and all are sentient; even
when unconscious they are therefore never purely mechanical, but always
organical" (*PLM, Physical Basis of Mind,* 390).

In drawing a distinction between organisms and machines (in the gross
sense of man-made objects like steam engines), Lewes imputed unique
properties to the "vital mechanism" in order to differentiate between it
and a mere "system of forces." Although an organism is "also a system of
forces," it responds less directly than a machine to external impulses;
rather, it responds to its own internal impulses: "Secondly, . . . its mechanism or structural adaptation, becomes *modified,* and consequently its
motors rearranged, under varying stimulations, so that its reactions are
not uniformly the same. The organism has a history, and is the expression
of experiences. On these two points of difference rests the marked contrast between the spontaneity of organisms and the fatality of machines.
No machine is educable. All its actions may be predicted. What it does
today it will do to-morrow, and without variation in the way of doing it"
(*PLM,* 3rd series, 2:85). He further distinguished between vital entities
and pure mechanisms on the basis of evolution: not only individual organisms but entire species have histories and are the expression of connected experiences—adaptable, mutable, and various. The phrase that

keeps reappearing in Lewes's work is "fluctuating spontaneity" or its alternative, "fluctuating variety." In his view it describes the fundamental properties of life.

When Lewes writes about the theater, he relies on example rather than extended exposition, but if his theatrical specimens are checked against his scientific principles, clear patterns begin to emerge. He boldly sets out to discriminate "the sources of theatrical emotion" (*On Actors*, 9), for he views expressiveness as the crux of the actor's art. The great performer must first possess "plasticity of organisation" (175). This means a fluid interdependence of body and mind, muscle and imagination, including a physique free from muscular tension, rigidity, and superfluity of motion and a technical mastery of voice in tone, cadence, and tempo. The physical organizations of great actors all share one characteristic: an "animal" physiology manifested in its energy, responsiveness, flexibility, and grace. Lewes's favorite performers spring from the pages of his criticism as if from the center ring at the circus. "Rachel was the panther of the stage; with a panther's terrible beauty and undulating grace she moved and stood, glared and sprang" (35). Edmund Kean was a lion (159). Lemaître burned with the "great energy of animal passion" (89). Shakespeare probably failed as an actor, Lewes speculates, because he lacked "weighty animalism" (101).

Animal physique or no, Lewes refused to credit "impulsive" or "inspired" acting as a way of communicating emotion: "It is not enough for an actor to *feel*, he must *represent*" (*On Actors*, 30). The craft of acting must be mastered by conscientious training and study. Unmediated emotion is not the source of great performances. The poet, as Lewes repeatedly says, may feel the emotions he describes, but he cannot read his poem in a way that would convey those emotions to others. Stage emotions must be enlarged or, for practical purposes, they will not exist. Only the actor has the appropriate instrument to magnify a mental *tremor* or *vibration*—clinical terms routinely used by Lewes in his drama criticism—into a theatrical image or symbol. "Voice, looks, and gestures are the actor's symbols" (30), and the finest actors are those who can choose the symbols that will most effectively represent the characters they are trying to portray. A symbol drained of its inner content of feeling, however, will not suffice for Lewes. He continually distinguishes the great actor who convincingly embodies the emotion he conveys from the conventional actor whose symbols lack vividness. "Either because in truth there is no strong feeling moving him, or because he is not artist enough to give it genuine expression," the conventional actor repeats merely pantomimic formulas—ready-made "signs," clichés, as "unlike nature as the gestures of a ballet-dancer" (176, 185). Though such hieroglyphic demonstrations may on occasion awe the uncultivated, for the most part Lewes stigmatizes them as "mechanical," barren of the textures and supple gradations of real life.

As a working critic Lewes reserved his most brutal analyses for those performers who failed to command what he called "the fluctuating physiognomy of passion" (*On Actors*, 180). In his view the actor had two givens with which to work—the character's emotions as conceived by the dramatist and the potentiality of his own bodily instrument. The actor's goal was to bring these elements into expressive juxtaposition, attaining the variegated responsiveness of a living organism. After surveying the several promising possibilities for vital characterization in Shakespeare's Macbeth, Lewes's surgical eye fell upon Charles Kean's inadequacies in this department: "When the witches accost him, his only expression of 'metaphysical influence' is to stand still with his eyes fixed and his mouth open, in the way you know. The *fluctuating* emotions which Macbeth must be undergoing all that time are expressed by a *fixed* stare."[21] Lewes, in his criticism of Charles Dickens's novels, develops a parallel idea. As truthful characterization in a realistic novel requires wholeness and roundness to capture the organic conditions of life, so characterization in the theater requires a completeness of response from the actor—body and mind together. In his remarks on mechanical characterization in Dickens, Lewes introduces an illuminating analogy between flat characters and maimed laboratory animals, whose centers of reflex coordination have been excised. When he thinks of mere catchwords personified as characters, Lewes

> is reminded of the frogs whose brains have been taken out for physiological purposes, and whose actions henceforth want the distinctive peculiarity of organic action, that of fluctuating spontaneity. Place one of these brainless frogs on his back and he will at once recover the sitting posture; draw a leg from under him, and he will draw it back again; tickle or prick him and he will push away the object, or take *one* hop out of the way; stroke his back, and he will utter *one* croak. All these things resemble the actions of the unmutilated frog, but they differ in being *isolated* actions, and *always the same:* they are as uniform and calculable as the movements of a machine. The uninjured frog may or may not croak, may or may not hop away; the result is never calculable, and is rarely a single croak or a single hop.[22]

Unimpaired frogs respond with the flexibility and variety of life itself, which are organic. Altered frogs react with uniformity and predictability, which are mechanical. In the eighteenth century similar alterations had emphasized the mechanical nature of artists like the *castrati* and had been praised as such; in the new context of the nineteenth century, anything less than organic completeness was considered less than human. Like Charles Kean's Shakespearean performances generally—for Lewes did not single out Macbeth for special condemnation—such decorticated characters are "utterly without physiognomical play; one stolid expression, immoveable as an ancient mask, is worn throughout a scene which demands fluctuating variety" (*On Actors,* 28). In short, according to Lewes, "Charles Kean has an organisation which excludes him from the artistic *expression* of complex or subtle emotions" (30–31).

At the opposite niche in Lewes's pantheon was Edmund Kean, Charles's father and the leonine hero of *On Actors and the Art of Acting.* Like Rachel and Lemaître, Edmund Kean was endowed with "mimetic flexibility of organisation" (100–01). In acting of this physical calibre, inner impulse and outer expression coincided with astonishing ease. They "found no difficulty in the most rapid transition; they could one moment chat calmly and the next explode. The imaginative sympathy instantaneously called up the accessories of expression; one tone would send vibrations through them powerful enough to excite the nervous discharge" (115). Lewes as a drama critic did not necessarily approve of these explosions because they dangerously resembled the mechanical "points" of old. As a scientist, however, he was fascinated by the reciprocity of mind and body demonstrated by such displays.

Discharge and *vibrations*—the terms Lewes used to describe the performances of Rachel, Edmund Kean, and Lemaître—are clinically defined in *The Physical Basis of Mind:* the former means a dynamic liberation of energy in nervous tissue, a sudden release of accumulated tension; the latter means the communication of a nervous impulse to adjacent tissue. "Laws of Discharge" and closely related "Laws of Arrest," Lewes theorizes, govern the function of the entire nervous mechanism. A state of nervous tension, for instance, is increased by every stimulation that falls short of discharge. Liberated tension in the form of energy discharges itself along "the lines of least resistance" in the pathways of the nervous system. Frequency of use helps to determine ease of traverse, but overstimulation may lead to arrest caused by fatigue of the organ at the end of the pathway.

Lewes applied his "Laws of Discharge and Arrest" directly to a theatrical phenomenon he called *subsiding emotion.* Like the observations Newton made on optical traces, Lewes's research proved that each nervous impulse "leaves behind it a tremor which does not immediately subside." Even after the stimulus has been withdrawn, the nervous activity or "agitation" that it caused continues. Lewes restates in abstract terms the basic idea that had led one hundred years before to the doctrine of sensibility: "We know by accurate measurements that the excitation of a nerve lasts much longer than the *stimulus*, a momentary impact producing an enduring agitation. We know that the excitation of a centre lasts longer than the muscular contraction it has initiated" (*PLM, Physical Basis of Mind,* 303, 176). Such experiences are familiar to everyone: the eyes, staring at a single lamp in an otherwise darkened room, continue to "see" the image after the light goes out; the bitter taste remains after the bitter substance has been removed; the arm muscles still tremble after the weight has been set down. These residual nervous tremors, increased in complexity and greatly amplified, form the physical basis of a complex psychic event—the gradual subsiding of emotion after a massive discharge. Again Lewes singles out Kean and Rachel, who also possessed the powers of nearly instantaneous transformation, as masters of the gradual physiology of subsiding emotion. He identified it as Kean's most conspicuous virtue and the clinching proof of his greatness:

> Kean was not only remarkable for the intensity of passionate expression, but for a peculiarity I have never seen so thoroughly realized by another, although it is one which belongs to the truth of passion, namely the expression of *subsiding emotion*. Although fond, far too fond of abrupt transitions—passing from vehemence to familiarity, and mingling strong lights and shadows with Caravaggio force of unreality—nevertheless his instinct taught him what few actors are taught—that a strong emotion, after discharging itself in one massive current, continues for a time expressing itself in feebler currents. The waves are not stilled when the storm has passed away. There remains a groundswell troubling the deeps. In watching Kean's quivering muscles and altered tones you felt the subsidence of passion. The voice might be calm, but there was a tremor in it; the face might be quiet, but there were vanishing traces of recent agitation. (*On Actors,* 20)

Emotion thus anatomized and finely delineated reproduces the behavior of a living being. Abrupt transitions, while "theatrically" effective in startling the philistines from their naps, mirror only the machine. According to Lewes, Rachel eventually began to neglect her talents, showing her most damaging carelessness by rushing to make old-fashioned "points." In isolated moments her former power burst forth, but without meaning, because her interim emotion had degenerated into empty noise and gesticulation. "The secondary emotions of subsiding passion," Lewes notes sadly, "she no longer represents, and that is what I indicate in saying she has become mechanical."[23]

Lewes's criterion of subsiding emotion offers yet another instance of a now familiar phenomenon. A transformed concept of the body had again revolutionized standards of theatrical truth. The mechanical passions like Garrick's astonishment, once accepted as the scientific representation of nature, had given way to organic transitions of evolving emotions. This marked the success of a new "semiotics of affects" founded on a new physiological paradigm. Naturally enough, Lewes the drama critic championed the interpretation of nature advanced by Lewes the biologist. The life of the role must, like the life of the organism, be marked by subtle gradations and complex adjustments. Both have identities shaped by their spontaneous capacity to adapt to changing circumstances. Both have histories formed by their memories of those adaptations. "Kean's quivering muscles and altered tones" attested to his sense of the character's integrity and the continuity of his experiences.

Kean could not have reproached Lewes, of course, as one of those amateurs who praised his impulsive genius and depreciated his craftsmanship. This drama critic at least wrote of Kean's technique from the position of an acting theorist who had often lowered his bucket into the wells of Diderot's *Paradoxe* and Talma's *Lekain*. As a physiologist at work on the phenomenon of conditioned reflexes, he understood the importance of second nature. His use of "mechanical" as a pejorative adjective obviously referred to the disappointing effect produced when body and mind cease to function in coordination onstage, when the actor's expressions lose the power to amplify the exquisite play of feeling in a sensitive organism. It did not refer in a negative sense to the creation of a character-model and the attendant rehearsal *process:*

> [Edmund Kean] was an artist, and in Art all effects are regulated. The original suggestion may be, and generally is, sudden and unprepared—"inspired," as we say; but the alert intellect recognizes its truth, seizes on it, regulates it. Without nice calculation no proportion could be preserved; we should have a work of fitful impulse, not a work of enduring Art. Kean vigilantly and patiently rehearsed every detail, trying out tones until his ear was satisfied; and having once regulated these he never changed them. The consequence was that, when he was sufficiently sober to stand and speak, he could act his part with the precision of a singer who has thoroughly learned his air.

Counting the steps for each cross was but one of the "mechanisms" of his art whereby Kean "was always the same" (*On Actors,* 18–19). There is a qualitative difference between "fitful impulse," which is without reflex coordination, and "fluctuating spontaneity," the illusion of which is achieved by artful calculation and sufficient rehearsal to develop a score of the role.

On Actors and the Art of Acting, therefore, like Talma's *Lekain* and Archer's *Masks or Faces?*, increases in specificity and coherence as it approaches the paradigmatic text, Diderot's *Paradoxe*. "The rarity of fine acting," Lewes writes, "depends on the difficulty there is in being at one and the same moment so deeply moved that emotion shall spontaneously express itself in symbols universally intelligible, and yet so calm as to be perfect master of effects . . . with a mind in vigilant supremacy controlling expression, *directing* every intonation, look, and gesture" (105–06). The psychophysiological solutions Lewes proposes to this dilemma derive from Diderot's central techniques for the creation and execution of the inner model: memory of emotion, observation of emotion in others, subconscious stimuli, imagination, and, above all, double consciousness. Like Diderot, Lewes supplies each of these techniques with a physical basis drawn from the best available knowledge of the body and its inner workings.

In "Subjective Analysis and the Introspective Method," a chapter from the penultimate volume of *Problems of Life and Mind*, Lewes defends introspection as a valid form of scientific inquiry. Although he regrets the vagueness of such terms as the *inner eye*, he believes that self-contemplation may hold insights that are impossible to achieve through the application of purely objective methods. The mind may stand outside itself, observe itself in operation, and retrieve those operations through memory: "states of consciousness, whatever their origin, are feelings capable of being *re*-felt in the forms of images and memories" (*PLM*, 3rd series, vol. 1, *Study of Psychology*, 88). Therefore, he strongly urged actors to practice "introspection of their own means" (*On Actors*, 107). The boldness of such inner vision characterizes great artists. It defines their powers. "We are all spectators of ourselves," he wrote, "but it is the peculiarity of the artistic nature to indulge in such introspection even in moments of all but the most disturbing passion, and to draw thence the materials of art" (113). Lewes quotes Talma to the effect that however cruel the actor's loss or sorrow in real life, his mental gaze turns inward to allow the artist to eavesdrop on the man. Only by becoming intimately familiar with the nature of his own emotions can the actor interpret analogous passion in creating a character, but, as Diderot and Wordsworth had also noted, time must intervene between the feeling and the artistic expression of feeling. Memory provides the storehouse to which introspection holds the key. Emotion must be processed. Lewes applies the neurophysiological term *tremor* and the psychological term *image* to the process whereby the artist can "select" those emotional memories that fit his design: "It is from the memory of past feelings that he draws the beautiful image with which he delights us. He is tremulous again under the remembered agitation, but it is a pleasant tremor, and in no way disturbs the clearness of his intellect" (113).

In a chapter from the final volume of *Problems of Life and Mind* called "Double Consciousness," Lewes offers an innovative explanation of this important phenomenon. His absolute mind-body monism will not permit him to follow Diderot in depicting the division of consciousness into several channels, parallel streams running along simultaneously. Rather, Lewes sees a rapid alternation of attention from one level of consciousness to another, not unlike alternating current in standard electrical devices. In searching out a metaphor for this version of double or multiple consciousness, Lewes shows that at least one sort of theatrical performance was foremost in his mind: "When Ducrow rode six horses at once he pressed the reins of each alternately, now checking, now redirecting. Attention in like manner shifts from one series to another." Earlier he had advanced a definition of *attention* that anticipates currently popular conceptions of breathing and body states as the basis for concentration: "The acquisition of the power of attention is the learning how to alternate mental adjustments with the rhythmic movements of respiration" (*PLM*, 3rd series, 2:220, 189n). The complex interplay of voluntary and automatic control over breathing illustrates his idea that levels of consciousness advance and recede alternately.

Ducrow's six-horse gallop improves on Diderot's model because it describes the phantasmagoric multeity of theatrical performance. It also does justice to the adaptive complexity of organisms. At any given moment the actor's mind must retain his cues, his lines, his blocking, his gestures, some idea of the similar assignments of his cohorts (lest they forget), audience reaction, the location of properties and their heft, the precise timing of complex business, and, if he works that way, his motivation. As in the case of Ducrow, it is easier to believe that the actor does one thing at a time in rapid succession than it is to believe that he does everything at once. It would seem that the more elements he can render automatic through repetition, the more control he can exert over the variables that do arise. Archer records several instances of multiple levels of consciousness, which he quaintly calls "The Brownies of the Brain," thereby allowing for the automation of at least some of them. He catalogues the ornate mosaic of Fanny Kemble's mind as she colors with a virgin blush, minds not to fall over her train, prevents the tears from dropping on her silk bodice, avoids setting herself on fire with the funeral torches, checks herself from leaning her full weight on the canvas balcony, and speaks iambic pentameter interpretively. "There is sometimes a difficulty, of course," says Archer, putting it mildly, "in distinguishing between automatic action and . . . conscious or subconscious mental activity" (*MF,* 185–87). Lewes's metaphor allows room for just this sort of psychophysical complexity, a consciousness not only doubled but polygonally multiplied like the inside of an insect's eye.

Dilating on Fechner's law of *Schwelle* or the "threshold" of consciousness, Lewes writes that "our mental activity is for ever alternating between the upper and under levels of excitation; and for every change in consciousness there is needed a rise in intensity on one side which involves a fall on the other. There is thus a stream of Consciousness formed out of the rivulets of excitation" (*PLM,* 3rd series, 2:366). The subterranean tributaries to the "stream of Consciousness" (Lewes used the phrase a decade before William James) have an important place in his concept of theatrical creativity. Actors such as Rachel and Edmund Kean possessed a volatile and prolific "imaginative sympathy," buried deep in their physical constitutions, which "instantaneously called up all the accessories of expression" (*On Actors,* 115). That an inner impulse can ignite an outward manifestation as "spontaneously" powerful as "the lurid flame of vengeance flashing from [Kean's] eye" (160) obviously intrigued Lewes. To his way of thinking, imagination has a recombinant power of linking heretofore discrete entities, but it also has a vivifying power of "reinstatement," in which images become irradiated with the energy of sensations. In *The Physical Basis of Mind,* he noted that inner mental activity in everyday life can influence involuntary physical responses: the mention of a lover's name will cause a blush; the thought of an absent infant will cause a flow of milk in the mother's breast (*PLM,* 288). He divides consciousness into regions of "special sensation" (the five senses) and "systemic sensation," the subconscious, the submerged world of the involuntary sensations. The operation of the subconscious region continually replenishes the sources of outward behavior: beneath the realm of sense experience, a "groundswell of systemic sensation, emotion, or ideal preoccupation" is ready to emerge into consciousness. Even when submerged "below the waves," this systemic sensation is "silently operating, determining the direction of the general current, and obscurely preparing the impulses which burst forth into action" (*PLM,* 3rd series, 2:366-67).

Lewes's excursion into the subconscious represents the "subjective aspect" of his theory of mind-body unity. In this aspect an impulse moves from interior to exterior, from subjective to objective: a psychic tremor stirs a physical act. In the "objective aspect" the direction of the process is reversed: the physical act excites the psychic tremor. The objective aspect of acting begins with the detached observation of nature: "[Passion] must be watched in others, the interpreting key being given in our own consciousness. Having something like an intellectual appreciation of the sequences of feeling and their modes of manifestation, the actor has next to select out of those such as his own physical qualifications enable him to reproduce effectively" (*On Actors*, 114). The physical enactment of these outward manifestations of emotion, Lewes believed, inexorably reacts on the inner fibres of the sensorium, producing the emotion itself. His examples, as Archer noted, included Macready, who shook a ladder to work up Shylock's rage, and Liston, who sputtered to himself backstage to attain the right tone of befuddlement for a comic entrance (50–51).

By his insistence on the essential unity of psychological and physiological processes, Lewes helped to prepare the way for the James-Lange theory of emotion. James first published his views in *Mind* (1884) and then recapitulated them in his *Principles of Psychology* (1890). Carl Lange announced similar findings in his *On the Emotions* (1885). Théodule Ribot digested the views of both psychologists in *La psychologie des sentiments* (1896), which Stanislavski cites in connection with memory of emotion, but whose service as a disseminator of the James-Lange theory has been overlooked. "The doctrine which I have called physiological," notes Ribot in acknowledging his own indebtedness to nineteenth-century English psychophysiology, "connects all states of feeling with biological conditions."[24] This fairly summarizes Lewes's position from *The Physiology of Common Life* in 1859 and throughout his career. In biologizing the passions, James goes on to observe that the physiological manifestation of the emotion *is* the emotion. He reorders the commonplace assumption that "I see the bear, I feel terrified, I run" to the innovative assertion that "I see the bear, I run, I feel terrified." Similarly, he argues that it is because we weep that we feel sad, that it is because we lash out that we feel angry, and that it is because we tremble that we feel afraid. In every case perception follows expression. A "necessary corollary" to James's theory would be that the voluntary enactment of the symptoms of emotion will bring forth the emotion itself—a point that has influenced theatrical theory profoundly. By the time he published *The Principles of Psychology*, James was aware that the testimony of actors on this point was mixed, and he cites from Archer's *Masks or Faces?* the material that most helps his case.[25] Lewes seems to have had his share in the formulation of the James-Lange theory, though his contribution is forgotten today. When James reviewed the second volume of *Problems of Life and Mind* (1874), a book he predicted would provide "a most important ferment in the philosophical thought of the immediate future," he employed a phrase that later echoes in his physiological definition of emotion: "Mr Lewes affirms the psychic event which accompanies a tremor in the brain to *be* that tremor in a different aspect."[26]

When Diderot wrote the *Paradoxe*, important advances in contemporary science remained within the grasp of the literate layman, in their breadth if not their depth. In his article "Encyclopédie" Diderot acknowledged that he undertook his editorial task at a most propitious time, at the dawn of the age of science or, at least, of publication, "before a superabundance of books should have accumulated to make its execution extremely laborious." By the close of the nineteenth century, however, as actors and theatrical theorists confronted the proliferating complexities of science, a combination of specialties such as that possessed by G. H. Lewes had become a valued rarity. In recognition of the range of his mind, he enjoyed a wider readership among actors than is generally appreciated today. Joseph Jefferson, Edwin Booth, and E. H. Sothern cited his authority (*AA*, 556, 560, 572), and Mrs. Fiske told her biographer that *On Actors and the Art of Acting* should be renamed "The Science of Acting" and required as a standard textbook.[27] The most significant evidence of his prestige as a scientific writer and his consequent contributions to acting theory, however, concerns his readership among his scientific contemporaries in Russia.

Historians of science have stressed the importance of the 1861 publication of Lewes's *Physiology of Common Life* in Russian translation. Appearing shortly after Darwin's *Origin of the Species* and sharing the same translator, Lewes's book precipitated a violent clash between reactionary idealists, who wanted it suppressed, and progressives, who took it as a rallying point for the general revolution in the biological sciences. Dostoyevski names it in the second chapter of *Crime and Punishment,* and it inspired young Ivan Pavlov to give up theology and take up the study of digestion. Pavlov memorized passages from Lewes and could repeat them verbatim.[28] The uncompromising monism of *The Physiology of Common Life,* its arguments for the wholeness of living creatures and for the continuity of nature, inevitably attracted scientists whose research probed the physical basis of mind and illuminated the increasingly dominant concept in the physiology of mental life—the reflex.

In 1863, the year that Stanislavski was born, Ivan Mikhailovich Sechenov completed his decisive essay, "An Attempt to Establish the Physiological Basis of Psychical Processes." The Tsarist censors thwarted its publication in a popular magazine. They permitted it to appear only in a medical journal under a revised title, "The Reflexes of the Brain," which actually describes its contents more specifically. Sechenov, who is known as the "father of Russian physiology," shared Lewes's view of the brain as the coordinating center of an integrated system. Sechenov also located the foundation of all higher processes in reflex action. He concluded that the living organism is a kind of self-acting "machine," responding to stimuli according to natural laws. As his intellectual predecessors, Sechenov cited the "French sensualists"—Holbach, Condillac, and Diderot.[29] The development of a physiologically based psychology by Sechenov and his successors, Pavlov and Vladimir Bekhterev, prepared the ground for the extraordinary flowering of acting theories in the Russian theater of the 1920s and 30s. The same development insured the ultimate triumph of Diderot's *Paradoxe* as a paradigmatic text. The very conflation of the word *Biomechanics* bespeaks Meyerhold's indebtedness to the central dialectic of modern life science; and, as we shall see in detail, Stanislavski based important elements of his System on the theory of spontaneity supplied to him by psychophysiology.

The full significance of the *übermarionette* may now perhaps be revealed in a clearer historical light. Craig's distrust of life is real but qualified. Pressed from all sides on the extent to which he meant to be taken seriously, he allowed that the precision of living Oriental actors might fulfill his dream of automation because their gestures had been amplified and their egos diminished by rigorous physical training. Moreover, the nearest thing to the superpuppet that Craig ever saw was not a puppet at all but Henry Irving, Diderot's self-professed antagonist in the *summa contra* Coquelin, whose "designed" motions transcended organism and achieved dance.[30] Although he hardly resembled a puppet in any other way, Irving did fulfill Craig's mechanical criterion for Diderot's *grand acteur*. Diderot's posthumous answer to Craig's challenge was supplied on behalf of psychophysiology by G. H. Lewes. He pointed out that an organism "becomes *modified*, and consequently its motors rearranged under varying stimulations. . . . No machine is educable." The actor-organism is not doomed to exist always within the same "structural adaptation." His body is educable, capable of acquiring a second nature more governable than the first. The *übermarionette*, therefore, symbolizes what the actor might achieve when his motors have been appropriately rearranged.

The search for a physical system of actor training, a process, a technique, a discipline whereby the body may be reliably mastered, characterizes the best thinking about the art of acting in the twentieth century. Craig's early enthusiasm for the flesh-and-blood actors of the Moscow Art Theatre suggests the direction his revolutionary idealism might have taken if only he could have gotten along with anyone long enough: "They give hundreds of rehearsals to a play," he wrote admiringly, "they rehearse, and rehearse, and rehearse."[31] Through disciplined application of a conscious process based on scientific principles, the Russians set out to resolve the mystery of the player's passion in light of modern biology. They knew that life was mutable, and they believed that it might be improved.

6

The *Paradoxe* as Paradigm:
The Structure of a Russian Revolution

Art should be based on scientific principles; the entire creative
act should be a conscious process. . . . Since the art of the actor
is the art of plastic forms in space, he must study the mechanics
of his body. This is essential because any manifestation of a
force (including the living organism) is subject to the constant
laws of mechanics.
—Meyerhold, "The Actor of the Future and Biomechanics"
(1922)

We are far from Pavlov's level, but his teaching is applicable to
our science of acting.
—Stanislavski, quoted in P. V. Simonov, *The Stanislavski
Method and the Physiology of Emotion* (1962)

In the summer of 1914, Stanislavski spent his holiday at Marienbad in the
company of a collection of excerpts from classical acting texts. They had
been assembled and translated for him by the dramaturg Lyubov
Gurevich, drawing upon the libraries of St. Petersburg. Stanislavski's
purpose was to define and clarify the emerging System of acting with
which he had been experimenting at the Moscow Art Theatre and its
recent offshoot, the First Studio. To this end he intended to measure the
best of previous theory against his tentative solutions to the problems that
he and his colleagues had encountered, chief among them organic spontaneity and the physical control of emotion and action. In surveying the
excellence of the great actors whose work he had especially revered—
Duse, Salvini, Chaliapin, Rossi—he asked: "What was this quality, com-

195

mon to all great talents?" He answered: "Their bodies were at the call and beck of the inner demands of their wills."[1] In essence he wanted to know by what methods and techniques, if any, this essential quality could be systematized, for that which defies method must be relegated to Apollo. In searching for the language that would allow him to formulate an intelligible system, Stanislavski markedly favored the French critics. His reading included Luigi Riccoboni's essay on declamation ("I could kiss him"), François Riccoboni's dissenting *L'art du théâtre*, the memoirs of Clairon and Dumesnil, and François-Joseph Talma's *Réflexions sur Lekain, et sur l'art théâtral.* Above all, it included Diderot.[2]

In his study of the *philosophe,* Stanislavski anticipated a trend, though one that would develop in the next few years more swiftly and more radically than he or anyone else could have foreseen. Diderot's special relationship to Russia dated from the reign of Catherine the Great, who acquired his personal library by lavish purchase and who in return accepted his manuscripts, including some of his more progressive writings, as his gift to the Imperial collection at St. Petersburg. Here they slumbered through the nineteenth century in sealed archives, like a time capsule in the cornerstone of a building overdue for demolition.

Following the Russian revolution, several editions of the *Paradoxe sur le comédien* and a substantial body of criticism on Diderot's theory appeared in the Soviet Union. Anatoly Lunacharskii, Commissar of Education and Enlightenment, provided the first of these editions (1922) with an admiring and ideologically significant foreword. Two methods of acting historically contend, Lunacharskii observed: one, turning inward, draws on the actor's own inner psychological "resources of *self*" and leads to "subjective impressionism"; the other, drawing on the actor's powers of detached observation, opens outward on the objective world, on nature and society.[3] That both Marx and Engels had professed admiration for Diderot no doubt disposed Lenin's culture minister to encourage general interest in the *philosophe* as a scientific writer and theatrical thinker. But the affinities ran more deeply here. As a university student in Zurich in the late 1890s, Lunacharskii made a special study of the classics of eighteenth-century French materialism. Later his ministerial charge was to review many of the same revolutionary ideas set forth in Diderot's *Plan of a University for the Government of Russia,* written in 1775 at the request of Catherine and long suppressed. The theme of the *philosophe* in his role as universal scientific educator, inscribed in the Soviet cultural pantheon under "the service of progressive mankind," still resounds in the entry "Diderot" of the *Bol'shaia Sovetskaia Entsiklopedia,* itself a lineal descendant of the *Encyclopédie.*[4]

Diderot's materialism, atheism, and revolutionary science seemed smartly in step with the new order. To commemorate this foresightedness with a suitable memorial, Lunacharskii's acquaintance, Bertolt Brecht, made a proposal. In 1937 he drew up a prospectus for an organization dedicated to scientific research in theatrical art that he would have called "The Diderot Society." Though eventually nothing came of this effort, Brecht used the occasion of the prospectus to sum up his debt and that of twentieth-century acting theory to Diderot's scientific muse: "In recent decades, however, a new kind of theatre has developed—one which sets itself the goal of an exact picture of the world and which admits of objective, non-individualistic criteria." The theatrical artist no longer presents *"his own world"* or "portraits of the portrayer." Rather, this mimetic automaton creates "images of the world" beyond him.[5] Brecht's proposal reflects his desire to gather together a group of thinkers engaged in a common pursuit. Presaging his call for a "theatre for a scientific age" in *Kleines Organon für das Theatre* of 1948, Brecht's "Diderot Society" self-consciously aspired to the model of a scientific community. An informal version of such a community emerged in the Soviet theater of the 1920s and 30s. Supported by current psychophysiological research, it was led by Stanislavski and Meyerhold, each of whom advanced a system of actor training guided ultimately by the principles originally propounded in Diderot's revolutionary text of 1773.

Brecht discerned with enviable clarity and fair-mindedness that the broad foundations of scientific materialism supported Stanislavski's position, especially as it evolved toward the end of his life, as well as it did his own. Throughout his experimentation with actors and in his writings, Stanislavski sought to objectify the phenomenon of spontaneity. From the formative years of the System to the years of its maturity, Stanislavski and his rebellious son Meyerhold would grapple with the issue of second nature. In the 1920s Meyerhold dismissed the acting methods of the Moscow Art Theatre, aimed at recreating lived experience onstage, as entirely too subjective, a form of self-hypnotic narcosis. Stanislavski's teachings during this period were exported by various emigrés and eventually this early stage in his thinking formed the basis of the American Method. His name became associated with the doctrine of "affective memory" whereby the actor, following in a tradition founded by Diderot and developed by Talma and Lewes, subjectively revived his own past emotions in the circumstances demanded by the role. The Stanislavski System, however, did not fully mature until the 1930s, and it was by no means a closed book at the time of the master's death in 1938. It culminated in the development of the "method of physical actions," based on what G. H. Lewes had termed the "objective aspect" of the mind-body continuum. Stanislavski's revisions stemmed not only from his

The Player's Passion

daily work with live actors and singers in his Studio, but also from his changing appreciation of current science. Brecht himself sympathetically analyzed the Stanislavski System as a synthesis of the struggle between the ancient "cult" of subjectivism and spontaneous self-transformation, of which Brecht was thoroughly skeptical, and the "progressiveness" of the method of physical actions, which he approvingly attributed to the "influence of Soviet life and its materialistic tendencies."[6]

The materialistic tendencies to which Brecht referred centered on the revolutionary transformation of psychology into an objective science of behavior. Underlying this new science resided the ideological assumptions that external conditions determine human nature and that objectively controlled manipulation of the physical environment will alter the inward man. This science denies, in short, that a meaningful distinction can be drawn between the psychological and the physical or, for that matter, between the vital and the mechanical. Thus it happened that materialistic doctrines of second nature prophesied by Diderot and reiterated by nineteenth-century science swiftly found a highly receptive audience in twentieth-century Russia.

Ivan Sechenov's collected *Works*, celebrating the primacy of the reflex as the essential mechanism of organic response, appeared posthumously in 1908. By that date Vladimir Bekhterev, director of the St. Petersburg Military-Medical Academy, had published *Foundations of Knowledge about the Functions of the Brain* (1903–07) and had begun his exploration of the science he later called "objective psychology" or "Reflexology." By that date Pavlov had won a Nobel Prize for his study of the digestive process in dogs, and he had newly devoted his laboratory, adjoining Bekhterev's at the Academy, to the central issue framed by Sechenov: reflex excitation and inhibition as the physiological basis of all behavior.

This research explained all psychological phenomena by reducing them to physiological laws. Sechenov, for instance, demonstrated the operation of *central inhibition,* the repressive effects of the thalamic nerve centers on spinal reflexes. His concept of reflex inhibition resembles G. H. Lewes's vague "Laws of Arrest," but there is nothing vague in Sechenov. All manifestations of brain function can be reduced to muscular movement propelled or repressed by reflex. Emotions are merely intensified reflexes. Thoughts are merely reflexes, from those of a girl trembling at the first awakening of love to those of Newton enunciating the universal laws of motion. Sechenov predicted that reflexes will someday present themselves to be studied with the exactitude that a physicist brings to the analysis of falling bodies. Long before Pavlov and Watson, Sechenov argued that "frequent repetition is the means by which capacity is acquired." Complex behaviors, moreover, consist of a "whole series of successive reflexes." The inevitable result of Sechenov's argument is to limit the role of what he terms "so-called voluntary actions." Reflexes run the bodily machine deterministically as "psychomotors." In an essay written in 1900 entitled "The Part Played by the Nervous System in Man's Working Movements," Sechenov sets down the basic psychophysiological principles that inform such familiar theatrical concepts as motivation and action. The essential view of will has not advanced significantly beyond Diderot's *Eléments de physiologie:*

> Things will be different if, remaining on the ground of psychology, we replace the meaningless concept of will by the real concept of desire in the form of a sensation with a definite content. Vital requirements engender desires, and the desires give rise to action; in this case, the desire is the motive or the aim, while the movements are the action or the means of attaining the aim. When a man performs a so-called voluntary movement the latter appears in his consciousness after the desire. Without the desire, which plays the role of a motive or impulse, the movement would be senseless. In accordance with this point of view, the motor centers located on the surface of the brain are known as the psychomotor centers.[7]

Reflex action thus constitutes the basis of all behavior, spontaneous and acquired, muscular and mental. In fact, the convenient terms *mental* and *physical* simply describe two aspects of an indivisible phenomenon—life. Appropriately, therefore, when Stanislavski asked rhetorically in 1924 if there could be a system for acting founded on "organic laws," his answer construed organism materialistically in light of the prevailing scientific optimism about what could be discovered in the tangible, physical reality of the body: "In certain parts of the system, like the physiological and the psychological, such laws exist for all, forever, and in all creative processes. They are indubitable, completely conscious, tried by science and found true, and binding on all" (*My Life in Art*, 483).

It was against this scientific backdrop, as well as in the midst of a political revolution whose leadership starkly dictated materialism, that Vsevolod Meyerhold called for a Biomechanical method of actor training in 1922. Biomechanics offered the actor preparatory exercise routines. The obvious goal of such exercises was to condition his neuromuscular responses to peak efficiency. Their ultimate purpose was to induce in his body the appearance of second nature. The profundity of Meyerhold's understanding of science was sharply questioned at the time,[8] but in light of what has been said here about the psychophysiological doctrines common to Diderot, Lewes, James, Sechenov, Bekhterev, and Pavlov, his grasp of the salient issue cannot be disputed: "All psychological states," he wrote in his biomechanical manifesto, "are determined by specific

FIGURE 26. Meyerhold, Biomechanical exercises. *(Courtesy of Washington University Libraries.)*

physiological processes." Above all, his new theatrical technique was to be predicated on the actor's *"innate capacity for reflex excitability."*[9]

The biomechanical exercises developed by Meyerhold followed a three-fold pattern, consistent, he claimed, with "the natural laws of movements" (*AA*, 502). First there was to be a moment of preparation (intention) for the action, then the physical performance of the action itself (realization), and finally the moment of reaction in which the sensations caused by the action in turn caused a new moment of preparation (intention). Igor Ilinsky, an actor under Meyerhold's direction when the biomechanical exercises were developed, explained them by way of this familiar example: "an actor representing fear must not experience fear first and then run, but must first run (reflex) and then take fright from that action" (*AA*, 504). Meyerhold's indebtedness to psychophysical science for such a formulation may be attributed to various influences. Sechenov had observed in 1863 that the "sensation of fright" constitutes an "integral reflex" following, not preceding, the exterior muscular movement or startle response. Bekhterev's theory of "associated motor reflexes" reduces all living behavior to reflexive responses to environmental stimuli. Ribot's digest of the James-Lange theory in *The Psychology of the Emotions* was also readily available to Meyerhold in Pavlenkov's Russian translation of 1898, which Stanislavski had already utilized for his own purposes as early as 1914.[10] These sources reflect the modern awakening of a long-slumbering radicalism in the theory of feeling, volition, consciousness, and behavior. "Life," said Diderot, biologizing mechanics in 1769, "is a series of actions and reactions" (*Rêve de d'Alembert*, 125).

In 1927 Ivan Pavlov summed up the trends in nerve physiology bearing on what Meyerhold had crudely termed "the natural laws of movements." In *Conditioned Reflexes: An Investigation of the Physiological Activity of the Cerebral Cortex*, Pavlov defines behavior as sequences of reflex responses to stimuli, the smaller reflex units adhering together to form links in the psychophysical chain. "Instincts" such as nest-building, for instance, are actually complex reflex re-actions connected in chains: "To look upon this as reflex we must assume that one reflex initiates the next following—or, in other words, we must regard it as a chain reflex." Pavlov goes even further: "But this linking up of activities is not peculiar to instincts alone. We are familiar with numerous reflexes which most certainly fuse into chains."[11] Slow-motion cinematography had revealed to Pavlov the elaborate reflex sequence that takes place when a cat lands on its feet after being dropped from a high place. First the cat's head, responding to stimuli created by its disturbed equilibrium, begins to right itself; then, following in a ripple effect along the entire length of its body, the muscle groups of the shoulders, trunk, and haunches respond in turn, each nerve in the "chain" contracting or inhibiting the appropriate muscles in reply to the stimulus provided by the actions of its predecessors. In this manner complex behaviors can be analyzed as mechanical sequences of simple reflexes. An animal's stirring restlessly in a cage Pavlov called the "freedom reflex." Likewise, he labeled curiosity the "What-is-it? reflex" (11–12).

Pavlov's mechanization of biological responsiveness, his organization of complex behaviors into chains with single reflex links, recalls the theory of *enchainement* as described in the *Eléments de physiologie*. Diderot derived from associationist psychology the idea of trains of sensations that naturally become linked in complex sequences. These are spontaneous in the sense that one leads automatically to the next. As secondary automatic sensations they can also be acquired by habit. Similarly, in Meyerhold's biomechanical scheme, discrete units of *preparation-action-reaction* may be linked together and organized into "chains of movements" propelled along by reflexes, rendered supple and apparently spontaneous by repetition, like those of a gymnastic routine.

A principal difference between the acting theories of Meyerhold in his biomechanical period and Stanislavski resides in their relative attitudes towards organic spontaneity, the degree to which they permitted "bio-," vitalistically interpreted, to figure in their "mechanics." Meyerhold had less interest than Stanislavski in the psychological content of motion. During the 1920s, in the climate that brought forth the experimental choreographer Nikolai Mikhailovich Foregger's "Dance of the Machines" and the Constructivist glorification of technology, Meyerhold was not being merely eccentric when he conceived of human movement by mechanical design. Elsewhere at the same time, Ernst Juenger in *The Glass Bees* (1923) dreamed Vaucanson's old dream of a stage peopled by performing automata. Enrico Prampolini in "Futurist Scenography" (1915) called for the replacement of living actors with colored "actor-gases." At the Bauhaus, Oskar Schlemmer designed his mechanical ballets and L. Moholy-Nagy joined Craig and the radical mechanists in proclaiming the inadequacy of "organism" as a theatrical medium.[12] In such company Meyerhold may actually seem moderate by comparison. After all, he retained the human body center stage, even if only as a reflex-machine.

Outlining a "Program of Biomechanics" for acting workshops in 1922, Meyerhold listed the essential topics to be covered with his actors. Chief among them are:

The human organism as an automative mechanism
Mimeticism and its biological significance (Bekhterev)

Complex of movements of the whole organism or chain of movements
Acts of inhibition (not doing)
Study of mechanism of reaction in the nervous system
Psychic reactions as the object of scientific study
Psychic phenomena, simple physico-chemical reactions . . . purely
   physiological reflexes
Reflex instinct
Reflexes, their connection, sequence, mutual dependence
Mechanization, subconsciously habitual acts[13]

Along with his citation of Bekhterev by name, Meyerhold recapitulates the essential content of reflexology as it had evolved since the publication of Sechenov's *Reflexes of the Brain* in 1863. In the name of Biomechanics he reifies the mind as a vital machine. He is also aware of the idea of reflex inhibition, which is essential to muscular coordination and locomotion. He conceives of the reflexes functioning in sequential "chains," the neurophysiological basis of complex behaviors. Finally, he underscores the importance of subconscious automatization, thus updating Diderot's *habitude* and the paradoxical spontaneity of second nature.

Under attack for exaggerating the scientific legitimacy of Biomechanics, Meyerhold brought to his defense a "brochure by Coquelin."[14] His *riposte* was more to the point than may appear at first glance. Coquelin built his case solidly on Diderot's science, notably on the indispensable premise of double consciousness. Meyerhold rather pretentiously reduced Coquelin's "dual personality" to a mathematical formula: "$N = A_1 + A_2$ (where N = the actor; A_1 = the artist who conceives the idea and issues the instructions necessary for its execution; A_2 = the executant who executes the conception of A_1)."[15] Diderot disdained abstract descriptions of natural phenomena and thought mathematics overrated as a tool of modern science, but in Meyerhold's pseudo-algebra he doubtless would have recognized a version of his metaphor of harpsichordist and harpsichord, of a dispassionate intelligence making a responsive instrument vibrate.

Reflexology, of course, had broad implications for the Soviet program of rapid industrialization during the 1920s. Advocating a strong director-centered theater, Meyerhold also familiarized himself with the motion economy studies set forth in *Principles of Scientific Management* by Frederick Winslow Taylor, whose efficiency theories attracted an odd mix of enthusiasts from the Bolsheviks to the engineering department of the Ford Motor Company. In his biomechanical period Meyerhold regarded his actors as workers whose motions in time and space could be objectively analyzed and mechanically improved. He had them dress in overalls and put them to work on Constructivist settings, machines for acting, featuring ramps, slides, and moving parts, which he treated as theatrical assembly lines. The best method of acting was the one that most effectively simplified the actor's industrial task. The movements of the well-drilled worker were the dance of the twentieth century. "Biomechanics," Ilinsky concluded, "shows the actor how to control his acting" (*AA*, 506), just as Diderot, in his article "Encyclopédie," recognized that the expert who has mastered a "mechanical craft" will "grasp the whole nature of a process, no motion of the hand will escape him, for he will easily distinguish a meaningless flourish from an essential precaution."

Whereas Meyerhold makes the objective physiological claims of biomechanics explicit in his workshop program of 1922, Stanislavski's relationship to science evolved over several decades with substantially more depth and complexity. His thirst for a system, a method, a science of his profession reached an early point of crisis in 1906. He had been playing his roles at the Moscow Art Theatre long enough and, in the case of Dr. Stockman in *An Enemy of the People,* successfully enough to have been bored by them. As Craig had admiringly observed, the Moscow Art Theatre rehearsed its productions at prodigious length and kept them in the repertoire indefinitely: indeed, some of them are still there. Without a reliable method of keeping a role fresh, fossilization had begun to set in. Unlike that unnameable paralysis afflicting the characters who people the Chekhovian *mise en scène* that Stanislavski had created, his own ennui permitted him to make a trenchant self-diagnosis: "From performance to performance I had merely made a mechanical habit of going through all this [*sic*] technical gymnastics, and muscular memory, which is so strong among actors, had powerfully fixed my bad theatrical habit" (*My Life in Art*, 460). In contradiction to the assurances of the mechanistic side of the *Paradoxe*, Stanislavski's mental machine was running down while his body kept right on ticking away. As his spontaneity drained away, his sense of crisis deepened. He despised in himself the automatization implied by his ability to perform gymnastics. He seems to have resented the surrender of consciousness implied by his mechanical habit. It represented a kind of spiritual death. This intense, even obsessive interest in the inner psychological content of an action, marked by the tendency to immerse himself in the nature of consciousness itself, may set Stanislavski apart from Meyerhold. But it does not set him apart from Diderot.

Stanislavski and Diderot evolved their theories about actors and acting in strikingly similar ways. Both began as uncritical believers in *ad hoc* inspiration. Having experienced disillusionment with unmediated emotion, both formulated psychophysical techniques whereby emotions may be processed into art through memory, imagination, and physical action. Both came to the conclusion that true emotion lay beyond the direct reach of the will. Both attributed major powers of artistic creativity to the unconscious mind, which they similarly interpreted as a subconscious repository in a pre-Freudian physiological sense. Both regarded the actor's creativity highly, but conceived of an inner model of character brought forth collaboratively with the playwright. Both believed in lengthy rehearsal periods to prepare a role meticulously. Both emphasized the need for absorption in the stage task. Both regarded the role as a score or inner model of physical actions overseen by the dispassionate half of a divided consciousness. In short, both Diderot and Stanislavski had final recourse to science and, within science, to essentially the same set of modern assumptions about the human body. With these premises in common, they attempted to solve the ancient riddle of theatrical aesthetics: To what extent is the player's bodily passion spontaneous?

Like the body itself, Stanislavski's theory of acting forms an indivisible whole, which may be analyzed in two aspects, physical and psychical. He views the actor's art as a rigorous process of "working on himself." It has been assumed that the process begins with work on the psychical aspect of the instrument, then emphasizes the preparation of its physical aspect, and finally brings both together in the creation of a role. At least this is the pattern that suggested itself to the unwary by the vexed publication history of his English-language trilogy. *An Actor Prepares* (1936) treats what Lewes would have recognized as the "subjective aspect" of the actor's process, including the celebrated doctrine of emotion memory and the all-important subconscious. *Building a Character* (1949), as the architectural metaphor of its title suggests, defines more objective techniques, including physical characterization, plasticity of motion, diction and singing, and tempo-rhythm in movement. *Creating a Role* (1961) offers practical analyses of three major roles and reworking of earlier materials. In Stanislavski's practice, both aspects—objective and subjective, psychical and physical—come into play from the outset, since in fact they exist simply as a convenient way to describe with different emphases the same set of phenomena. Stanislavski explains in *An Actor Prepares:* "The bond between body and soul is indivisible. . . . In every physical act there is a psychological element and a physical one in every psychological act" (132, 136). The law of the unity of the physical and psychological, derived from the paradigm framed by contemporary science, provides the basis for the method of physical actions on which Stanislavski was at work when he died and which he regarded as the final synthesis of all his theories. At every stage of the development of his System, however, he accepted the premise of dual-aspect monism: "Conscious or unconscious objectives are carried out both inwardly and outwardly, by both body and soul. Therefore they can be both physical and psychological."[16]

Significantly, the implied division is not between body and mind, but between conscious and unconscious states.

The Stanislavski System is a means of manipulating levels of consciousness to achieve certain specific effects on the body, especially the illusion of spontaneity. It promises to give the actor expressive control over a living organism, his own body, in all its mercurial diversity and surprising obstinacies. Among the techniques that Stanislavski proposes toward this end are the relaxation of the muscles, concentration of attention, public solitude, adaptation, units and objectives, emotion memory, tempo-rhythm, the score of the role, and, definitively, the method of physical actions. Stanislavski's theories defy tidy summary because they take into account the complexity of higher organisms, including the phenomenon of double or multiple consciousness. As he clarified the implications of contemporary psychophysiological theory in his own mind, Stanislavski adjusted his emphases to suit the emerging facts of life. His System, therefore, cannot be comprehended without his science.

"So infinitely complex, so continuously in flux, are the conditions in the world around," wrote Ivan Pavlov, "that that complex animal system which is itself in living flux, and that system only, has a chance to establish dynamic equilibrium with the environment."[17] Part of this living flux consists of the alternation between conscious and unconscious adaptations to circumstances. Another related part consists of an alternation of attention between external and internal stimuli. This is life as Stanislavski also construed it. *"Mechanical* or *motor* adjustments," he wrote in *An Actor Prepares,* "are subconscious, semiconscious, and conscious in origin. They are normal, natural, human adaptations that are carried to a point of becoming purely mechanical . . . without sacrificing their quality of naturalness. Because they remain organic and human, they are the antithesis of the rubber stamp" (224). It is significant that Stanislavski allowed for actions that are at once mechanical and organic, thereby reiterating the fundamental paradox within the *Paradoxe.* By "rubber stamp" he means a theatrical cliché, a gesture made for the sake of a gesture. It is not, as in life, an adaptive adjustment designed to mediate between the organism and its environment; it is drained of its purposive content. A "rubber stamp" can exist on stage and nowhere else in the world known to science, except perhaps in the purely mechanical spasms of a decorticated animal, and perhaps not even there. Lewes, after all, allowed the spinal frog a sentience that he could not locate in Charles Kean's Macbeth.

Pavlov views the reflex as the central phenomenon of psychic life. He became particularly interested in the learned or conditioned reflex, which he regarded as an improved adaptive mechanism. It consists of a tempo-rary nervous connection linking the inner functions of the organism, such as digestion, to the senses and through them to the external world. Perhaps Pavlov's greatest achievement was to devise scientific methods of studying these mechanisms in higher animals without vivisection, the trauma of which radically disturbs the behavior of the organism. In a series of famous experiments, he juxtaposed four basic elements of reflex: unconditioned stimulus and unconditioned response, conditioned stimulus and conditioned response. Unremarkably, he discovered that an unconditioned stimulus (say a drop of dilute acid) placed on a dog's tongue automatically produced an unconditioned response (salivation) in measurable quantities. Each time this simple transaction occurred, however, Pavlov saw to it that a sound (bell) or visual effect (slide) immediately preceded the administration of the acid. After a certain number of repetitions, the sound or visual effect alone, now the conditioned stimulus, proved sufficient to produce the same amount of salivation, now the conditioned response. A learned mental reflex had been substituted for an innate physical one, suggesting that higher adaptive responses had important characteristics in common with the knee-jerk. Pavlov banned all subjective terminology and interpretations of data from his physiological laboratory and stoutly refused to recognize psychology as a science, but his methods, infinitely replicable and controllably variable, yielded results that could reasonably be supposed to have important implications for such psychological issues as motivation and the spontaneity of purposive actions.

The reflexive linkage between inner motivations and outer world is a continuous process. It may be interrupted only by trauma, total unconsciousness, or death. Along closely parallel lines, Stanislavski believed that in life the process of adaptation is continuous. He believed that an "inner dialogue" runs within us without interruption—a stream of consciousness sustained and constantly redirected by subconscious impulses and sensory stimuli. To both Pavlov and Stanislavski, behavior consists of chains of physical adaptations, continuous transitions in the direction of the stream of consciousness caused by physical stimuli. This is the life that the actor attempts to emulate by "living the role."

The unnatural experience of stepping out onto the stage, however, is, like vivisection, a trauma that impinges upon this free-flowing continuity of stimulus and spontaneous response. Stage fright—itself an adaptation to stress—threatens even the natural reciprocity of mind and body, which may be taken for granted under normal circumstances; it engenders a psychophysical paralysis, which frustrates the natural completion of even the most commonplace tasks. It flattens out the variegated textures of life into the characteristic rigidities of mortification.

Several techniques proposed by Stanislavski seek to overcome the unnatural stimuli emanating from the "black hole," the audience, and to replace them with natural stimuli more directly under the actor's control. These techniques exist to alter the actor's consciousness so that he can induce the spontaneous reappearance of life. One such technique Stanislavski termed "concentration of attention," the ultimate goal of which is to create a state of heightened consciousness called "public solitude." Once, when he was given the simple task of counting the nails in the stage floor, Stanislavski discovered that his self-consciousness before the public decreased and his sense of reality on stage increased markedly. He was, in Diderot's terminology, absorbed within a perimeter from which the audience was excluded. Stanislavski concluded that the only way for the actor to create a sense of public solitude is to absorb himself in the stimuli generated by the physical reality of his immediate stage environment. He should narrow his attention to the physical objects around him and the physical tasks he is performing. Stanislavski proposed that the actor focus his concentration in "circles of attention." The smallest circle encloses the actor himself and his immediate surroundings, such as the chair in which he is seated. The largest circle encompasses the entire stage. The wider the aperture, the harder it is to maintain the intensity of concentration—the harder, that is, to displace the audience from the center of attention and to banish it beyond the perimeter of consciousness measured by Diderot's fourth wall.

Relaxation and concentration of attention are preliminary techniques leading toward the experience of living the part. This process involves approximating on stage the conditions of psychophysical normalcy that prevail off it, the state, as Pavlov called it, of "dynamic equilibrium with the environment." Under normal conditions organisms act purposively. The actor, however, requires extensive training and elaborate preparation before he can create the illusion of this phenomenon in the theater. Specifically, creating a role requires the actor to analyze the large actions of the character or "super-objective" into smaller "units and objectives." Like Pavlov's analysis of complex behaviors as chains of reflexes, Stanislavski's formulation defines individual units and objectives as "bits" in what will eventually, after sufficient rehearsal, become "the unbroken line of action" or "the score of the role." This line is a chain of mutually interdependent reflex desires and reflex actions. Engendered by powerful stimuli, such desires or strong motivations recall Sechenov's maxim: "vital requirements engender desires, and the desires give rise to action." Stanislavski himself explained: "Life on stage, as well as off it, consists of an uninterrupted series of objectives and their attainment" (*Creating a Role*, 51). By laws of this "psychotechnique"—for that is how Stanislavski referred to his System—the actor can "reach the spiritual life of a role reflexively through its physical life" (*Creating a Role*, 206). Emotions, feelings, thoughts, and desires do not arise without a cause, and the cause is physical. It cannot be otherwise.

In the formulation of his psychotechnique, Stanislavski experimented with various means of creating stimuli that would reliably excite the appropriate reflexive responses. He was particularly interested in a method that promised to open up the deepest levels of the subconscious for the actor's use. It brought into play the actor's memory and imagination, which can be consciously manipulated, to trigger his emotions, which are not at the beck and call of his will. "Through conscious means," Stanislavski promised in *An Actor Prepares,* "we reach the subconscious" (166). This, the most notorious concept in the subjective aspect of the System, is affective memory or memory of emotion: "We cannot directly act on our emotion," Stanislavski wrote, "but we can prod our creative fantasy in a necessary path, and fantasy, as scientific psychologists have discovered, stirs up our *affective memory,* calling up from its secret depths, beyond reach of consciousness, elements of already experienced emotions, and regroups them to correspond with the images which arise in us."[18] Foremost among the scientific psychologists to whom Stanislavski alludes was Théodule Ribot, whose chapter "The Memory of Feelings" from *The Psychology of the Emotions* he drew upon for the "Emotion Memory" chapter in *An Actor Prepares.* Ribot discussed the intimate reciprocity of memory of sensation and memory of emotion, and he deliberately chose the word *feelings* for its ambivalence. Stanislavski seized upon this authority for the co-revivability of sensation and emotion in equal parts, but Ribot was somewhat less sanguine: "The emotional memory is *nil* in the majority of people" (171). Complete revivability is a special gift—or affliction—enjoyed by a few. Stanislavski was acutely aware of the capricious nature of parallel memory of sensation and emotion, even in the most sensitive person: "They may seem to be beyond recall, when suddenly a suggestion, a thought, a familiar object will bring them back in full force" (*An Actor Prepares*, 158).

This passage offers an eerie echo of Diderot's *Eléments de physiologie:* "The sound of a voice, the presence of an object, a certain place, and behold, an object recalled—more than that, a whole stretch of my past—and I am plunged again into pleasure, regret, affliction" (*Eléments*, 248). But, more importantly, Stanislavski closely intertwines imagination with memory in the manner described in the *Paradoxe.* As the years pass, imagination refines memory of emotion into art. The resulting impressions are "more condensed, compact, substantial and sharper than the actual happenings"—not in pain but in clarity (*An Actor Prepares*, 163).

As Diderot put it, after the passage of time, impressions vibrate ever more distantly in the subconscious, "memory and imagination unite, one to retrace the other to accentuate" (*PC*, 36). In the creative process, according to Stanislavski, "Time is a splendid filter for our remembered feelings—besides it is a great artist. It not only purifies, it also transmutes even painfully realistic memories into poetry" (*An Actor Prepares*, 163). This is the meaning behind Stanislavski's observation that emotion memory re-groups impressions into sequences of images. Like Diderot, he was heir to associationist psychology, which viewed memory as Hobbesian *traynes* of thought, normally revived in the order that they were received, but capable of being reordered through imagination into new sequences. The line of descent traveled by this idea may have been roundabout—Hartley to Lewes to Ribot and/or the Russian reflexologists to Stanislavski. Or it may have been more direct—Diderot to Stanislavski. The creation of Diderot's inner model, after all, requires the regrouping of memories into revivable patterns of sensation and action.

Following the doctrine of reflex conditioning, Stanislavski said that the actor uses affective memory to revive the physiological manifestations of an emotional response in the absence of the original stimulus. It is, strictly speaking, a conditioned reflex substituting the stimuli provided by memory of certain sensations, locations, or physical objects for the first reaction to actual events. It is the bell without the acid. These conditioned responses may prove useful if they are analogous to those required by the role, but in this matter the human mind shows considerably more subtlety than the dog's in its response to the bell. Stanislavski's suggestible Kostya recalls that he once came upon an old Italian organ-grinder, who wept as he knelt over the body of a dead monkey lying in the gutter. As the man wept, he kept trying to shove a little piece of orange into the dead animal's mouth, coaxing it, pleading with it to eat. This deeply engrained memory struck Kostya as a more vivid image with which to unlock his subconsciousness than that of a horrible street accident he had seen much more recently. Moreover, he found that his reaction to the image of the old Italian intensified rather than diminished with time and with repetition. "I wonder why that is?" Kostya asked with unconvincing naiveté (*An Actor Prepares*, 162–63).

The use of affective memories live and on stage, as opposed to during leisurely rehearsals as favored by Diderot, places double stress on the actor's ability to concentrate narrowly on his task, to step within his magic circle and to achieve a sense of public solitude. The first problem Stanislavski ran into with this doctrine of the affective memory, a problem that also rebounded on the use of emotion memory at the Actor's Studio in America, was a basic one: speed. A play, even a supposedly actionless play like *A Month in the Country*, is a rapidly shifting kaleido-scope of action and emotion. The scientific psychologists offered no succor on this point. Ribot, who usually qualifies everything he says by counterexamples, was emphatic: "A characteristic peculiar to emotional affective revivability is the slowness with which it develops and the time required." He explains that "emotional representation" depends on the completion of two stages, one intellectual and one emotional, and that the second stage "requires organic conditions, a difference in the organism, an excitement of the motor, vascular, respiratory, secretory, and other centres" (*Psychology of the Emotions,* 157 n). The second problem that Stanislavski discovered with affective memory was one of mental hygiene. In nature, emotions do not appear without a reason. They are prompted by the appropriate physical stimuli. As Sechenov taught, there are no voluntary actions. Certainly the fugitive emotions are the least likely phenomena to be forced into public existence at will. Squeezing the emotions defies nature and threatens the actor's mental equilibrium. On this point the American Method and the Stanislavski System parted company. The chapter on "Memory of Emotion" in Richard Boleslavsky's influential *Acting: The First Six Lessons* (1933) cites Ribot but does not address this thorny point. The Group Theatre employed its own famous "minute of preparation" to work up affective memories. The reputation acquired by Method actors as self-indulgent and moody, whether deserved or not, derives at least in part from this introspective practice. Stanislavski, however, moved on to confront the issue in what Lewes would have called its "objective aspect" with his method of physical actions.

Stanislavski's search for appropriate stimuli led him outward from the subjective world of memory and emotion and into the concrete physical world of actions and events. These too, he believed, can influence the actor's creativity indirectly. "There is no *direct approach* to our subconscious," he reiterates; "therefore we make use of various stimuli that induce a process of living the part" (*An Actor Prepares,* 225). Such stimuli can be purely fortuitous, like the sound of nervous fingers scratching on a wooden bench that electrified him in rehearsal for *The Three Sisters:* "A spiritual spring was touched and I at last understood the nature of the something that was missing. I had known it before also, but I had known it with my mind and not my emotions" (*My Life in Art,* 373). But in the absence of happy accidents, appropriate physical actions can act on the subconscious to create the "inner truth of feeling" by "psychotechnical" means. Stanislavski calls the interdependence of physical action and mental experience "organic activity." The petulant Grisha, who is always giving Tortsov a bad time in *An Actor Prepares,* asks: "How can you call activity based on thin air *physical* or *organic?*" (128). In Tortsov's view mind is not based on thin air but on reflex action. He replies with the example of an actor called upon to "drink" water from an empty glass. Swallow air, he advises, swallow your saliva—the physical processes will create a sense of truth reflexively in the absence of the water. The all-knowing Director concludes, "Mind you, only physical actions, physical truths, and physical belief in them! Nothing more!" (134).

As Stanislavski's emphasis on physical actions increased, questions of reflex conditioning and automatization played an ever more decisive role in his theories. In Chapter 4 of *Building a Character*, "Making the Body Expressive," Tortsov, accompanied by a famous circus clown, arrives at acting school in time for the Swedish gymnastic class. He announces that tumbling and acrobatics will henceforth provide a mainstay of the school curriculum. There is one reason for this: "Decisiveness." The acrobat's nerves and sinews, on which his life depends everyday, must be structured into patterns of unreflecting response. Flying high above the netless void below, "there is no room for indecision; he must, without stopping to reflect, give himself into the hands of chance and his skill. He must jump, come what may. This is exactly what an actor must do when he comes up to the culminating point of his part. In such moments as when Hamlet says 'Why, let the stricken deer go weep' or Othello cries 'Oh, blood, blood, blood!' the actor cannot stop to think, to doubt, to weigh considerations, to make ready and test himself. He must act, he must clear the jump at full gallop."[19] Opera fascinated Stanislavski, and the material that later coalesced into *An Actor Prepares* and *Building a Character* was first read as lectures to the students in his Opera Studio.[20] A singer-actor, of course, would be ill-advised to explain to the conductor that his entrance will be so many measures late because he needs a private moment to get into the creative mood. Stanislavski knew that in opera the score of the role is the score of the role, and like the acrobat, the singer-actor "must jump, come what may." Taking the great basso Chaliapin as his model, Stanislavski perfected his System in accordance with the needs of operatic production because he believed that the same laws must inevitably apply on the regular stage.

In the chapter on "Tempo-rhythm in Movement" in *Building a Character*, Rakhmanov, Tortsov's assistant, introduces an "electrical conductor for plays." This device consists of two silently blinking lights that could be placed in the prompter's box and altered to blink like a silent metronome at different tempi as noted in the prompt book. Tortsov and Rakhmanov demonstrate this device by playing scenes in accordance with tempi set randomly by the electrician, yet justifying each tempo with proper motivations (212). A gifted actor with proper training, Stanislavski believed, should be able to respond to external tempo-rhythm without violating the law of inner justification. How can that be?

The tempo-rhythm itself allegedly stimulates the correct inner feelings. Rhythmic patterns of muscular movement work themselves inward, reacting on the psyche in the form of a "mechanical stimulus to emotion memory and consequently to innermost experience." Stanislavski invited the actor to ask any singer what it is like to sing under the direction of a conductor who understands the correct tempo-rhythm to bring out the emotion of a score (*Building a Character*, 236). This technique recommends itself because the actor's memory pervades his entire body; it is not the function of his brain alone. Physical action stirs memory and *muscle sense*, as Lewes and Sechenov called it, with a speed and certainty not obtainable from mental images induced by subjective means. Heart rate fluctuates, respiration quickens and slows, body chemistry subtly alters, driven by changing outer rhythms, which inexorably react on the inner sensorium. Organism and mechanism coexist, two aspects of the reflex machine.

Stanislavski regarded the method of physical actions as the culmination of his life's work. It rests on the now familiar principle that every thought and feeling is connected to a physical action, that mind is merely the subjective aspect of an objective process called body. The method of physical actions begins with structured improvisations in which the actor defines his role as a sequence of psychophysical objectives and events. As he builds his character by accretion, he consciously constructs a chain of stimulating actions. This is his inner model—a conscious artistic construction automatized into his muscles and nerves. When he has fixed the sequence or score through many repetitions, spontaneity returns. As Kostya notes of Tortsov's demonstration: "The more often he repeated this sequence of so-called physical actions—or, to be more exact, the inner stimuli to action—the more his involuntary motions increased" (*Creating a Role*, 229). In summarizing his method of physical actions in *Creating a Role,* Stanislavski explains exactly how the score will be composed:

With time and frequent repetition, in rehearsal and performance, this score becomes habitual. An actor becomes so accustomed to all his objectives and their sequence that he cannot conceive of approaching his role otherwise than along the line of the steps fixed in the score. Habit plays a great part in creativeness: it establishes in a firm way the accomplishments of creativeness. In the familiar words of Volkonski it makes what is difficult habitual, what is habitual easy, and what is easy beautiful. Habit creates second nature, which is a second reality. The score automatically stirs the actor to physical action. (*Creating a Role*, 62)

Here Stanislavski takes up Diderot's meaning of *spontaneity*—an activity repeated so often that it becomes automatic and therefore free. Reflexology firmly supported this position. Sechenov, in a book-length essay entitled "The Elements of Thought" (1878), expanded on G. H. Lewes's definition of intuition as "organised reasoning" by noting that "Lewes wanted to point out its similarity with a very habitual movement which has become automatic and in which the mechanism of its assimilation is imperceptible owing to the rapidity and easiness of the action."[21] This is second nature, looking for all the world like the first.

The advantage to the actor of such physical automatism is that it liberates his critical faculties to observe, assess, and correct his performance in accordance with the pre-established score. Stanislavski's wide-eyed Kostya marveled at the power and control that this dual consciousness gave to his acting: "I divided myself, as it were, into two personalities. One continued as an actor, the other was an observer. Strangely enough this duality not only did not impede, it actually promoted my creative work. It encouraged and lent impetus to it" (*Building a Character*, 19).

The task of the inner critic might be compared to an editor whose goal is to trim away all that is superfluous and to maintain the clarity of the model and the dynamic accents of the score. "Unrestrained movements," notes Tortsov, "natural though they may be to the actor himself, only blur the design of his part, make his performance unclear, monotonous and uncontrolled." Tortsov goes on to compare the unrestrained performer to the narrator who surrenders his narrative art to the personal emotions of the story he has to tell: "A person in the midst of experiencing a poignant emotional drama is incapable of speaking of it coherently," he insists. Under the stress of unmediated emotion, his voice breaks, choked with tears; his grimaces and spasms distract his listeners and prevent them from understanding the story he is telling. Only after the passage of "time, the great healer," can the storyteller come to grips with his sorrow, give it shape and solemnity, and speak of it in artful cadences calmly wrought "while those who listen weep." All the references to feeling the part and getting into character and inner truth finally come down to this, Tortsov's summing up of the goal of the Stanislavski System:

Our art seeks to achieve this very result and requires that an actor experience the agony of his role, and weep his heart out at home or in rehearsals, that he then calm himself, get rid of every sentiment alien or obstructive to his part. He then comes out on the stage to convey to the audience in clear, pregnant, deeply felt, intelligible and eloquent terms what he has been through. At this point the spectators will be more affected than the actor, and he will conserve all his forces in order to direct them where he needs them most of all: in reproducing the inner life of the character he is portraying. (*Building a Character,* 69–70)

Such "emotion recollected in tranquillity" requires even more method and control than Wordsworth demanded of the poet, but the goal in both cases is the same: "clear, pregnant, deeply felt, intelligible and eloquent" artistic expression.

Stanislavski's search for truth brought him round again to the point at which he had begun in 1906, but with a new respect for habit. The strong muscular memory he had distrusted in actors survived in his thinking to become a crucial element in the System as it stood at the end of his life. That which remembers bad habits may also remember good ones. Impulse may create the score in rehearsal, but the score creates the impulse in performance—that was his final word.

Around the work of Stanislavski there developed a community of dedicated practitioners. Dividing into various studios and schools, they explored different phases of the System, probing its anomalies and testing the reach of its applications in a process analogous to what Thomas Kuhn describes as the workings of normal science. Stanislavski's foremost legatee, Eugene Vakhtangov, devoted his short life to the synthesis of Meyerholdian theatricality and Stanislavskian realism—an anomaly poised between the mechanics of external form and the organic content of inner feeling. B. E. Zakhava, among other practitioners, continued Stanislavski and Vakhtangov's inquiries into the "Unity of the Physical and Psychological, of the Objective and the Subjective in the Actor's Art." Similarly, Vasili O. Toporkov recorded the foundation of the method of physical actions on "the *Law* of *Unity of the Physical and the Psychical* in man's nervous system" (*AA,* 524). The greatest actor to emerge from this circle, Michael Chekhov, went on to develop the *psychological gesture,* a physical delineation of complex expressive sequences. Those practitioners who, like Chekhov, left Russia to settle abroad carried various elements of the System with them. In 1924 Richard Boleslavsky and others founded the American Laboratory Theatre, which taught the principles of Stanislavski as they had evolved at the First Studio until 1919. Boleslavsky's own textbook on acting emphasized the actor's inner technique, "which works unconsciously by itself

and for itself."[22] His teaching at the Lab Theatre influenced a new generation of American actors and directors, including Lee Strasberg, Harold
Clurman, and Stella Adler.

The common point of reference among the various schools within the
larger international community remained the paradigm established by
Diderot and reinforced by scientific psychology. As Lee Strasberg observed in summing up the doctrine of emotion memory as it appeared in
the American Method: "The emotional thing is not Freud, as people
commonly think. Theoretically and actually, it is Pavlov."[23] The complex
interplay of the organic and mechanical, of the unconscious and the
conscious, of the objective and the subjective in the System demonstrates
beyond question the pervasiveness of materialistic science in modern theatrical aesthetics. "Influenced by the materialist world view and by I. M.
Sechenov and I. P. Pavlov's theory of higher nervous activity," runs the
recent entry on the System in the *Bol'shaia Sovetskaia Entsiklopedia*,
"Stanislavski came to recognize the fundamental importance of physical
actions in the mastering of the inner meaning of a role" (24:465). The
atheistical editor-in-chief of the *Encyclopédie* himself could not have
hoped for a more resounding vindication by his progeny. He could not
have proposed a more succinct attribution of material causes to the great
mysteries of the player's passion—spontaneity, consciousness, and inspiration—nor could he have penned a more unambiguous explanation of a
craftsman's physical instrument in the clear light of progressive science.

Yet Stanislavski does not seem to have been entirely at ease with this
formulation. As described by V. O. Toporkov, an actor who worked with
him during his last years, the method of physical actions entailed the
extensive use of improvisation. Stanislavski had his actors improvise
physical tasks in order to capture—or rather liberate—the organic motivations, objectives, and actions of their characters before they incorporated the lines in the text. The goal of improvisation is spontaneous
creation from which theoretically indeterminant impulses can emerge.
Sometimes it is hard to determine where, according to Stanislavski, improvisation was supposed to have ended and the fixed score to have
begun. To this day spontaneity is stressed by all those who promote the
Stanislavski System. The word *sincerity* also frequently recurs in Toporkov's memoirs in contexts that exalt it as the requisite attribute for stage
performance, as something more than a term from stage ethics, perhaps
traceable to Leo Tolstoy's ideal of moral redemption through spiritual
simplicity. Toporkov attributes to Stanislavski the observation that the
"ability to be sincere onstage—that is talent."[24] In fact, the reader will
search Stanislavski's trilogy in vain for any such fatuity.

At the same time, however, there does exist a strong element of paradox in all Stanislavski's writings. He sought to create a religion of art, in which the theater was a temple, the audience worshippers, and the actors celebrants at a mysterious rite. A mystic and idealist, he tolerated his own mechanization of the art he loved only within definite limits, and such sonorities as the "inner life of the human spirit" rolled off his tongue far more naturally than technical terms like *cerebral reflexes.* Although Stanislavski is a state hero, Soviet psychologists have expressed uneasiness with some of the more unscientific passages in his writings,[25] and the censors felt compelled to prune a number of sentimental animisms out of the Russian edition of *My Life in Art.* For the inexplicable, the fugitive, and the enigmatic, Stanislavski invoked "inspiration" and "spiritual truth" from the realm of "Apollo," the last presence of the *visiones* of the rhetors, now paved over by Soviet science, but stubbornly pushing up between the cracks in odd places, sustained by roots more ancient than history. Nevertheless, when his views are digested by less orphic voices than his own, Stanislavski's paradox flattens out into a materialism as far left as La Mettrie's, a bald equation of organism and machine. Of Stanislavskian actors Sonia Moore writes: "The System teaches them to function on the stage automatically as live human beings."[26] Such an apparent contradiction makes sense only when it is read in the context of the psychophysical doctrines foreseen by Diderot and developed by Russian science during Stanislavski's lifetime, doctrines that define man as a machine who remembers and dies.

Epilogue:
The Vitalist Twilight

Were Pavlov's dog improvising, he would still salivate when
the bell rang, but he would feel sure it was all his own doing:
"I'm dribbling," he would say, proud of his daring.
—Peter Brook, *The Empty Space* (1968)

Our current views of acting seem to reverse the anxiety that seventeenth-
century rhetoricians expressed with regard to the flow of the passions:
instead of worrying about how to cap the gusher, as they did, modern
actors wonder where to drill. Contemporary psychology has utterly
transformed our image of the body. We believe that spontaneous feelings,
if they can be located and identified, must be extracted with difficulty
from beneath the layers of inhibition that time and habit have deposited
over our natural selves, selves that lie repressed under the rigidifying
sediment of stress, trauma, and shame. We tend, therefore, to see our
bodies as damaged by the kinds of lives we have lived.

In response to this powerful idea, acting theorists have come to believe
that before an actor can learn to act, to use his bodily instrument expres-
sively in vital characterization, he must himself learn to move and feel and
live anew because in growing up he has disordered his musculature,
misshapen his bones, and dulled his sensitivities. The goal at the end of a
training program in acting today is natural expressiveness; its enemy is
inhibition. Under the rubric of "the re-awakening of the oral zone," to
take but one instance, today's acting student is liable to learn that "this
zone and modality bear a heavy burden of repression from early days. It
is important to realize that the tongue, the teeth, the lips, the throat must
be re-activated in the service of communication. Necessary inhibitions of
biting, sucking, licking, etc. cannot be allowed to undermine the key-

stone of the dramatic language."[1] In such accounts, the Freudian equation of sexuality and mental life becomes a new equation of sexuality and performance.

Sexology naturally interests the modern acting theorist. This is so because the question of the spontaneous bodily expression of inner emotions—supposedly threatened on all sides by society, upbringing, and even by language itself—has taken on a particular urgency in both fields. The psychologist Wilhelm Reich has exerted a considerable influence on international theatrical theory through such works as *The Function of Orgasm* (1942). Reich acknowledged his indebtedness to La Mettrie for his mind-body monism, but he went on to define the mechanization or rigidification of the body as the essential symptom of neurosis. He believed that character can be deduced from body alignments. He spoke of "character armor" as a carapace that the mind-body constructs to protect itself against the threat of psychological damage, but the armor inexorably becomes a scar. He spoke of the "physiological anchoring" of neuroses in the muscles, an induced bodily rigidity that also paralyzes the mind. Correspondingly, he believed that the cure for neurosis is a change in muscular habits, a casting off of the hard outer shell to reveal the soft inside. Reviving the doctrine of the irascible and concupiscible passions, he characterized neurosis as contracting the body and sex as expanding it outward, increasing its plasticity and sensitivity. Rejecting the mentalistic free association of Freudian psychoanalysis, he sought therapeutic results through physical means.

A physicality of approach similar to Reich's appears in various programs of body awareness, sensitivity training, and actor education.[2] Not all the inventors and advocates of self-use systems would feel comfortable in the company of Reich, whose eccentricities eventually isolated him from respectable science, indeed, from society as a whole. Nevertheless, authors of systems of psychophysical improvement share the Reichian premise that the body has to be therapeutically liberated from the tensions and distortions that bind it, that it has to be exercised and manipulated in order to be whole again and restored to its natural plasticity. F. M. Alexander based the "Alexander Technique" on aligning the head-neck reflex of "primary control." Surveying a human landscape blighted by hunched shoulders, compacted spines, drooping jowls, and sagging breasts, Alexander's followers conclude that the oppressor is not gravity, but civilization. The technological and social terrain has changed more rapidly than man's ability to adapt to it. Elevators, automobiles, mattresses, brassieres, and office furniture conspire with anxiety and Puritan conscience to disfigure the body and wither the mind. The supposed "degenerative influence that civilized living has exerted upon the human organism" is the etiological cliché of the self-use movement.[3] Ida Rolf, whose "Rolfers" practice "Structural Integration," advocates the restoration of the body to proper alignment through the separation of the muscle fasciae that have allegedly become knotted through physical and psychic trauma. When a subject is "Rolfed," he is "processed" back into prelapsarian plasticity. Perhaps most impressively, the extensive biomechanical exercises developed by Moshe Feldenkrais seek to reintegrate the body-mind impulses that have become disorganized through disuse or misuse, a state of affairs he blames on the aggressive regimentation of our culture. "Education provided by society," he writes in *Awareness through Movement,* exists to compel the individual "to overcome and discard spontaneous desires."[4]

In some of the performance training exercises of the 1970s, the line society draws between physicality and sexuality was crossed with a boldness that would have no doubt exceeded the specifications of a respectable biomechanical clinician like Feldenkrais, but it was done in the same spirit, if not with the same erudition, of the self-use concept of releasing the body from its acquired bondage, of sensitizing it to itself. In the climate of the times, learning "to let go" seemed of paramount importance to the actor, who doubted his capacity to feel what he should. Desperate circumstances engendered desperate measures. Ann Halprin in *The Drama Review* suggested the following exercise, entitled "Hip Roll: Reinforcing" under the general heading of "breakthrough movements":

Objective: To open and loosen the pelvic region. To use breathing as automatic reflex and allow intuitive responses.
Description: Do very slowly.
Person I: Lie on back with legs apart, knees bent and soles of feet on ground. Breathe into lower abdomen and follow your partner's touch with hips and sounds.
Person II: Kneel between partner's legs. Press your middle finger in the perineum and tilt upwards as your partner breathes out. Glide your hands over top rim of hip bone and tilt pelvis forward as partner breathes in. Go with the breath and allow movement to gradually increase in range. Repeat for one hour—let the movement take over and flow with it.
Questions: Feedback your immediate experience. Did you hold back? Where? What can your partner do to reinforce?[5]

Sparing the reader little but a final defeatist direction such as "Repeat if necessary," this exercise captures the similar paradox inherent in sex manuals, whose recipes for spontaneous intimacy inevitably end by mechanizing the mysteries that they promise merely to organize. "Auto-

matic reflex" looms large in Halprin's conception of feeling and responsiveness. Even more revealingly, she appropriates the term *feedback* from
the language that machines use when they talk to other machines.

The elusive ideal of spontaneous expression, like Goethe's eternal
feminine, continues to lead us thither and yon. The *avant-garde* theater
of the 1960s and 70s, in all its diverse energies and passions, might be
generally interpreted as a reversion to vitalism in revolt against the relentless advance of the *homme machine*, in revolt, that is, against the
definition of spontaneity supplied by Diderot. Romantic vitalism invests
the flesh with a special energy, a life force that exceeds the sum of its
interdependent mechanisms. An impulse rather than a reflex, this autonomous force accounts for "true" spontaneity. Feeling is supposed to be
created from within the self, not called into existence in response to
stimuli from without. It is a kind of impromptu soul, a paradise innocent
of the destructive habits that have corrupted its body.

Predictably, the idea of improvisation dominates much of the contemporary literature on the actor's art. It promises a creative escape from pre-
established patterns. In class and in rehearsal, the theory runs, the actor
improvises—invents his actions and words *ex tempore*—in order to free
his creativity from the deadening influence of acquired behaviors. Peter
Brook calls the sum total of these mechanized acquisitions "The Deadly
Theatre," and he identifies improvisation as a means of revitalization
(*Empty Space*, 102). He views it as a possible route of escape from the
closed system of false routines, a route that leads inward to an implied
source of vital truth. Yet Brook is ultimately wary of the liberating powers attributed to improvisation, and he carefully qualifies their practical
limits. His ironic interpretation of the response of Pavlov's dog to the bell
as an improvisation (101) testifies to the precision of his skepticism. In the
casual parlance of contemporary acting classes, however, the soft-edged
haze of romantic vitalism more often prevails over such scrupulosity:
impulses are to be trusted and cherished while habits are shunned and
maligned.

In the 1960s theatrical vitalism took on an added burden of political
meaning. It came to represent a utopian ideal of revolutionized behavior
deployed against the tyranny of the *homme machine*. The Living Theatre,
for example, taking its name from a reactionary mystification of organism, demonstrated an unyielding and ennobling hatred of the maceration
of flesh by technocracy, as most eloquently argued in *Frankenstein*. Judith
Malina and Julian Beck taught by physical example and vitalistic
sloganeering:

Don't enact. Act.
Don't re-create. Create.

Don't imitate life. Live.
Don't make graven images. Be. (*AA*, 658)

They taught the dissolution of structure into performance event. They taught collective improvisation, mutually fluctuating responsiveness without prior calculation. They taught unrehearsed transactions between performer and spectator, whose existence was once again rhetorically acknowledged—indeed, in *Paradise Now*, violently insisted upon—fiery eye to eye. They taught bodily resistance against the rigidifying conventions of the mechano-literary theater in all its repressive manifestations—complexity of production technology, for instance, and scripts. Diderot's paradigm, from the *Paradoxe* to Stanislavski's trilogy, assumes the existence of a text, which by its nature imposes upon the actor's spontaneity, as Diderot himself realized in his early advocacy of improvised pantomime independent from a text. The *avant-garde* movement, of which the Living Theatre was a part, generally exalted the actor's bodily impulse, the happening, over the polished automatism, the selection.

Like the latter-day proponents of the self-use systems, Antonin Artaud, the prophet of the *avant-garde*, thought that man's vital spontaneity falls victim to civilization, but in his case the instrument of civilized oppression is language itself. Like destructive habits of physical ill-use, language is an acquired encrustation over the fertile loam of original feeling. For Artaud language represents a network of preexisting categories and established structures that denature an emotion even as it is being expressed. It is conditioned behavior, corrupted by habit. Therefore, the text must be replaced by some form of spontaneous utterance.

Artaud contemplated a number of solutions to the problem of spontaneity. As one-time director of the Bureau de Recherches of the Surrealist movement, he explored automatic writing, the supposedly free-flowing ejaculations of the unconscious onto the page, a kind of Ouija board for the emission of dreams. Automatic writing is the poet's version of the actor's improvisation, but the end result is a stream of words coalescing into a text. This threatens to ossify the pure resilience of spontaneous feeling before the ink is dry on the page. The poem, if it is to be read at all, should be read once and then quickly burned.

To rescue himself from the deadly threat of replicability, Artaud turned to the theater. In "No More Masterpieces" he argued that its efficacy exists not in a literary structure, infinitely reproducible, but in the "*action* of what is gesticulated and pronounced, and which is never made the same way twice."[6] The conventional literary text has no place in such a conception of the theater. Artaud seized upon the immediate and continuous physical presence of the actor to the spectator. In the actor the word is made flesh. His expressiveness, Artaud emphasized, has a concrete physiological basis: just as the snake uncoils its length to receive the message of the snake-charmer's flute, so the spectator experiences the signals from the actor's soul in the form of physical vibrations. Not a word need pass between them. The kinship of inspiration and disease had not escaped the notice of the Galenists who wrote on the *visiones* of the actor/rhetor, and Artaud vivified this relationship by comparing the physiology of the theatrical event to the onset of the plague. The signs in his Theatre of Cruelty, like the plague germs of old, would possess a concrete physical existence and potency. They would consist of gestures, sobs, cries, moans, and mysterious vibrations. They would carry the physical experience of the passions, like an infection, a kind of spontaneous generation of pain, from the bodies of the actors to those of the spectators.

The more that the romantic vitalists struggled against mechanism, however, the more it devoured them. Artaud's tormented visions of the actor consume themselves in the violence of this struggle. Recapitulating Diderot's movement from inspiration to automation, he condenses the entire history of the science of acting into expository paradoxes with the density of verse. Repelled by the lack of rigor in improvisation, he advocated the thorough automatization of the actor's expressions. Flatly contradicting his erstwhile advocacy of spontaneity, he proposed sufficient preparation so that the actor's performance "would proceed like a music role in a player piano," attaining the perfection of "fatality and the most precise predetermination."[7] His idealization of the Balinese theater included his particular enthusiasm for its "methodically calculated effects which forbid any recourse to spontaneous improvisation" (*Theatre and its Double*, 55). In his love-hate for the theater, in his loathing of repetition and his contradictory adoration of precision, he kept returning to the enigma within the paradox, the body of the actor, whom he called "an athlete of the heart." What he found in the actor's body was the sort of machine with which we are now quite familiar. "The soul," he wrote in a phrase that La Mettrie or Diderot would have found commonplace, "can be physiologically reduced to a skein of vibrations" (135). For the words that he suspected of killing the actor's vitality, Artaud substituted a physical score of gestural hieroglyphs. As the piano roll of habit runs through the strings of the passions, the inner model vibrates the sensible instrument in accordance with the score.

Beyond his rejection of literary texts, which supposedly doom the theater to derivation, Artaud rooted his version of the paradox in the actor's breathing. His whole complex Cabalistic theory, with its baffling elaboration of modes and colors, is sustained by a simple physiological fact: respiration, while fundamentally automatic, is subject to voluntary influence. While its rate and rhythm may be altered to a certain extent, the physiological consequences of those alterations are fully automatized: if we breathe too fast, one set of sensations will automatically ensue; if we breathe too slowly, another set appears whether we will its existence or not. "It is certain that since breathing accompanies effort," Artaud reasons, "the mechanical production of breath will engender in the working organism a quality corresponding to the effort." Succumbing at last to the mechanist's definition of spontaneity as automatism, Artaud concludes: "What voluntary breathing provokes is a spontaneous reappearance of life." He shares with James, Lange, and the reflexologists a confidence in the unity of the physiological expression of emotion and its inner experience: "an actor can arrive by means of breath at a feeling which he does not have" (136–37). Divested of its pulsating shock effects and exotic imagery, Artaud's "athlete of the heart" is safely within the mainstream of opinion on the science of acting.

In a more pragmatic and less theoretical realm than Artaud, the remarkable career of Jerzy Grotowski—a career that may not be over—could be interpreted as an unfinished struggle with the anomaly of spontaneity. As founding director of the Polish Laboratory Theatre, Grotowski achieved international recognition in the 1960s through a series of innovative productions of classical plays, such as *Akropolis, Dr. Faustus,* and *The Constant Prince.* In these his acting ensemble created theatrical scores based on the texts but not subservient to them in the usual sense. Stripped of all the opulent effects of what he calls the "Rich" theater, Grotowski centered his "Poor" theater on the body of the actor. His Laboratory Theatre—the name itself betokens an attitude and an ambition—experimented with a method of training the actor that would enable him to accomplish almost sacrificial acts of self-discovery and self-revelation. Grotowski defined this method as "a *via negativa*—not a collection of skills but an eradication of blocks," a psychic stripping away of disguises analogous to the radical simplification of his settings. In proposing a laboratory for "Methodical Exploration" founded vaguely on the model of the Bohr Institute for physics, Grotowski identified three conditions of the actor's art as the objectives of speculation and experiment:

a) To stimulate a process of self-revelation, going back as far as the subconscious, yet canalizing this stimulus in order to obtain the required reaction.

b) To be able to articulate this process, discipline it and convert it into signs. In concrete terms, this means to construct a score whose notes are tiny elements of contact, reactions to the stimuli of the outside world: what we call "give and take."

c) To eliminate from the creative process the resistances and obstacles caused by one's own organism, both physical and psychic (the two forming a whole).[8]

The idea of the score of the role was woven into the fabric of Grotowski's work at this stage, as were the representatively modernist concepts of mind-body monism, creative subconscious, and the conditioned ("canalized") stimulus and response. Whatever "give and take" may have meant to him, he rejected improvisation during performance. A search for spontaneity without discipline, he believed, ended with confusion. A confession spoken by an inarticulate voice goes unheard.

As was the case with Stanislavski, however, the religious impulse in Grotowski's thought qualifies the scientific. He has ritualized his Laboratory procedures. The act of sacrificial self-revelation has darkly mystical shadings that obscure its technical nature even as it promises to discover more significant truths. His is an odd kind of faith, which, because it is without God or even gods, turns man inward upon himself and his own mysteries and potencies. Celebrating the introverted union of flesh and spirit, as Peter Brook explains, the Laboratory Theatre believes that "acting is mediumistic—the idea suddenly envelops the whole in an act of possession—in Grotowski's terminology the actors are 'penetrated'—penetrated by themselves" (99). It would seem that this time-honored idea has yet to run its course in theatrical theory. Yet even at his most mystical, in his description of the "Holy Actor," Grotowski falls back upon the assumptions that materialistic science liberated from religious interpretations only with great difficulty in the not-too-distant past. When the actor has mastered the technique of self-penetration, when he has removed the "blocks" inhibiting his powers of self-revelation, Grotowski believes, he commands inner and outer self as one entity: "The result is freedom from the time-lapse between inner impulse and outer reaction in such a way that the impulse is already an outer reaction. Impulse and action are concurrent: the body vanishes, burns, and the spectator sees only a series of visible impulses" (*Towards a Poor Theatre*, 16). G. H. Lewes made much the same point a century earlier when he spoke of an actor's imaginative impulse instantaneously exciting a palpable nervous discharge, but he expressed himself in the decidedly less incantatory language of Victorian science.

Perhaps it is this confrontation with mechanism that has repelled his religious nature and led Grotowski away from the disciplined score and toward organic paratheatrical events such as *The Tree of People.* In this production a group of invited spectators/performers lived and worked in the Laboratory for days, reacting to one another and evolving a miniature society, the order and structure of which were, to use Lewes's term, *emergent,* spontaneous in a way that a conventional performance could never truly be. Perhaps in these surroundings acts of sincere self-discovery, self-revelation, and self-penetration are possible. It is hard to judge, however, what prior calculations the participants may have made on their own, what faces they have studiously fashioned to wear underneath their masks. The uncertainty principle undermines theories of emotional spontaneity more thoroughly than it does those of modern physics: just as an act of observation must alter the nature of the observed phenomenon, so an act of public expression must alter the nature of the feeling expressed. As Quintilian realized long ago, when you choose to reveal your innermost emotions in the public forum, the act of revelation itself elaborates the true feeling into a kind of fiction that is, for better or worse, a work of art. What physiology and psychology since the eighteenth century have done is to define this process of elaboration in terms of the body as a physical instrument, demystifying some of its most sacred totems at great cost to the actor's sense of his own spirituality. Even as Grotowski bases his theories of acting on current scientific conceptions of the body, he is tempted to make detours into the realm of ineffable mystery. Like the ancients, he yearns for the unquestionable authenticity of inspired revelation. At present the outcome of his journey is uncertain, but if the historic pattern continues to hold true, Grotowski will reach its end only to find Diderot waiting for him there, his patient face enlivened by the irritating smile of reason.

Notes

Note on Citations

The following works are cited in the text, using the abbreviations noted here:

AA *Actors on Acting*, ed. Toby Cole and Helen Krich Chinoy (1949; New York: Crown, 1970).

AT Denis Diderot, *Oeuvres complètes*, ed. J. Assézat and M. Tourneux, 20 vols. (Paris: Garnier, 1875–77).

MF William Archer, *Masks or Faces?* in *The Paradox of Acting and Masks or Faces?* intro. Lee Strasberg (New York: Hill and Wang, 1957).

PA *Papers on Acting*, ed. Brander Matthews (New York: Hill and Wang, 1958).

PC Denis Diderot, *Le paradoxe sur le comédien*, trans. W. H. Pollock in *The Paradox of Acting and Masks or Faces?* (MF).

Frequently quoted works are noted here on their first appearance and automatically cited in the text thereafter.

Chapter 1. Changeling Proteus

1. *Institutio Oratoria*, 6. Preface, 5–12; translator's gloss on *animam recipere*.
2. Artistotle, *Works* 3:431. For the significance of this reference, I am indebted to McMahon, "Images as Motives," 465–67.
3. Abrams, *Mirror and the Lamp*, chap. 1.
4. Oesterreich, *Possession*, 313–15.
5. Onians, *Origins of European Thought about the Body*, 35–65.
6. Hall, *Ideas of Life and Matter* 1:155; see also *Galen on the Passions*, 15.
7. T. Wright, *Passions of the Minde*, 301–06.
8. Doran, *Endeavors of Art*, 38.
9. Marker, "Nature and Decorum," 87–107; see also Mullin, "Methods and Manners," 5–22.
10. Heywood, *Apology for Actors*, 45.
11. Joseph, *Elizabethan Acting*, 100. Joseph's thanks for bringing to light a great deal of useful information on the relationship between oratory and stage performance was a series of hostile essays attacking his book on crypto-scientific grounds; i.e., what emotion in acting is really like: Rosenberg ("Elizabethan Actors: Men or Marionettes?" 915–27) would dismiss John Bulwer's rhetorical studies of "formal" gesture because "he had nothing to say to actors" and immortalize Richard Flecknoe's description of Richard Burbage because it

"sounds like an earlier Stanislavski"; J. R. Brown ("On the Acting of Shakespeare's Plays"), commenting on the ample evidence that the Shakespearean actor was "emotionally identified" with his role, argued: "Such absorption in one's part has nothing to do with oratory; it is closer to the acting techniques of Stanislavsky. It suggests that an Elizabethan actor sunk himself in his part and did not merely declaim his lines with formal effectiveness" (481). As we have seen, absorption in one's part had everything to do with oratory. Joseph, in the second edition of *Elizabethan Acting*, offered a needless concession to his antagonists by deleting his account of rhetoric in humanist education and clarifying his views in light of "methods still used in the modern theatre and advocated by Stanislavski and his followers" (vi). The formalist position on the subject of "symbolic" acting has been applied to the latter half of the seventeenth-century by Hugh Hunt, "Restoration Acting" in *Restoration Theatre*, ed. Brown and Harris: "An overdose of contemporary naturalism coupled with a mistaken belief that acting is necessarily based on psychology has resulted in an all-too ready condemnation of . . . the grand manner . . . [which] was frankly artificial" (191). But acting has always been based on psychology or its historical equivalents, just not on our psychology; to my knowledge no seventeenth-century theorist ever demanded an acting style that was "frankly artificial." Holland, in *The Ornament of Action* (55–98), sees the continuity in the seventeenth-century rhetorical tradition of tragic acting, but usefully distinguishes comic dramaturgy in the Restoration by its tendency to build characters around audience expectations of the individual personalities of popular actors, thus reversing the ancient idea of possession by the role.

12. On Gildon's plagiarism, see Howell, "Sources of the Elocutionary Movement," 1–18; Gildon, *Life of Betterton*, 41; T. Wright, 131. The full title of Gildon's pastiche bespeaks its oratorical provenance: *The Life of Mr. Thomas Betterton, The Late Eminent Tragedian Wherein the Action and Utterance of the Stage, Bar, and Pulpit are distinctly considered*. In a cagey preface Gildon preemptively answers the charge of "plagiory" with this accurate if evasive statement: "I first allow, that I have borrow'd many of [my instances] from the French, but then the French drew most of them from Quintilian and other Authors" (ix). He does not, however, similarly acknowledge his indebtedness to Thomas Wright.

13. Bacon, *Works* 2:567, 568, 570.

14. Bulwer, *Chirologia and Chironomia*, 5.

15. Bulwer, *Pathomyotomia*, 147. The full title projects Bulwer's ambitious scope: *Pathomyotomia or a Dissection of the Significative Muscles of the Affections of the Minde. Being an Essay to a New Method of observing the most Important movings of the Muscles of the Head, as they are the nearest and Immediate Organs of the Voluntarie or Impetuous Motions of the Mind. With the Proposall of a new Nomenclature of the Muscles.*

16. For the following material on Galenic physiology, I am variously indebted to Hall, *Ideas of Life and Matter* 1:141–63; Foster, *Lectures on the History of Physiology*, 11–14; Singer, *Evolution of Anatomy*, 58–62, 115–19; J. Miller, *Body in Question*, 144–212, 290–94.

17. Burton, *Anatomy of Melancholy*, 131.

18. Randolph, "To his friend, Thomas Riley," cited in Joseph, *Elizabethan Acting* (2d ed.), 4; Heywood, "Prologue to the Stage at the Cock-pit" in Marlowe, *Jew of Malta*, ed. Bennett, 28.

19. *Thesaurus Dramaticus* 1:223–24.

20. Cibber, *Apology*, 62.

21. *Laureat*, in Nagler, *Sourcebook*, 219.

22. Fulman's transcription of a letter by Henry Jackson dated 24 September 1610 in Tillotson, "*Othello* and *The Alchemist* at Oxford," 494.

23. A. L. Walker, "Convention in Shakespeare's Description of Emotion," 52 n.

24. Gayton, *Pleasant Notes upon Don Quixot*, 144–45.

25. Grant, *Essay on the Science of Acting*, 19–20.

26. Gayton, *Art of Longevity*, 15–17.

27. Bulwer, *Anthropometamorphosis*, prefatory verse.

28. Anthony Aston, *Brief Supplement to Colley Cibber*, in Nagler, 216.

29. Richard Cumberland, *Memoires*, in Nagler, 363–64.

Chapter 2. Nature Mechanized

1. *Biographical Dictionary of Actors* 6:72. For particulars about Perkins and the mechanical wig, see Burnim, *David Garrick, Director,* 160.

2. *Monitor,* no. 11, 24 October 1767, cited in Sprague, *Shakespearean Players,* 181.

3. Foucault, *Order of Things,* 127–28.

4. See Dijksterhuis, *Mechanization of the World Picture,* and Rosenfield, *From Beast-Machine to Man-Machine.*

5. J. Miller, *Body in Question,* 187–89; see also Jaynes, "Problem of Animate Motion in the Seventeenth Century" in *Historical Conceptions of Psychology,* ed. Henle, Jaynes, and Sullivan, 166–79.

6. For an account of Heron, see Vartanian, "Man-Machine," *Dictionary of the History of Ideas* 3:134.

7. Baur-Heinhold, *Baroque Theatre,* pl. 58.

8. Descartes, *Treatise of Man,* 21–22.

9. Descartes, *Passions of the Soul,* art. 1.

10. Levi, *French Moralists,* 249.

11. T. Brown, "Physiology and Mechanical Philosophy," 25–54.

12. Cheyne, *English Malady,* 49.

13. Du Bos, *Critical Reflections on Poetry* 2:179–81.

14. La Mettrie, *Man a Machine,* 140–41. For the use of automata in the theater, see Visser, "Scenery and Technical Design," *London Theatre World,* ed. R. Hume, 102–03.

15. Hogarth, *Analysis of Beauty,* 138.

16. Lee, *Ut Pictura Poesis,* 28.

17. Heriot, *Castrati in Opera,* 48.

18. Smart, "Dramatic Gesture and Expression in the Age of Hogarth," 90–97; McKenzie, "The Countenance You Show Me," 758–73.

19. Downer, "Nature to Advantage Dressed," 1028.

20. Barnett, "The Performance Practice of Acting," *passim.*

21. See Schechner, "Kinesics and Performance" in his *Essays on Performance Theory,* 100–01.

22. Lessing, *Hamburg Dramaturgy,* 19.

23. Garrick, *Letters* 1:82–83.

24. Noverre, *Works* 1:7, 59–60.

25. Lavater, *Essays on Physiognomy* 1:19.

26. Siddons, *Practical Illustrations,* 92.

27. Burgh, *Art of Speaking,* 65; J. Walker, *Elements of Elocution,* 308–79.

28. A. Hill, *Prompter,* no. 64, 20 June 1735, 82–83. The provenance of Hill's various essays on acting has been clarified by Hughes, "The Actor's Epitome," 306–07; Descartes's influence on Hill's system was first noted by Wasserman, "Sympathetic Imagination," 266–67.

29. L. Hunt, *Dramatic Criticism,* 113; A. Hill, *Works* 4:392, 400.

30. Riccoboni, *General History of the Stage,* 24.

31. Robertson, *Lessing's Dramatic Theory,* 258–59, 31.

32. Sainte-Albine, *Le comédien,* 108.

33. For the relationship of Descartes and Malebranche to the James-Lange theory, see Gardiner, Metcalf, and Beebe-Center, *Feeling and Emotion,* 161–62; also James, *Emotions by Carl Georg Lange and William James,* 83–90.

34. James, "What is an Emotion?" 194–97.

35. William Ball cited in Benedetti, *Actor at Work,* 212.

36. Koestler, *Act of Creation,* 148.

37. *Lichtenberg's Visits to England,* 10–11.

38. *Dictionary of Scientific Biography* 8:321.

39. Lichtenberg cited in Stern, *Lichtenberg,* 89.

40. Garrick's "Autograph Notebook" in the Harvard Theatre Collection, cited in the preface to A. Hill's *Prompter*, xii.

41. Noverre, *Works* 1:26–27.

42. Vartanian, *La Mettrie's L'Homme Machine*, 74–75.

Chapter 3. Crisis of Sensibility

1. Cited by Hanna, "Polinière and the Teaching of Experimental Physics at Paris," in *Eighteenth Century Studies*, ed. Gay, 31–32.

2. Cheyne, *English Malady*, 51.

3. Rousseau, "Nerves, Spirits, and Fibres," *Studies in the Eighteenth Century*, ed. Brissenden and Eade, 135–57. See also the same author's essay "Science" in *The Eighteenth Century*, ed. Rogers, 153–207.

4. See Rothschuh, *History of Physiology*, 125.

5. Gaub, "The Harmony of Mind and Body," in *De regimine mentis*, in Rather, *Mind and Body in Eighteenth Century Medicine*, 34.

6. Battie, *Treatise on Madness*, 78–79.

7. Sainte-Albine, *Le comédien*, 96.

8. Rousseau, "John Hill, Universal Genius *Manqué*," in his *Renaissance Man in the Eighteenth Century*, 45–129; Redmond, "Tobacco and Cancer," 21; *Dictionary of Scientific Biography* 6: 400–01; Proust, *Diderot et L'Encyclopédie*, 521.

9. J. Hill, *The Actor*, 1. This and subsequent references in the text are to the revised and enlarged version of 1755.

10. Riccoboni, *General History of the Stage*, 9–10.

11. Carnall, *Mid-eighteenth Century*, 495, 505–06.

12. Mandeville, *Hypochondriack and Hysterick Diseases*, 135.

13. Boring, *History of Experimental Psychology*, 197.

14. Newton, *Opticks*, 353–54.

15. D. Hume, *Treatise on Human Nature*, 440–41.

16. Siddons, *Practical Illustrations of Rhetorical Gesture*, 344–45.

17. Brook, *Empty Space*, 99.

18. Lewes, *Biographical History of Philosophy*, 605. See also: Warren, *History of Association Psychology*, 50–64, 168–75.

19. Hartley, *Observations on Man*, 67.

20. The relationship between Associationist psychology and *The Actor* has been explored by Taylor in " 'Just Delineation of the Passions,' " *Eighteenth-Century Stage*, ed. Richards and Thomson, 51–72. I believe that Taylor, in an otherwise excellent essay, reads John Hill far too Whiggishly in light of "Stanislavsky's search for 'an inner spiritual technique,' " praising the eighteenth-century physician for "groping" toward psychotechnique but taxing him for falling short of "a systematic examination of the subconscious creativity of the actor, which [he] seems to recognize but cannot explain" (68–69). Hill cannot explain biochemical photosynthesis either, but this is not a meaningful criterion by which to judge the significance of his *Vegetable System*.

21. Swammerdam, *Book of Nature*, 131.

22. D. Hume, *Human Understanding;* Lichtenburg, *Aphorismen;* both cited in Whyte, *Unconscious before Freud*, 111–14.

23. *Biographical Dictionary of Actors* 3: 262–82.

24. Nash, *Provoked Wife*, 89.

25. Joseph, *Tragic Actor*, 113. See also his index entries for *points* and *transitions*. For an account of Garrick's exhibition, see Hedgcock, *Garrick and his French Friends*, 232–34.

26. J. Hill, *Hypochondriasis*, 16–17, 20–21.

27. Kuhn, *Structure of Scientific Revolutions*, 67.

Chapter 4. Diderot

1. For my purposes the work of Bonnichon (*La psychologie du comédien*, 40–54), which tests Diderot's views against modern psychophysiology, and Beleval (*L'esthétique sans paradoxe de Diderot*, passim), which argues for the overall cohesiveness of the *Paradoxe* within Diderot's *oeuvre*, provide an informative starting point, particularly when read in conjunction with Dieckmann, "Le thème de l'acteur dans la pensée de Diderot," 157–72; Wilson (*Diderot*, 618–28) updates his own still useful essay, "Biographical Implications of Diderot's *Paradoxe sur le comédien*," 369–83; more recently Tort (*L'origine du Paradoxe sur le comédien*) has reexamined Diderot's opus in light of the treatises of Luigi and François Riccoboni, Sainte-Albine, and Antonio Fabio Sticotti.

2. Wilson, *Diderot,* 173.

3. Vartanian, *Diderot and Descartes,* 245.

4. See Roger, *Les sciences de la vie,* 585–682.

5. Duerr, *Length and Depth of Acting,* 262.

6. See Wilson, *Diderot,* 622–25.

7. For the place of *Le neveu de Rameau* in the general context of Diderot's thought, see Josephs, *Diderot's Dialogue of Language and Gesture.*

8. *Rameau's Nephew and Other Works,* 47.

9. Gaub, "Mind-Body Interaction in States of Disturbance," in *De regimine mentis,* in *Mind and Body in Eighteenth Century Medicine,* ed. Rather, 54.

10. Hedgcock, *Cosmopolitan Actor,* 214–37.

11. *Eléments de physiologie,* ed. Mayer, lxxii–lxxvii. I am responsible for the translations, but I am indebted to Prof. Laura T. Buckham for her helpful emendations.

12. Vartanian, "The Enigma of Diderot's *Eléments de Physiologie,*" 300.

13 *D'Alembert's Dream* in *Rameau's Nephew and Other Works,* 126–27.

14. *Dictionary of Scientific Biography* 6:64; on Buffon, see Mayer's commentary, *Eléments,* 37 n.

15. Chouillet ("Une source anglaise du 'Paradoxe sur le comédien,'" 209–26) attributes *The Actor* to Aaron Hill. There are many reasons why this could not have been so, not the least of which is that Aaron Hill died in 1750 and the extensively revised edition of *The Actor,* "written by the Author of the former," appeared in 1755.

16. For a reading of the *Paradoxe* in light of Rousseau's *Lettre à d'Alembert contre les spectacles* (1758), see Sennett, *Fall of Public Man,* 110–22.

17. Le Brun's heads found their way into the *Encyclopédie* and influenced Diderot's conception of expression: see Proust, "Diderot et la physiognomonie," 317–29.

18. McGraw, for instance (*Acting is Believing,* 16), confidently assures the student that "the objective of this exercise from *The Sea Gull* is not to pretend your foot is asleep. It is to make yourself *believe* your foot is asleep through the actions you take to ease the numbing sensation."

19. Bonneville, "Diderot's Artist: Puppet and Poet" in *Literature and History in the Age of Ideas,* ed. Williams, 244–52.

20. Ribot, *Psychology of the Emotions,* 140–71; cf. Stanislavski, *An Actor Prepares,* 156–58, and Boleslavsky, *Acting,* 29–48.

21. T. Braun, "Diderot, Wordsworth, and the Creative Process," 151–58.

22. Bonnichon, *La psychologie,* 47; Belaval, *L'esthétique,* 251.

23. Further relationships between musician and actor in Diderot's thought have been elaborated by Cartwright in "Diderot and the Idea of Performance and the Performer," *Studies in Eighteenth-Century French Literature,* ed. Fox, Waddicor, Watts, 31–42.

24. Whytt, *Essay on the Vital and Other Involuntary Motions of Animals,* 1–2, 280.

25. For example, Grotowski, *Towards a Poor Theatre,* 211–13.

26. Taylor, "'Just Delineation of the Passions,'" 62.

27. Olivier, "Staging Shakespeare," in *Directors on Directing,* ed. Cole and Chinoy, 412. Cf. Brook, *Empty Space:* "Olivier repeats lines of dialogue to himself again and again until

he conditions his tongue muscles to a point of absolute obedience—and so gains total freedom" (125).

28. See Diderot, *Oeuvres esthétiques,* ed. Vernière, xvii, 311 n.

29. Fried, *Absorption and Theatricality,* 93–105.

30. Trudgian, "Claude Bernard and the 'Groupe de Médan,'" 273–76.

31. This is conspicuously true of double consciousness. "The actor should feel," says Aumont, as if in crushing refutation of Diderot, "but he must have a kind of 'radar'" (*Paradoxe sur le comédien avec recueilles présentées par Marc Blanquet,* 169).

32. Binet, "Réflexions sur le paradoxe de Diderot," 243–53.

33. Kuhn, *Structure of Scientific Revolutions,* 10.

Chapter 5. Second Nature

1. Craig, "Actor and the Übermarionette," 3, 9–10.

2. Wordsworth, Preface to *Lyrical Ballads* (1802) in *Prose Works* 1 : 127.

3. Kleist, "On the Marionette Theatre," 22–26.

4. See Vasco, *Diderot and Goethe, passim.*

5. Lewes, *Life of Goethe,* 345, 359.

6. Staël, *De L'Allemagne,* 136.

7. Goethe, *Rules for Actors,* cited in Carlson, *Goethe and the Weimar Theatre,* appendix, 314–18.

8. Freer, "Talma and Diderot's Paradox on Acting," 23–76. Freer makes a good case for Talma's acquisition of a ms. of the *Paradoxe* before its publication in 1830. The actor also paraphrased and directly plagiarized passages from the "Observations sur *Garrick*" in his essay on Lekain.

9. Donohue, *Dramatic Character in the English Romantic Age,* particularly "Kemble and the 'Science' of Shakespearean Acting," 243–53.

10. Bell, *Anatomy and Philosophy of Expression,* 125.

11. Darwin, *Expression of the Emotions in Man and Animals,* 351.

12. Schechner, "Ethology and Theatre," in his *Essays,* 157–201.

13. See Sulloway, *Freud, Biologist of the Mind,* 238–76.

14. Whyte, *Unconscious before Freud,* 164, 153–76.

15. Kjerbühl-Peterson, *Psychology of Acting,* 175.

16. Archer, "George Henry Lewes and the Stage," 230; Ribot, *English Psychology,* 255; Hearnshaw, *Short History of British Psychology,* 46–53.

17. Lewes, *On Actors and the Art of Acting,* 103.

18. Lewes, *Problems of Life and Mind,* Third Series, 2 : 290. The publishing history of *Problems of Life and Mind* is complicated. In order to simplify matters, the following volumes will be cited in the text as *"PLM"*—

  1st series: *Foundations of a Creed,* 2 vols.
  2nd series: *Physical Basis of Mind.*
  3rd series: *Problem the First: The Study of Psychology; Problem the Second: Mind as a Function of the Organism.*

19. For Lewes's concept of *image* and *symbol,* see Kaminsky, "George Henry Lewes," *Encyclopedia of Philosophy* 4 : 452–53; Lewes, *Physiology of Common Life* 2 : 351–52.

20. Fearing, *Reflex Action,* 162–73.

21. Lewes, *The Leader,* 19 February 1853, in *Victorian Dramatic Criticism,* ed. Rowell, 94–95.

22. Lewes, "Dickens in Relation to Criticism," in *Literary Criticism of George Henry Lewes,* 101.

23. Quoted in Kitchel, *George Lewes and George Eliot,* 123.

24. Ribot, *Psychology of the Emotions,* vii.

25. James, *Principles of Psychology* 2 : 464–65.

26. James [unsigned], "Problems of Life and Mind," 362–63.

27. Fiske, *Mrs. Fiske, Her Views on the Stage,* 104.

28. Koshtoyants, *Essays on the History of Physiology in Russia*, 145; Vucinich, *Science in Russian Culture*, 300.
29. Sechenov, *Reflexes of the Brain*, 8, 118 n.
30. Lyons, "Gordon Craig's Concept of the Actor," 267–69.
31. Craig, *On the Art of the Theatre*, 133.

Chapter 6. *Paradoxe* as Paradigm

1. Stanislavski, *My Life in Art*, 463.
2. Magarshack, *Stanislavsky*, 337.
3. Lunacharskii, quoted in A. Miller, "Annexation of a *Philosophe*," 118.
4. *Great Soviet Encyclopedia* 8:214.
5. Brecht, "Prospectus of the Diderot Society," 114.
6. Brecht, "Notes on Stanislavski," in *Stanislavski and America*, ed. Munk, 124–29.
7. Sechenov, "The Part Played by the Nervous System in Man's Working Movements," in *Selected Physiological and Psychological Works*, 484.
8. E. Braun, *Theatre of Meyerhold*, 167.
9. Meyerhold, "Actor of the Future and Biomechanics," in *Meyerhold on Theatre*, 199.
10. Sechenov, *Reflexes of the Brain*, 53; Gordon, "Meyerhold's Biomechanics," 77; Gray, "A Critical Chronology," in *Stanislavski and America*, ed. Munk, 142.
11. Pavlov, *Conditioned Reflexes*, 9–10.
12. Gordon, "Foregger and the Dance of the Machines," 68–73; Prampolini, "Futurist Scenography," in *Total Theatre*, ed. Kirby, 98; Moholy-Nagy, "Theatre, Circus, Variety," in *Theatre of the Bauhaus*, ed. Gropius, 52–54.
13. Meyerhold, "Program of Biomechanics," in Hoover, *Meyerhold*, 312.
14. E. Braun, *Theatre of Meyerhold*, 167.
15. "Actor of the Future and Biomechanics," *Meyerhold on Theatre*, 198.
16. Stanislavski, *Creating a Role*, 54.
17. Pavlov, *Conditioned Reflexes*, 15.
18. Stanislavski, "Art of the Actor and Director," in *Stanislavski's Legacy*, 187.
19. Stanislavski, *Building a Character*, 37–38.
20. Stanislavski, *Stanislavski on Opera*, 3.
21. Sechenov, "Elements of Thought," in *Selected Physiological and Psychological Works*, 391.
22. Zakhava, "Mastery of the Actor and the Director" in *Stanislavski Today*, ed. Moore, 4: Chekhov, *To the Actor*, 63–84; Boleslavsky, *Acting*, 36.
23. Strasberg, "Working with Live Material," *Stanislavski and America*, ed. Munk, 198.
24. Toporkov, *Stanislavski in Rehearsal*, 158.
25. See Bassin, "Consciousness and Unconsciousness," in *Handbook of Soviet Psychology*, ed. M. Cole, 399–420.
26. Moore, *Stanislavski System*, 20.

Epilogue: Vitalist Twilight

1. Freed, *Freud and Stanislavsky*, 58.
2. Clay, "Self-Use in Actor Training," 16–22.
3. Barker, *Alexander Technique*, 22–23.
4. Feldenkrais, *Awareness through Movement*, 6.
5. Halprin, "Community Art as Life Process," 69.
6. Artaud, *Theatre and Its Double*, 78.
7. Artaud, *Oeuvres complètes* 2:47.
8. Grotowski, *Towards a Poor Theatre*, 17, 128.

Works Consulted

Abrams, M. H. *The Mirror and the Lamp: Romantic Theory and the Critical Tradition.* 1953. New York: Norton, 1958.

Addison, Joseph. *The Spectator.* 5 vols. Oxford: Clarendon Press, 1965.

Archer, William. "George Henry Lewes and the Stage." *Fortnightly Review* 59 (1896): 216–30.

———. *Masks or Faces? A Study in the Psychology of Acting.* London: Longmans, Green, and Co., 1888.

———. *Masks or Faces?* In *The Paradox of Acting and Masks or Faces?* Introduced by Lee Strasberg. New York: Hill and Wang, 1957.

Aristotle. *The Rhetoric.* Edited by Lane Cooper. New York: Appleton-Century-Crofts, 1933.

———. *Works.* Edited by W. D. Ross. Vol. 3. Oxford: Clarendon Press, 1931.

Armstrong, William A. "Shakespeare and the Acting of Edward Alleyn." *Shakespeare Survey* 7 (1954): 82–89.

Artaud, Antonin. *Oeuvres complètes.* Paris: Gallimard, 1956–.

———. *The Theatre and Its Double.* Translated by M. C. Richards. New York: Grove Press, 1958.

Austin, Gilbert. *Chironomia; or a Treatise on Rhetorical Delivery.* 1806. Reprint. Edited by M. M. Robb and Lester Thonssen. Carbondale and Edwardsville: Southern Illinois University Press, 1966.

Babkin, B. P. *Pavlov: A Biography.* Chicago: University of Chicago Press, 1949.

Bacon, Francis. *The Works of Francis Bacon.* Edited by James Spedding, R. L. Ellis, and D. D. Heath. Vol. 2. New ed. London: Longmans, 1887.

Barish, Jonas. *The Anti-Theatrical Prejudice.* Berkeley: University of California Press, 1981.

Barker, Sarah. *The Alexander Technique: The Revolutionary Way to Use Your Body for Total Energy.* New York: Bantam, 1978.

Barnett, Dene. "The Performance Practice of Acting." *Theatre Research International.* Part 1: "Ensemble Acting." *TRI* 2 (1977): 157–85; Part 2: "The Hands." *TRI* 3 (1977): 1–19; Part 3: "The Arms." *TRI* 3 (1978): 79–93; Part 4: "The Eyes, the Face, and the Head." *TRI* 5 (1979–80): 1–13.

Bassin, F. V. "Consciousness and Unconsciousness." In Cole, M., and Maltzman, *Handbook of Contemporary Soviet Psychology*, 399–420.

Battie, William. *A Treatise on Madness.* 1758. Edited by Richard Hunter and Ida Macalpine. London: Dawson, 1962.

Baur-Heinhold, Margarete. *The Baroque Theatre: A Cultural History of the 17th and 18th Centuries.* New York: McGraw-Hill, 1967.

Beckerman, Bernard. *Shakespeare at the Globe 1599–1609.* 1962. New York: Collier, 1966.

Beleval, Yvon. *L'esthétique sans parodoxe de Diderot.* 2d ed. Paris: Gallimard, 1950.

Bell, Charles. *The Anatomy and Philosophy of Expression.* 1806. 7th ed. London: George Bell and Sons, 1880.

Benedetti, Robert. *The Actor at Work.* Englewood Cliffs, N.J.: Prentice Hall, 1976.

[Betterton, Thomas.] *The History of the English Stage.* London: Printed for E. Curl, 1741.

Binet, Alfred. "Réflexions sur le paradoxe de Diderot." *Année psychologique* 3 (1897): 279–95.

Biographical Dictionary of Actors, Actresses, Musicians, Dancers, Managers and Other Stage Personnel in London, 1600–1800. Edited by Philip H. Highfill, Kalmin A. Burnim and Edward Langhans. Carbondale and Edwardsville: Southern Illinois University Press, 1973–.

Boleslavsky, Richard. *Acting: The First Six Lessons.* New York: Theatre Arts Books, 1933.

Bonaparte, Laura. *La psicologia dell'attore.* Milan: Contemporanea, 1976.

Bonifacio, Giovanni. *L'arte de'cenni.* Vicenza: Francesco Grossi, 1616.

Bonneville, Douglas. "Diderot's Artist: Puppet and Poet." In Williams, *Literature and History in the Age of Ideas*, 244–52.

Bonnichon, André [André Villiers]. *L'art du comédien.* 4th ed. Paris: Presses Universitaires de France, 1968.

———. *La psychologie du comédien.* 1942. Paris: O. Lieuter, 1946.

Boring, E. G. *A History of Experimental Psychology.* 1929. 2d ed. New York: Appleton-Century-Crofts, 1950.

Braun, Theodore E. D. "Diderot, Wordsworth, and the Creative Process." York: Drama Book Specialists, 1979.

Braun, Theodore, E. D. "Diderot, Wordsworth, and the Creative Process." *Comparative Literature Studies* 11 (1974): 151–58.

Brecht, Bertolt. *Brecht on Theatre.* Edited by John Willet. New York: Hill and Wang, 1964.

———. "Bertolt Brecht's Prospectus of the Diderot Society." Translated by Mordecai Gorelik. *Quarterly Journal of Speech* 47 (1961): 113–17.

———. "Notes on Stanislavski." In Munk, *Stanislavski and America*, 124–36.

Brett, George. *History of Psychology.* Edited by R. S. Peters. London: Allen and Unwin, 1953.

Brissenden, R. F., and J. C. Eade, eds. *Studies in the Eighteenth Century*, 3. Toronto and Buffalo: University of Toronto Press, 1976.

Brook, Peter. *The Empty Space.* 1968. Reprint. New York: Avon, 1969.

Brown, John Russell. "On the Acting of Shakespeare's Plays." *Quarterly Journal of Speech* 34 (1953): 477–84.

Brown, John Russell, and Bernard Harris, eds. *Restoration Theatre.* 1965. New York: Capricorn, 1967.

Brown, Theodore M. "From Mechanism to Vitalism in Eighteenth-Century English Physiology." *Journal of the History of Biology* 7 (1974): 179–216.

————. "Physiology and the Mechanical Philosophy in Mid-Seventeenth-Century England." *Bulletin of the History of Medicine* 51 (1977): 25–54.

Buffon, Georges. *Oeuvres complètes.* 14 vols. Paris: Vasseur, 1884.

Bugard, Pierre. *Le comédien et son double; psychologie du comédien.* Paris: Stock, 1970.

Bulwer, John. *Anthropometamorphosis: Man Transformed; or, the Artificial Changeling.* London: Printed for J. Hardesty, 1650.

————. *Chirologia: or the Natural Language of the Hand and Chironomia: or the Art of Manual Rhetoric.* 1644. Edited by James W. Cleary. Carbondale and Edwardsville: Southern Illinois University Press, 1974.

————. *Pathomyotomia: Or, a Dissection of the Significative Muscles of the Affections of the Minde.* London: Printed by W. W. for Humphrey Mosely, 1649.

Burgh, James. *The Art of Speaking* [with] *An Index of the Passions.* London: T. Longman, 1761.

Burnim, Kalman A. "Aaron Hill's *The Prompter:* An Eighteenth-Century Theatrical Paper." *ETJ* 13 (1961): 74–81.

————. *David Garrick, Director.* 1961. Reprint. Carbondale and Edwardsville: Southern Illinois University Press, 1973.

Burton, Robert. *The Anatomy of Melancholy.* 1621. Reprint. New York: Da Capo, 1971.

Campbell, Lily B. *Shakespeare's Tragic Heroes: Slaves of Passion.* 1930. Reprint. New York: Barnes and Noble, 1967.

Canguilhem, G. *La formation du concept de réflexe aux XVIIᵉ et XVIIIᵉ.* Paris: Presses Universitaires de France, 1955.

Carlson, Marvin. *Goethe and the Weimar Theatre.* Ithaca and London: Cornell University Press, 1978.

Carnall, Geoffrey, ed. *The Mid-eighteenth Century*, by John Butt. Oxford: Clarendon, 1979.

Cartwright, Michael. "Diderot and the Idea of Performance and the Performer." In *Studies in Eighteenth-Century Literature*, ed. Fox, Waddicor, and Watts, 31–42.

Chekhov, Michael. *To the Actor.* New York: Harper and Row, 1953.

Cheyne, George. *The English Malady; or, a Treatise of Nervous Diseases of all Kinds.* London and Dublin: S. Powell, 1733.

Chouillet, Jacques. "Une source anglaise du 'Paradoxe sur le comédien.'" *Dix-Huitième Siècle* 2 (1970): 209–26.

Cibber, Colley. *An Apology for the Life of Colley Cibber.* 1740. Edited by B. R. S. Fone. Ann Arbor: University of Michigan Press, 1968.

Clay, Jack. "Self-Use in Actor Training." *TDR* 16 (1972): 16–22.

Cleary, James W. "John Bulwer: Renaissance Communicationist." *Quarterly Journal of Speech* 45 (1959): 391–98.

Cole, Michael, and Irving Maltzman, eds. *A Handbook of Contemporary Soviet Psychology.* New York and London: Basic Books, 1969.

Cole, Toby, and Helen Krich Chinoy, eds. *Actors on Acting: The Theories, Techniques, and Practices of the Great Actors of all Times as Told in Their Own Words.* 1949. Rev. ed. New York: Crown Publishers, 1970.

———. *Directors on Directing.* Rev. ed. Indianapolis: Bobbs-Merrill, 1963.

Craig, Edward Gordon. "The Actor and the Übermarionette." *The Mask* 1 (1908): 3–15.

———. *On the Art of the Theatre.* 1911. Reprint. New York: Theatre Arts Books, 1956.

Darwin, Charles. *The Expression of the Emotions in Man and Animals.* 1872. New York: D. Appleton and Co., 1894.

Descartes, René. *The Passions of the Soul.* In *The Philosophical Works of Descartes.* Translated by E. S. Haldane and G. R. T. Ross. Vol. 1. 1911. Reprint. Cambridge: Cambridge University Press, 1967.

———. *Treatise of Man.* Edited and translated by T. S. Hall. Cambridge, Mass.: Harvard University Press, 1972.

Dictionary of the History of Ideas. Edited by Philip P. Wiener. 5 vols. New York: Scribners, 1973.

Dictionary of Scientific Biography. Edited by C. C. Gillispie. 16 vols. New York: Scribners, 1970–80.

Diderot, Denis. *Eléments de physiologie.* Edited by Jean Mayer. Paris: Didier, 1964.

———. *Oeuvres complètes.* Edited by J. Assézat and M. Tourneux. 20 vols. Paris: Garnier, 1875–77.

———. *Oeuvres esthétiques.* Edited by Paul Vernière. Paris: Garnier, 1965.

———. *The Paradox of Acting.* Translated by W. H. Pollock. 1883. In *The Paradox of Acting and Masks or Faces?* Introduced by Lee Strasberg. New York: Hill and Wang, 1957.

———. *Le paradoxe sur le comédien avec recueilles présentées par Marc Blanquet.* Paris: Editions Nord-Sud, 1949.

———. *Rameau's Nephew and Other Works.* Translated by Jacques Barzun and Ralph H. Bowen. Indianapolis: Bobbs-Merrill, 1964.

Dieckmann, Herbert. "Le thème de l'acteur dans la pensée de Diderot." *Cahiers de l'association internationale des études françaises,* no. 13 (1961): 157–72.

Dijksterhuis, E. J. *The Mechanization of the World Picture.* Translated by C. Dikshorn. Oxford: Clarendon, 1961.

Donohue, Joseph W., Jr. *Dramatic Character in the English Romantic Age.* Princeton: Princeton University Press, 1970.

Doran, Madeleine. *Endeavors of Art: A Study of Form in Elizabethan Drama.* Madison: University of Wisconsin Press, 1954.

Downer, Alan S. "Nature to Advantage Dressed: Eighteenth-Century Acting." *PMLA* 58 (1943): 1002–37.

Du Bos, Abbé. *Critical Reflections on Poetry, Painting and Music with an Inquiry into the Rise and Progress of Theatrical Entertainments of the Ancients.* Translated by Thomas Nugent. 3 vols. London: Printed for John Nourse, 1758.

Duerr, Edwin. *The Length and Depth of Acting.* New York: Holt, Rinehart and Winston, 1962.

Edwards, Christine. *The Stanislavsky Heritage: Its Contribution to the Russian and American Theatre.* New York: New York University Press, 1965.

Ekman, Paul. "Darwin and Cross-Cultural Studies of Facial Expression." In his *The Face of Man: Expressions of Universal Emotions in a New Guinea Village.* New York and London: Garland, 1980, 91–138.

Ellenberger, Henri F. *The Discovery of the Unconscious.* New York: Basic Books, 1970.

The Encyclopedia of Philosophy. Edited by Paul Edwards. 6 vols. New York: Macmillan, 1967.

Encyclopédie, ou Dictionnaire raisonné des sciences, des arts et des métiers. 17 vols. Paris: Briasson, 1751–65. With *Recueil de planches, sur les sciences, les arts libéraux, et les arts mechaniques.* 11 vols. Paris: Briasson, 1762–72.

Engel, Johann Jakob. *Ideen zu einer Mimik.* Berlin, 1812.

English Theophrastus. 1702. 3rd ed. London: B. Lintott, 1708.

Esslin, Martin. *Antonin Artaud.* Harmondsworth, Middlesex: Penguin, 1977.

Fearing, Franklin. *Reflex Action: A Study in the History of Physiological Psychology.* Baltimore: Williams and Wilkins, 1930.

Feldenkrais, Moshe. *Awareness through Movement: Health Exercises for Personal Growth.* New York and Evanston: Harper and Row, 1972.

Fenichel, Otto. "On Acting." *Psychoanalytic Quarterly* 15 (1946): 144–60. Reprinted in *Tulane Drama Review* 4 (1960): 148–59.

Fiske, Minnie Maddern. *Mrs. Fiske, Her Views on the Stage Recorded by Alexander Woollcott.* 1917. Reprint. New York: Benjamin Blom, 1968.

Foakes, R. A. " 'The Player's Passion': Some Notes on Elizabethan Psychology and Acting." *Essays and Studies of the English Association* (1954): 62–77.

[Foote, Samuel.] *A Treatise on the Passions so far as they regard the Stage.* London: C. Corbett, 1747.

Forest, Louise Turner. "A Caveat for Critics against Invoking Elizabethan Psychology." *PMLA* 61 (1946): 651–72.

Foster, Michael. *Lectures on the History of Physiology during the Seventeenth and Eighteenth Centuries.* Cambridge: Cambridge University Press, 1901.

Foucault, Michel. *The Archeology of Knowledge.* Translated by A. M. Sheridan Smith. New York: Pantheon Books, 1972.

————. *The Order of Things: An Archeology of the Human Sciences.* New York: Pantheon Books, 1970.

Fox, J. H., M. H. Waddicor, and D. A. Watts, eds. *Studies in Eighteenth-Century French Literature.* Exeter: University of Exeter Press, 1975.

Freed, Donald. *Freud and Stanislavsky: New Directions in the Performing Arts.* New York: Vantage Press, 1964.

Freer, Alan J. "Talma and Diderot's Paradox on Acting." *Diderot Studies* 8 (1966): 23–76.

Fried, Michael. *Absorption and Theatricality: Painting and Beholder in the Age of Diderot.* Berkeley: University of California Press, 1980.

Galen. *On Anatomical Procedures.* Edited and translated by C. J. Singer. London and New York: Wellcome Historical Medical Museum, Oxford University Press, 1956.

Galen on the Passions and Errors of the Soul. Translated by Paul W. Harkins. [Columbus]: Ohio State University Press, 1963.

Galloway, David, ed. *The Elizabethan Theatre, 2.* Waterloo, Ontario: Archon Books, 1970.

Gardiner, H. M., Ruth Clark Metcalf, and John G. Beebe-Center. *Feeling and Emotion: A History of Theories.* New York: American Book Company, 1937.

Garrick, David. *Letters.* Edited by David M. Little and George M. Kahrl. 3 vols. Cambridge, Mass.: Belknap Press, 1963.

Gaub, Jerome. *De regimine mentis.* In Rather, *Mind and Body,* 34–204.

Gay, Peter, ed. *Eighteenth Century Studies Presented to Arthur M. Wilson.* Hanover, N.H.: University Press of New England, 1972.

Gayton, Edmund. *The Art of Longevity; or, A Diaeteticall Institution.* London: Printed for the Author, 1659.

————. *Pleasant Notes upon Don Quixot.* London: Printed for W. Hunt, 1654.

Gildon, Charles. *The Life of Mr. Thomas Betterton.* 1710. Reprint. New York: Augustus M. Kelly, 1970.

Goldman, Michael. *The Actor's Freedom: Toward a Theory of Drama.* New York: Viking Press, 1975.

Gorchakov, Nikolai M. *Stanislavsky Directs.* N.p.: Funk and Wagnalls, 1954.

Gordon, Mel. "Foregger and the Dance of the Machines." *TDR* 19 (1975): 68–73.

————. "Meyerhold's Biomechanics." *TDR* 18 (1974): 73–88.

Grant, George. *An Essay on the Science of Acting.* London: Cowie and Strange, 1828.

Gray, Paul. "A Critical Chronology." In Munk, *Stanislavski and America,* 137–77.

Great Soviet Encyclopedia. Edited by A. M. Prokhorov. London and New York: Macmillan, 1970.

Gropius, Walter, ed. *The Theatre of the Bauhaus.* Middletown: Wesleyan University Press, 1961.

Grotowski, Jerzy. *Towards a Poor Theatre.* New York: Simon and Schuster, 1968.

Gurr, Andrew. *The Shakespearean Stage 1574–1642.* 2d edition. Cambridge: Cambridge University Press, 1980.

Hall, Thomas S. *Ideas of Life and Matter: Studies in the History of General Physiology.* 2 vols. Chicago and London: University of Chicago Press, 1969.

Halprin, Ann. "Community Art as Life Process." *TDR* 17 (1973): 64–80.

Hanna, Blake T. "Polinière and the Teaching of Experimental Physics at Paris: 1700–1730." In Gay, *Eighteenth Century Studies,* 15–39.

Hare, Arnold. *George Frederick Cooke: The Actor and the Man.* London: Society for Theatre Research, 1980.

Hartley, David. *Observations on Man, His Frame, His Duty and His Expectations.* 1749. Reprint. Gainesville, Fl.: Scholars' Facsimiles and Reprints, 1966.

Hartmann, Eduard von. *Philosophy of the Unconscious.* Translated by W. C. Coupland. 2d ed. London: K. Paul, Trench, Trübner, 1893.

Hearnshaw, L. S. *A Short History of British Psychology: 1840–1940.* New York: Barnes and Noble, 1964.

Hedgcock, Frank Arthur. *A Cosmopolitan Actor: David Garrick and His French Friends.* London: Stanley Paul and Co., 1911.

Henle, Mary, Julian Jaynes and John Sullivan, eds. *Historical Conceptions of Psychology.* New York: Springer, 1973.

Heriot, Angus. *The Castrati in Opera.* 1956. Reprint. New York: Da Capo, 1975.

Heywood, Thomas. *Apology for Actors.* 1612. London: Shakespeare Society, 1841.

Hill, Aaron. *The Works of the Late Aaron Hill, Esq. in Four Volumes. Consisting of Letters on Various Subjects, and of Original Poems, Moral and Facetious, With an Essay on the Art of Acting.* London: Printed for the Benefit of the Family, 1753.

——— and William Popple. *The Prompter: A Theatrical Paper (1734–1736).* Edited by William A. Appleton and Kalmin A. Burnim. New York: Benjamin Blom, 1966.

Hill, John. *The Actor: or, A Treatise on the Art of Playing.* Enlarged ed. London: R. Griffiths, 1755.

———. *Hypochondriasis, A Practical Treatise.* 1766. The Augustan Reprint Society Publication no. 135. Los Angeles: William Andrew Clark Memorial Library, 1969.

Hogarth, William. *The Analysis of Beauty.* Edited by Joseph Burke. Oxford: Clarendon, 1955.

Holland, Peter. *The Ornament of Action: Text and Performance in Restoration Comedy.* Cambridge: Cambridge University Press, 1979.

Holmes, Martin. *Shakespeare and Burbage.* London: Phillimore, 1978.

Hoover, Marjorie L. *Meyerhold: The Art of Conscious Theatre.* Amherst: University of Massachusetts Press, 1974.

Howell, William S. "Sources of the Elocutionary Movement in England, 1700–1748." *Quarterly Journal of Speech* 45 (1959): 1–18.

Hughes, Leo. "The Actor's Epitome." *Review of English Studies* 20 (1944): 306–07.

Hume, David. *A Treatise on Human Nature.* Edited by L. A. Selby-Bigge. Oxford: Clarendon Press, 1888.

Hume, Robert D., ed. *The London Theatre World, 1660–1800.* Carbondale and Edwardsville: Southern Illinois University Press, 1980.

Hunt, Hugh. "Restoration Acting." In *Restoration Theatre,* ed. Brown and Harris.

Hunt, Leigh. *Dramatic Criticism 1808–1831.* Edited by L. H. Houtchens and C. W. Houtchens. New York: Columbia University Press, 1949.

James, William. *The Principles of Psychology.* 2 vols. New York: Henry Holt, 1890.

———— [unsigned]. "Problems of Life and Mind." *Atlantic Monthly* 36 (1875): 362–63.

————. "What is an Emotion?" *Mind* 9 (1884): 188–205.

———— and C. G. Lange. *The Emotions by Carl Georg Lange and William James.* Edited by Knight Dunlap. Psychology Classics Reprints. Baltimore: Williams and Wilkins, 1922.

Jaynes, Julian. "The Problem of Animate Motion in the Seventeenth Century." In Henle, Jaynes, and Sullivan, *Historical Conceptions of Psychology,* 166–79.

Jorio, Andrea de. *La Mimica degli antichi.* 1832. Reprint. Naples: Associazione Napoletana, 1964.

Joseph, Bertram Leon. *Elizabethan Acting.* London: Oxford University Press, 1951.

————. *Elizabethan Acting.* 2d, rev. ed. London: Oxford University Press, 1964.

————. *The Tragic Actor.* London: Theatre Art Books, 1959.

Josephs, Herbert. *Diderot's Dialogue of Language and Gesture: Le Neveu de Rameau.* [Columbus]: Ohio State University Press, 1969.

Kirby, E. T., ed. *Total Theatre.* New York: Dutton, 1969.

Kitchel, A. T., *George Lewes and George Eliot.* New York: John Day, 1933.

Kjerbühl-Peterson, Lorenz. *Psychology of Acting: A Consideration of Its Principles as an Art.* Translated by S. T. Barows. Boston: Expression, 1935.

Kleist, Heinrich von. "On the Marionette Theatre." Translated by T. G. Neumiller. *TDR,* T-55, 16 (1972): 22–26.

Koestler, Arthur. *The Act of Creation.* New York: Macmillan, 1964.

Koffka, Kurt. "The Art of the Actor as a Psychological Problem." *American Scholar* 2 (1942): 315–26.

Koshtoyants, Kh. S. *Essays on the History of Physiology in Russia.* Edited by Donald B. Lindsay. Translated by David Boder and Kristan Hanes. 1946. Washington, D.C.: American Institute of Biological Sciences and American Psychological Association, 1964.

Kuhn, Thomas S. *The Essential Tension: Selected Studies in Scientific Tradition and Change.* Chicago: University of Chicago Press, 1977.

————.*The Structure of Scientific Revolutions.* 1962. Rev. enlarged ed. Chicago: University of Chicago Press, 1970.

La Mettrie, Julien Offray de. *Man a Machine.* Translated by G. C. Bussey. Chicago: Open Court Publishing Co., 1912.

Lange, Franciscus. *Dissertatio de actione scenica.* Munich: Society of Jesus, 1727.

Lavater, J. C. *Essays on Physiognomy: For the Promotion of the Knowledge and the Love of Mankind.* Translated by T. Holcroft. 3 vols. 2d ed. London: H. D. Symonds, 1804.

Le Brun, Charles. *A Method to Learn to Design the Passions.* 1734. Augustan Reprint Society, 200–1. Los Angeles: William Andrew Clark Memorial Library, 1980.

Lee, Rensselaer W. *Ut Pictura Poesis: The Humanistic Theory of Painting.* 1940. Reprint. New York: Norton, 1967.

Lemay, J. A. Leo, and G. S. Rousseau, eds. *The Renaissance Man in the Eighteenth Century.* Los Angeles: William Andrew Clark Memorial Library, 1978.

Lessing, Gotthold Ephraim. *Hamburg Dramaturgy.* Translated by Helen Zimmern. New York: Dover, 1962.

Levi, Anthony. *French Moralists: The Theory of the Passions 1585–1644.* Oxford: Clarendon, 1964.

Levitine, Georges C. "The Influence of Lavater and Giroudet's *Expression des Sentiments de l'Ame.*" *Art Bulletin* 36 (1954): 33–45.

Lewes, George Henry. *The Biographical History of Philosophy.* 1845. Rev. ed. New York: Appleton, 1857.

————. *The Life of Goethe.* 1855. Reprint. New York: Frederick Ungar, 1965.

————. *Literary Criticism of George Henry Lewes.* Edited by Alice R. Kaminsky. Lincoln: University of Nebraska Press, 1964.

————. *On Actors and the Art of Acting.* Leipzig: Bernhard Tauchnitz, 1875.

————. *The Physiology of Common Life.* 2 vols. 1859. New York: Appleton, 1860.

————. *Problems of Life and Mind.* 5 vols. in 3 series. 1st series: *The Foundations of a Creed.* 2 vols. Boston: James R. Osgood, 1874. 2nd series: *The Physical Basis of Mind.* London: Trübner, 1877. 3rd series: *Problem the First: The Study of Psychology.* Boston: Houghton, Osgood, 1879; *Problem the Second: Mind as a Function of the Organism.* Boston: Houghton, Osgood, 1880.

Lewis, Robert. *Method—or Madness?* New York: Samuel French, 1958.

Lichtenberg, Georg Christoph. *Lichtenberg's Visits to England.* Edited and translated by Margaret L. Mare and W. H. Quarrell. 1938. Reprint. New York: Benjamin Blom, 1969.

Lyons, Charles R. "Gordon Craig's Concept of the Actor." *ETJ* 16 (1964): 258–69.

McGraw, Charles. *Acting is Believing.* 1955. 4th ed. rev. New York: Holt, Rinehart and Winston, 1980.

McKenzie, Alan T. "The Countenance You Show Me: Reading the Passions in the Eighteenth Century." *Georgia Review* 32 (1978): 758–73.

McMahon, C. E. "Images as Motives and Motivators: A Historical Perspective." *American Journal of Psychology* 86 (1973): 465–90.

McNeir, Waldo. "Edmund Gayton on Elizabethan Acting." *PMLA* 56 (1941): 579–83.

Magarshack, David. *Stanislavsky, A Life.* New York: Chanticleer Press, 1951.

Mandeville, Bernard. *A Treatise of the Hypochondriack and Hysterick Diseases.* 1730. Reprint. New York: Scholars' Facsimiles and Reprints, 1976.

Marker, Lise-Lone. "Nature and Decorum in the Theory of Elizabethan Acting." In Galloway, *The Elizabethan Theatre,* 2, 87–107.

Marlowe, Christopher. *The Jew of Malta and The Massacre at Paris.* Edited by H. S. Bennett. New York: Dial Press, 1931.

Matthews, Brander, ed. *Papers on Acting.* New York: Hill and Wang, 1958.

Meyerhold, Vsevolod. *Meyerhold on Theatre.* Edited and translated by Edward Braun. New York: Hill and Wang, 1969.

————. "Program of Biomechanics, Meyerhold Workshop (1922)." In Hoover, *Meyerhold: The Art of Conscious Theatre,* 311–15.

Miller, Arnold. "The Annexation of a *Philosophe:* Diderot in Soviet Criticism, 1917–1960." *Diderot Studies* 15 (1971): 11–464.

Miller, Jonathan. *The Body in Question.* New York: Random House, 1978.

Moholy-Nagy, L. "Theatre, Circus, Variety." In Gropius, *The Theatre of the Bauhaus,* 49–70.

Moore, Sonia. *The Stanislavski System: The Professional Training of an Actor.* Rev. ed. New York: Viking, 1965.

————, ed. and trans. *Stanislavski Today: Commentaries on K. S. Stanislavski and his Method for the Theatre.* New York: American Center for Stanislavski Theatre Art, 1973.

Mullin, Donald C. "Methods and Manners of Traditional Acting." *ETJ* 27 (1975): 5–22.

Munk, Erika, ed. *Stanislavski and America: The "Method" and Its Influence on the American Actor.* New York: Hill and Wang, 1966.

Nagler, A. M., ed. *A Source Book in Theatrical History.* New York: Dover, 1952.

Nash, Mary. *The Provoked Wife: The Life and Times of Susannah Cibber.* Boston: Little, Brown, 1977.

Newton, Isaac. *Opticks: or, a Treatise of the Reflections, Refractions, Inflections, and Colours of Light.* 4th ed. 1730. Reprint. London: G. Bell, 1931.

Noverre, Jean Georges. *The Works of Monsieur Noverre.* 3 vols. 1782–83. Reprint. New York: AMS, 1978.

Oesterreich, Traugott K. *Possession Demonical and other among Primitive Races in Antiquity, the Middle Ages, and Modern Times.* 1921. Translated by D. Ibberson. Reprint. Hyde Park, New York: University Books, 1966.

Olivier, Laurence. "Staging Shakespeare: A Survey of Current Problems and Opinions." In Cole and Chinoy, eds., *Directors on Directing,* 412–13.

Onians, Richard Broxton. *The Origins of European Thought about the Body, the*

Mind, the Soul, the World, Time and Fate. Cambridge: Cambridge University Press, 1954.

Pavlov, Ivan Petrovitch. *Conditioned Reflexes: An Investigation of the Physiological Activity of the Cerebral Cortex.* Edited and translated by G. V. Anrep. London: Oxford University Press, 1927.

———. *Experimental Psychology and Other Essays.* New York: Philosophical Library, 1957.

Pisk, Litz. *The Actor and His Body.* New York: Theatre Arts Books, 1975.

Popper, Karl, and Sir John Eccles. *The Self and Its Brain.* New York: Springer, 1977.

Prampolini, Enrico. "Futurist Scenography (Manifesto)." In Kirby, ed., *Total Theatre,* 95–98.

Proust, Jacques. "Diderot et la physiognomonie." *Cahiers de l'Association internationale des études françaises* 13 (1961): 318–29.

———. *Diderot et L'Encyclopédie.* Paris: Armand Colin, 1967.

Quintilian. *The Institutio Oratoria of Quintilian.* Translated by H. E. Butler. 4 vols. London: William Heinemann, 1920.

Rather, L. J. *Mind and Body in Eighteenth-Century Medicine: A Study Based on Jerome Gaub's "De regimine mentis."* Berkeley and Los Angeles: University of California Press, 1965.

Redmond, Donald Eugene, Jr., M.D. "Tobacco and Cancer: The First Clinical Report, 1761." *New England Journal of Medicine* 282 (1970): 18–23.

Reich, Wilhelm. *Genitality in the Theory and Therapy of Neurosis.* New York: Farrar, Strauss and Giroux, 1979.

———. *Selected Writings.* New York: Farrar, Strauss and Giroux, 1973.

Ribot, Théodule-Armand. *English Psychology.* 1870. New York: Appleton, 1874.

———. *The Psychology of the Emotions.* Edited by Havelock Ellis. 1896. London: Walter Scott, 1897.

Riccoboni, Luigi. *A General History of the Stage.* 1754. Reprint. New York: AMS, 1978.

Richards, Kenneth, and Peter Thomson, eds. *The Eighteenth-Century English Stage.* London: Methuen, 1972.

Robertson, J. G. *Lessing's Dramatic Theory.* Cambridge: Cambridge University Press, 1939.

Roger, Jacques. *Les sciences de la vie dans la pensée française du XVIIIᵉ siècle.* Paris: Armand Colin, 1963.

Rogers, Pat, ed. *The Eighteenth Century.* Context in English Literature Series. London: Methuen, 1978.

Rogerson, Brewster. "The Art of Painting the Passions." *Journal of the History of Ideas* 14 (1953): 68–94.

Rorty, Amélie Oksenberg, ed. *Explaining Emotions.* Berkeley: University of California Press, 1980.

Rosenberg, Marvin. "Elizabethan Actors: Men or Marionettes?" *PMLA* 69 (1954): 915–27.

Rosenfield, Leonora Cohen. *From Beast-Machine to Man-Machine.* 1940. 2d ed. rev. New York: Octagon Books, 1968.

Rothschuh, Karl E. *History of Physiology.* Translated by Guenter B. Risse. New York: Robert E. Krieger, 1973.

Rousseau, G. S. "John Hill, Universal Genius *Manqué:* Remarks on His Life and Times, with a Checklist of his Works." In Lemay and Rousseau, *The Renaissance Man in the Eighteenth Century,* 45–129.

———. "Nerves, Spirits, and Fibres: Toward Defining the Origins of Sensibility." In Brissenden and Eade, *Studies in the Eighteenth Century,* 137–57.

———. "Science." In Rogers, *The Eighteenth Century,* 153–207.

——— and Roy Porter, eds. *The Ferment of Knowledge: Studies in the Historiography of Eighteenth-Century Science.* Cambridge: Cambridge University Press, 1980.

Rowell, George, ed. *Victorian Dramatic Criticism.* London: Methuen, 1971.

Sainte-Albine, Pierre Rémond de. *Le comédien.* 1749. Geneva: Slatkine Reprints, 1971.

Schechner, Richard. *Essays on Performance Theory 1970–1976.* New York: Drama Book Specialists, 1977.

Schofield, Robert E. *Mechanism and Materialism: British Natural Philosophy in an Age of Reason.* Princeton: Princeton University Press, 1970.

Sechenov, Ivan Mikhailovich. *Reflexes of the Brain.* Translated by S. Belsky. Cambridge: M.I.T. Press, 1965.

———. *Selected Physiological and Psychological Works.* Edited by Kh. Koshtoyants. Moscow: Foreign Language Publishing House, n.d.

———. *Selected Works.* Moscow: State Publishing House, 1935.

Sennett, Richard. *The Fall of Public Man.* New York: Alfred A. Knopf, 1977.

Siddons, Henry. *Practical Illustrations of Rhetorical Gesture and Action.* 1822. Reprint. New York: Benjamin Blom, 1968.

Simonov, P. V. "The Method of K. S. Stanislavski and the Physiology of Emotion." In Moore, *Stanislavski Today,* 34–41.

Singer, Charles Joseph. *The Evolution of Anatomy: A Short History of Anatomical and Physiological Discovery to Harvey.* New York: Alfred A. Knopf, 1926.

Smart, Alastair. "Dramatic Gesture and Expression in the Age of Hogarth." *Apollo* 82 (1965): 90–97.

Sprague, Arthur Colby. *Shakespearean Players and Performances.* Cambridge, Mass.: Harvard University Press, 1953.

Staël, Madame de. *De L'Allemagne.* 1815. Paris: Garnier, n.d.

Stanislavski, Constantin. *Acting, A Handbook of the Stanislavski Method.* Edited by Toby Cole. New York: Crown Publishers, 1955.

———. *An Actor Prepares.* Translated by Elizabeth Reynolds Hapgood. New York: Theatre Arts Books, 1936.

———. *Building a Character.* Translated by Elizabeth Reynolds Hapgood. New York: Theatre Arts Books, 1949.

———. *Creating a Role.* Translated by Elizabeth Reynolds Hapgood. New York: Theatre Arts Books, 1961.

———. *My Life in Art.* Translated by J. J. Robbins. 1924. Cleveland: World Publishing Company, 1956.

———. *Stanislavski on Opera.* New York: Theatre Arts Books, 1975.

———. *Stanislavski's Legacy: A Collection of Comments on a Variety of Aspects of an Actor's Art and Life.* Translated by Elizabeth Reynolds Hapgood. New York: Theatre Arts Books, 1958.

———. *Stanislavsky on the Art of the Stage.* Translated by David Magarshack. New York: Hill and Wang, 1961.

Steele, Richard. *The Tatler.* 4 vols. London: Duckworth, 1899.

Stern, J. P. *Lichtenberg: A Doctrine of Scattered Occasions.* Bloomington: Indiana University Press, 1959.

Stone, George Winchester, Jr., and George M. Kahrl. *David Garrick: A Critical Biography.* Carbondale and Edwardsville: Southern Illinois University Press, 1979.

Strasberg, Lee. "Working with Live Material." In Munk, *Stanislavski and America*, 183–200.

Sulloway, Frank J. *Freud, Biologist of the Mind.* New York: Basic Books, 1979.

Swammerdam, Jan. *The Book of Nature; . . . Revised and improved by Notes from Reamur and others, by John Hill, M.D.* London: Printed for C. G. Seyffert, 1758.

Taylor, George. " 'The Just Delineation of the Passions': Theories of Acting in the Age of Garrick." In Richards and Thomson, *The Eighteenth-Century English Stage*, 51–72.

Temkin, Owsei. *Galenism: Rise and Decline of a Medical Philosophy.* Ithaca and London: Cornell University Press, 1973.

Thesaurus Dramaticus. London: T. Butler, 1724.

Tillotson, Geoffrey. "*Othello* and *The Alchemist* at Oxford." *TLS* (July 20, 1933): 494.

Todd, Mabel Elsworth. *The Thinking Body.* Boston: Charles T. Branford, 1937.

Toporkov, Vasily Osipovich. *Stanislavski in Rehearsal: The Final Years.* Translated by Christine Edwards. New York: Theatre Arts Books, 1979.

Tort, Patrick. *L'origine du Paradoxe sur le comédien: La partition intérieure.* 2d ed. Paris: J. Vrin, 1980.

Trudgian, Helen. "Claude Bernard and the 'Groupe de Médan.' " International Federation for Modern Languages and Literatures, *Acta*, 6, *Literature and Science: Proceedings of the Sixth Annual Congress.* Oxford: Basil Blackwell, 273–76.

Vartanian, Aram. *Diderot and Descartes: A Study of Scientific Naturalism in the Enlightenment.* Princeton: Princeton University Press, 1953.

———. "The Enigma of Diderot's *Eléments de Physiologie.*" *Diderot Studies* 10 (1968), 285–301.

————. *La Mettrie's L'Homme Machine: A Study in the Origins of an Idea.* Princeton: Princeton University Press, 1960.

Vasco, Gerhard M. *Diderot and Goethe: A Study in Science and Humanism.* Geneva: Slatkine; Paris: Champion, 1978.

Visser, Colin. "Scenery and Technical Design." In R. Hume, *London Theatre World,* 66–118.

Vucinich, Alexander. *Science in Russian Culture, 1861–1917.* Stanford: Stanford University Press, 1970.

Walker, Albert L. "Convention in Shakespeare's Description of Emotion." *Philological Quarterly* 17 (1938): 26–66.

Walker, John. *Elements of Elocution: in which the Principles of Reading and Speaking are Investigated.* Boston: Mallory and Co., 1810.

Warren, Howard C. *A History of the Association Psychology from Hartley to Lewes.* Baltimore: Scribners, 1921.

Wasserman, Earl R. "The Sympathetic Imagination in Eighteenth-Century Theories of Acting." *Journal of English and Germanic Philology* 46 (1947): 264–72.

Weissman, Philip. *Creativity in the Theater: A Psychoanalytic Study.* New York: Delta, 1965.

Whyte, Lancelot L. *The Unconscious before Freud.* New York: Basic Books, 1960.

Whytt, Robert. *An Essay on the Vital and Other Involuntary Motions of Animals.* 1751. 2d ed. Edinburgh: Printed for John Balfour, 1763.

Williams, G. S., ed. *Literature and History in the Age of Ideas.* Columbus: Ohio State University Press, 1975.

Wilson, Arthur M. "The Biographical Implications of Diderot's *Paradoxe sur le comédien.*" *Diderot Studies* 3 (1961): 369–83.

————. *Diderot.* New York: Oxford University Press, 1972.

Wordsworth, William. *The Prose Works of William Wordsworth.* Edited by W. J. B. Owen and J. W. Smyser. Vol 1. Oxford: Clarendon Press, 1974.

Wright, John P. "Hysteria and Mechanical Man." *Journal of the History of Ideas* 41 (1980): 233–47.

Wright, Thomas. *The Passions of the Minde in Generall.* 1604. Reprint. Urbana: University of Illinois Press, 1971.

Zakhava, B. E. "The Mastery of the Actor and the Director." In Moore, *Stanislavski Today,* 1–21.

Index

Abington, Frances, 153

Acting styles: formalism vs. naturalism, 15, 30; and mechanical paradigm, 59–60; and mechanical physiology, 85–87; obsolescence of rhetorical style, 60, 155; and organism, 184–88; revolutions in, 2, 56–57; as semiotic codes, 12, 16

Actors: cultural role of, 11–12; intellect of, 138–39; as machines, 152; as orators, 24, 32–33; prejudice against, 27–28, 137; social psychology of, 136–38; unhealthiness of, 28, 48–50. *See also* Automata

Actor's Studio, 210

Addison, Joseph, 69

Adler, Stella, 216

Aeschylus, 76

Affective memory. *See* Emotion memory

Alembert, Jean Le Rond d', 127, 162, 166

Aleotti, Giovanni Battista, 62

Alexander, F. M., 219

Alleyn, Edward, 41–42

Andronicus, 32, 35

Animal electricity, 95

Animal magnetism, 180

Animal spirits, 15–16; action of, at a distance, 45–47; in Astonishment, 86; exhalation of, 40; in mechanical physiology, 63–65, 80; obsolescence of, 94, 104–5, 155; occult powers of, 40, 43–47

Antoine, André, 172

Apollo, 26, 196, 217

Archer, William, 16, 158; on autosuggestion, 179–80, 181; and Darwin, 177–79, 180–81; on double consciousness, 190; and von Hartmann, 179; on innervation, 16, 180–81; and Lewes, 181–82; *Masks or Faces?* 147, 162, 177, 192; on vaso-motor system, 43–44

Aristotle, 24; and Bulwer, 33; *De Anima,* 25; on imagination, 25, 40–41; *Poetics,* 151; *Problemata Physica,* 14, 53; *Rhetoric,* 25, 28–29

Artaud, Antonin, 222–24

Associationism, 106–7, 108, 143, 147, 151, 202, 210

Aston, Anthony, 54

Austin, Gilbert, 74

Automata, 65–66, 84; Garrick on, 91; history of, 61–63; Kleist on, 164–65; Meyerhold on, 202–3. *See also* Craig, Edward Gordon: *übermarionette*

Autosuggestion. *See* Archer, William: autosuggestion

Bacon, Francis, 38; on imagination, 46; influence of, on Bulwer, 33, 34; and significations of the passions, 31

Ballet: as mechanism, 74–75, 165

Barry, Spranger, 102

Barsanti, Jenny, 153

Battie, William, 98, 113

Bauhaus, 61, 202

Beck, Julian, 221

Beckford, William, 102

Bekhterev, Vladimir, 194, 198, 199, 201, 203

Bell, Charles, 162, 173–76

Bell, G. J., 173

Bernard, Claude, 158

Bernheim, Hippolyte, 180

Betterton, Thomas, 30–31, 69; and animal spirits, 43; calisthenic attributed to, 49, 55; and controlled gestures, 52–53, 54; and decorum, 52–53; diversity of roles of, 42; as Hamlet, 44–45; and rhetorical style, 56

Binet, Alfred, 158

Biomechanics. *See* Meyerhold, Vsevolod

Blood, 27, 39

Body: as actor's instrument, 11, 226; as automaton, 164; character body, 154; and contemporary psychology, 218; Galenic paradigm of, 38–40; as machine, 16, 57, 60–66, 71, 76, 129–30, 193–94, 202; and mind, 13, 49, 97–98, 112, 147, 152, 182, 205–6; as moving statue, 59, 63, 68–69; as musical instrument, 66, 105–6; as organism, 187–88. *See also* Actors: as machines

Boerhaave, Hermann, 94, 98

Bohr Institute, 224

Boleslavsky, Richard, 211, 215–16

Bonnet, Charles, 114, 143

Booth, Barton, 70–71, 73

Booth, Edwin, 193

Bordeu, Théophile, 132

Borelli, Giovanni, 65

Boucher, François, 119

Breath: Artaud on, 223–24; Lewes on, 190; of life, 25; and states of consciousness, 26. *See also* Inspiration; *Pneuma*

Brecht, Bertolt, 157, 197–98

Brook, Peter, 15, 106, 225

Buffon, Georges, 114, 121, 131

Bulwer, John, 33–38; *Anthropometamorphosis,* 50; *Chironomia and Chirologia,* 33, 34, 42, 50, 53, 72–73; on hand-wringing, 34–35; *Pathomyotomia,* 38, 40, 43, 44, 64; on physical exercises, 55; on physiological basis of gesture, 33–34, 38, 50

Burbage, Richard, 30, 41, 42, 43, 179

Burgh, James, 76–78, 79

Burton, Robert, 41, 64; *Anatomy of Melancholy,* 33, 39; and Bulwer, 33; on imagination, 41, 45; on sorrow, 39

Cartesianism. *See* Descartes, René: Cartesianism

Castrati, 68–70, 136, 165, 185–86

Caus, Salomon de, 62

Cervantes, Miguel de, 48

Chaliapin, Feodor Ivanovich, 195, 212

Chambre, Marin Cureau de la, 32, 64, 67

Changeling, 49–51

Charcot, Jean-Martin, 180

Chekhov, Michael, 215

Cheyne, George, 65, 94, 101, 113

Cibber, Colley, 43, 110

Cibber, Susannah, 110, 168

Cicero, 24, 33, 35, 79

Clairon, Claire-Joseph, 95–96, 97, 104; criticized by Garrick, 95–96; and Diderot, 135, 163, 167; and Dumesnil controversy, 109–10, 123, 124, 170, 196; and inner model, 142, 148, 154, 155, 171

Clurman, Harold, 216

Coleridge, Samuel Taylor, 163, 168

Condillac, Etienne Bonnot de, 76, 114, 120, 143, 194

Cooke, George Frederick, 49, 176

Copeau, Jacques, 158

Copernicus, 113

Coquelin, Constant, 157–58, 194, 203

Corneille, Pierre, 134

Craig, Edward Gordon, 62, 165, 202; "Actor and the *Übermarionette,*" 160–61; "Artist of the Theatre," 167; and Goethe, 167; and Stanislavski, 204; on *übermarionette,* 157, 160, 164, 194

Cumberland, Richard, 56

Darwin, Charles: Darwinism, 174–79; *Expression of the Emotions in Man and Animals,* 139, 162, 177, 180–81; *Origin of the Species,* 193

Decorum, 29–30, 52–56

Della Porta, Giambattista, 66, 139

Demosthenes, 32, 35

Descartes, René: Cartesianism, 65–66, 121, 163; and Aaron Hill, 80–81, 86; interactive dualism, 64, 78, 80, 83, 96; and Lessing, 82–85; and mechanical physiology, 62–65, 94, 183; and mechanization of the world picture, 60–61; *Passions de l'âme,* 63, 86, 87, 112, 130; *Traité de l'homme,* 62–63

Dickens, Charles, 185

Diderot, Denis, 13, 26, 89, 95, 164, 183, 189, 199, 221, 226; on absorption, 154–56, 179,

208; and Artaud, 223; as autobiographer, 118–19; and Brecht, 197; on conditioned reflexes, 150–52; and Craig, 194; and Darwin, 139, 174–79; on double consciousness, 142, 147–50, 151, 158, 162, 190–91, 203, 214; and emotion memory, 145–46, 209–10; as encyclopedist, 114–15, 116–17, 159, 192–93, 216; on evolution, 121, 130, 157, 174–79; formative scientific influences on, 120–21; and Freud, 179; and Garrick, 111, 127–28, 138, 177; and Goethe, 165–67; on the inner model, 125–28, 133–34, 139–42, 153–54, 168–69, 171, 173, 213, 223; and Lewes, 188, 189; and Lunacharskii, 196; on memory and imagination, 143–47; and Meyerhold, 201, 203; physiological theories of, 128–32; on rehearsal, 152–53; and Rousseau, 137; on scale of performance, 134; and Sechenov, 194; on sensibility, 113, 129; on diaphragmatic sensibility, 131–32, 135; favors sensibility, 119–20, 122; rejects sensibility, 122; on silence, 145; on social psychology of acting, 136–38; and Stanislavski, 196, 204–5, 208, 209–10, 216–17; and Talma, 169–72; on theory of the fourth wall, 154–55, 208; on three-stage process (observation, reflection, experimentation), 139–41; and transformism, 121; and vitalism, 121; and Wordsworth, 146, 163. Works: *Bijoux indiscrets*, 121; *Discours sur la poésie dramatique*, 154; *Eléments de physiologie*, 114, 128–31, 135, 139, 142, 143, 145, 146, 149, 150, 151, 157, 172, 174, 199, 202, 209; *Encyclopédie*, 97, 100, 114, 116, 121, 122, 135–36, 137, 157, 159, 196, 216; *Entretiens sur le fils naturel*, 120, 122; *Essais sur la peinture*, 126–27, 153; *Le fils naturel*, 76; *Lettre sur les aveugles*, 121; *Lettre sur les sourds et muets*, 121, 145, 153; *Mémoires sur différens sujets de mathématiques*, 120; *Le neveu de Rameau*, 122–25, 127, 132, 157, 179; "Observations sur . . . *Garrick*," 132–33, 169; *Paradoxe sur le comédien*, 14, 113, 117, 120, 122, 128, 129, 133–59, 161, 162, 169, 170, 172, 174, 189, 194, 196, 206, 209; *Pensées philosophiques*, 119; *Pensées sur l'interprétation de la nature*, 121, 122; *Plan of a University*, 196; "Réponse à . . .

Mme Riccoboni," 141; *Rêve de d'Alembert*, 114, 127, 129, 130, 132, 135, 142, 145, 147, 148, 149, 154, 157, 174; *Salon de 1767*, 127–28, 132, 153; *Salons*, 125, 126, 145, 153, 154

Dostoyevski, Feodor Mikhailovich, 193

Dryden, John, 42

Du Bos, Jean-Baptiste, 65, 76, 78, 82, 83, 101

Dullin, Charles, 158

Dumesnil, Marie-Françoise, 111; and Clairon, 109–10, 123, 124, 170, 196; and Diderot, 135, 136, 148. *See also* Clairon, Claire-Joseph: and Dumesnil controversy

Duse, Eleonora, 160, 195

Ekhof, Konrad, 82, 83

Emotion memory, 14, 173, 197; Boleslavsky on, 211; Diderot on, 145–46, 209–10; Lewes on, 189–90; Ribot on, 209, 211; Stanislavski on, 209–11; Strasberg on, 216; Talma on, 171; Wordsworth on, 163. *See also* Quintilian: *visiones*

Enargeia, 24–25, 44, 101, 102, 143

Engel, Johann Jakob, 76–77, 106

Engels, Friedrich, 196

Evolution, 161–62; Diderot on, 121, 130, 157, 174–79; Lewes on, 181, 183. *See also* Darwin, Charles

Fechner, Gustav Theodor, 191

Feldenkrais, Moshe, 220

Feuillet, R. A., 76

Fielding, Henry, 100

Fiske, Minnie Maddern, 193

Flaubert, Gustave, 160

Flecknoe, Richard, 41

Foregger, Nikolai Mikhailovich, 202

Foucault, Michel, 13, 72; and discontinuity, 13–14, 59; *episteme* of, 13; on life as mental category, 14, 95, 161

Fouquet, M., 97

Franklin, Benjamin, 102

Freud, Sigmund, 179, 180, 219

Futurism, 61, 157

Galen, 27, 41, 53, 61, 64; and Bulwer, 33, 53, 64; on grief, 38; and nerve physiology, 30, 39–40; physiological doctrines of, 38–40. *See also* Animal spirits

Galileo, 60

Galvani, Luigi, 95

Garrick, David, 12, 26, 30, 109, 114, 164, 177; as acting machine, 152; acting style of, 56–57, 69; and animal electricity, 95, 102; and Astonishment, 188; on Clairon, 95–96, 97, 104; and Diderot, 122, 135, 141, 142, 145; and *Encyclopédie*, 97; *Essay on Acting*, 59, 89, 95; fright wig of, 58–59; as Hamlet, 86–88, 112; on John Hill, 100; as Lear, 141; as Lothario, 56; as Macbeth, 89–90, 111, 127; on mechanical physiology, 89–91; as Othello, 73–74; on physics, 65, 71; on rehearsal, 153; and salon exhibition of passions, 111, 127, 138, 152, 164; on science, 59, 89–91; on sensibility, 95–96; on unconsciousness, 96, 108

Gaub, Jerome, 98, 104, 125

Gayton, Edmund, 48–50

Gesture: Artaud on, 223; Bulwer on, 34–38, 50–51, 53–55; decorous regulation of, 54–55; Diderot on, 76, 123–24, 145; Gildon on, 52; Goethe on, 167–68; notation of, 74–78; in painting, 53–54, 70–74, 126–27; obsolescence of ancient rules of, 79; of right hand, 53–54, 79; Stanislavski on, 206

Gildon, Charles, 38, 48, 49, 55; on gestures, 52; on Le Brun, 67; *Life of . . . Betterton*, 30–31, 67–68; on physical transformation, 43; and plagiarism of Wright, 30–31

Gillette, William, 171

Glisson, Francis, 94

Goethe, Johann Wolfgang von, 70, 161, 162, 221; on acting, 165–68; on biology, 166; and Diderot, 157; on rehearsal, 167–68; *Rules for Actors*, 70, 167

Greuze, Jean-Baptiste, 119

Grimm, Friedrich Melchior, 111, 114, 127, 132, 157, 169

Grotowski, Jerzy, 16, 162, 224–26; and canalizing the stimulus, 16, 224–25; and score of the role, 225; and Stanislavski, 225

Group Theatre, 211

Gurevich, Lyubov, 195

Haller, Albrecht von, 97, 100, 102, 114, 129, 131

Halprin, Ann, 220–21

Handel, George Frederick, 78, 110

Hartley, David, 114, 147, 152, 210; and Coleridge, 163; *Observations on Man*, 106, 107, 182; and psychophysiology, 106–7; and secondary automatic motions, 151, 163; on violent passions, 112. *See also* Associationism; Lewes, George Henry: and Hartley; Vibrations

Hartmann, Eduard von, 179, 181. *See also* Unconsciousness

Harvey, William, 61, 65

Hayman, Francis, 73

Hazlitt, William, 164

Helvétius, Claude-Adrien, 127

Heron, 61–62

Heywood, Thomas, 15, 30, 38, 48; on Edward Alleyn, 41–42; on animal spirits, 30, 43; *Apology for Actors*, 28, 32; on gesture, 52; on impersonation, 42–43

Hill, Aaron, 16, 60, 91, 165, 181; and animal spirits, 80, 86; "Art of Acting," 81, 82, 86; and Cartesian physiology, 80, 81–82, 86–87, 112; and Susannah Cibber, 110–11; and Descartes, 80–81, 86; on exercise, 82; and Garrick, 89; on imagination, 108; and Lessing, 82–83; *Prompter*, 78, 93; his system of acting, 78–82, 85–86; on vibrations, 104; *Walking Statue*, 68

Hill, John, 16, 110, 112, 117, 124; *Actor*, 103, 113, 114, 132; on dangers of sensibility, 112–13, and Diderot, 100, 132; and Garrick, 103, 111; and Hartley, 107; *Hypochondriasis*, 101; on imagination, 107–9; and Sainte-Albine, 100, 101, 132; as scientist, 100–101; on sensibility, 103–4, 112–13; and Sticotti, 114, 132–33; and Swammerdam, 100, 107; on vibrations, 104

Hobbes, Thomas, 107, 210

Hoffmann, E. T. A., 164

Hogarth, William, 66, 70, 74, 156

Holbach, Paul Thiry baron d', 89, 111, 127, 194

Hooke, Robert, 65

Horace, 24

Hume, David, 105–6, 109

Humours, 26; dangers of, 47–48; imbalance of, 39, 47, 49; obsolescence of, 65, 80

Hunt, Leigh, 79

Hypnosis, 180. *See also* Archer, William: autosuggestion

Hysteria: as nervous disorder, 98; as visceral disorder, 48

Ilinsky, Igor, 201, 204
Imagination: Archer on, 177; Aristotle on, 25, 40; Bacon on, 46; Burton on, 41; Coleridge on, 163; dangers of, 48–50; Diderot on, 143–44, 146–47, 154; Goethe on, 166; Hartley on, 107–9; Aaron Hill on, 80, 81; *imago animi*, 25, 41; Lewes on, 191, 225; and memory, 143, 209; occult powers of, 40–41, 44, 46–47; and organicism, 162–63, 166; Stanislavski on, 209–10; Talma on, 172–73. *See also* Quintilian: *visiones*
Improvisation, 221; Artaud on, 222, 223; Brook on, 221; Diderot on, 120, 123–24, 153, 222; Grotowski on, 225; and Living Theatre, 222; Stanislavski on, 216. *See also* Inspiration; Spontaneity
Inhibition, 52–55, 80, 218, 220. *See also* Reflex: reflex inhibition
Inner model. *See* Clairon, Claire-Joseph; Diderot, Denis: an inner model
Innervation. *See* Archer, William: innervation
Inspiration, 114; ancient superstitions about, 24–25, 26–27; Diderot on, 120, 124–25, 141, 144; and disease, 50, 223; Plato on, 46; as possession, 26–27, 40, 101–2, 112, 225; in Romantic acting, 168; Stanislavski on, 217; vs. technique, 25–26, 55–56, 83, 109–10. See also *Pneuma*
Interactive dualism. *See* Body: and mind; Descartes, René: interactive dualism
Irving, Henry, 136, 158, 169–70, 171, 194

James, Robert, 120
James, William, 11, 199; James-Lange theory, 84, 148, 162, 192, 201, 224; and Lewes, 191, 192; *Principles of Psychology*, 192; "What is an Emotion?" 11
James-Lange theory. *See* James, William
Jefferson, Joseph, 193
Jelgerhuis, Johannes, 74–75, 165
Johnson, Samuel, 58
Jones, Inigo, 48
Jonson, Ben, 48, 59
Jordaens, Jacob, 67–68
Joseph, B. L., 30

Jouvet, Louis, 158
Juenger, Ernst, 61, 202

Kames, Henry Home, Lord, 99
Kean, Charles, 106, 185–86, 206
Kean, Edmund, 49; on acting, 168–69; Lewes on, 106, 184, 186–88, 191; and subsiding emotion, 187–88
Kemble, Fanny, 190
Kinesics, 73
Kirkman, Francis, 50
Kleist, Heinrich von, 161, 164
Kuhn, Thomas, 13, 215; and paradigm, 13, 56–57; and paradigmatic texts, 14, 117, 158; and scientific revolutions, 13–14, 113–14

Lamarck, Jean-Baptiste de Monet, 161
Lamb, Charles, 164
La Mettrie, Julien Offray de, 71, 114, 223; and Diderot, 121, 129, 148; *homme machine*, 68, 89, 91, 221; *L'homme machine*, 60; and Wilhelm Reich, 219; on soul, 66, 97; and Stanislavski, 217; on terror, 90
Lange, Carl. *See* James, William: James-Lange theory
Lange, Franciscus, 70, 71
Lavater, Johann Casper, 76, 87
Lavoisier, Antoine-Laurent de, 117
Le Brun, Charles, 71, 72–73; and Cartesian passions, 66, 72; and Diderot, 139; and Gildon, 67; *Méthode pour apprendre à dessiner les passions*, 66–67, 70; and Wilkes, 70
Lekain, Henri-Louis, 135, 162, 169, 170–71
Lemaître, Frederick, 184, 186
Lenin, Vladimir Ilyich, 196
Leonardo da Vinci, 27, 61
Leroy, Julien, 91
Lespinasse, Julie-Jeanne-Eléonore de, 127, 132, 154
Lessing, Gotthold Ephraim, 60, 74, 76, 91, 112, 117; on acting, 73, 82–85; "Actor," 83; and Descartes, 82, 83–85; and Diderot, 153–54; and Du Bos, 82, 83–84; *Hamburg Dramaturgy*, 73, 78, 83, 181; and Aaron Hill, 78, 82; and James-Lange theory, 83–84; *Laocöon*, 73, 83, 153–54; on "transitory painting," 73, 87

Lewes, George Henry, 194, 197, 199, 206, 213, 214, 225, 226; on acting, 184–92; on actor's symbols, 184; and Diderot, 188, 189; and dual-aspect monism, 162, 182–83, 190, 191, 207; and emotion memory, 189–90; on evolution, 181, 183; on fluctuating spontaneity, 16, 184–88; and Goethe, 166; and Hartley, 107, 182; influence of, on Russian science, 193; and Charles Kean, 106, 185–86, 206; and Edmund Kean, 106, 184, 186–88, 191; his Laws of Discharge and Arrest, 186, 198; on reflex, 182–83; as scientific psychologist, 181–84; on stream of consciousness, 191; on subsiding emotion, 106, 186–87; and Talma, 162, 170, 189, 197; on vibrations, 106, 182; on vitalist-mechanist controversy, 182–84. Works: *Biographical History of Philosophy*, 181; *Life of Goethe*, 181; *On Actors . . .* , 170, 189; *Physical Basis of Mind*, 182, 191; *Physiology of Common Life*, 181, 182, 192, 193; *Problems of Life and Mind*, 181, 189, 192

Lichtenberg, Georg Christoph, 12, 58; on Garrick, 86–89; on the unconscious, 109

Linnaeus, Carl, 76, 100, 166

Living Theatre, 221–22

Lloyd, Robert, 111–12

Locke, John, 106, 120, 143

Loutherbourg, Phillipe Jacques de, 65–66

Lunacharskii, Anatoly, 196–97

Macklin, Charles, 71–72, 78, 100

Macready, William Charles, 170, 192

Malina, Judith, 221

Mandeville, Bernard, 101, 105, 113

Marmontel, Jean-François, 119, 127

Martersteig, Max, 180

Marx, Karl, 196

Mechanism. *See* Actors: as machines; Automata; Body: as machine; Vitalism: and mechanism

Memory of emotion. *See* Emotion memory

Mesmer, Franz Anton, 180

Method acting, 14, 197, 211, 216

Meyerhold, Vsevolod, 16, 162, 194; and biomechanics, 157, 194, 199–204; and constructivism, 202, 203–4; and Diderot, 203; and Stanislavski, 197, 202

Mills, John, 81

Milton, John, 103

Moholy-Nagy, Laszlo, 161, 202

Monism, 162. *See also* Lewes, George Henry: and dual-aspect monism

Montdory, 49

Moore, Sonia, 217

Morellet, André, 127

Moscow Art Theatre, 153, 194, 195, 204

Naturphilosophie, 162

Newton, Isaac, 60, 76, 117, 120, 136, 198; on vibrations of nerves, 105, 106

Nicolino (Nicolini Grimaldi), 68–69, 70, 78

Noverre, Jean Georges, 74–76, 87, 91

Olivier, Laurence, 153

Otway, Thomas, 42

Paganini, Niccolo, 165

Passions, 28–29; Descartes on, 64–65; destructive effects of, 47–48; Diderot on, 139–41; in Galenic physiology, 40; instruction manuals of, 66–67; significations of, 31; taxonomy of, 71–72, 78, 81–82, 139–41, 172; textbooks on, 76–78; as vibrations of nerves, 105–6; violent transitions of, 42

Pavlov, Ivan Petrovich, 194, 198, 199; *Conditioned Reflexes*, 201; and Lewes, 193; and Meyerhold, 201–2, on reflex, 206–7; and Stanislavski, 206–10; and Whytt, 151

Pflüger, Eduard, 182–83

Pickering, Roger, 70

Pigalle, Jean-Baptiste, 134

Plato, 46, 137

Pliny, 49

Plutarch, 32

Pneuma, 27, 38, 39, 45, 65, 155

Pneumatism, 27. *See also* Animal spirits

Points. *See* Transitions

Polinière, Pierre, 93, 94

Polish Laboratory Theatre, 224–26

Pope, Alexander, 29

Poussin, Nicholas, 53, 66

Powell, George, 52

Prampolini, Enrico, 202

Priestley, Joseph, 102

Pritchard, Hannah, 103

Proteus, 27, 41–42, 49–50
Proust, Marcel, 146

Quin, James, 30, 60, 78; and rhetorical acting style, 56–57
Quintilian, 23–26, 32, 44, 46, 53, 57, 101, 104, 226; on blood, 27; and Bulwer, 33, 34, 53; on impersonation, 24, 25; *Institutio Oratoria*, 23, 29, 53, 55, 79, 173; rejection of, by Aaron Hill, 79; his rules for delivery, 29; *visiones*, 24, 26, 28, 40, 223

Rachel, 186, 187, 191
Rameau, Jean Philippe, 68
Randolph, Thomas, 41
Reflex, 147, 164; Bekhterev on, 198, 201, 203; Bell-Magendie law of, 173; Descartes on, 63; Diderot on, 150–51; Lewes on, 182–83, 193; Meyerhold on, 201, 203; Pavlov on, 201–2, 206–7; Pflüger on, 182–83; and reflex chains, 151–52, 201, 202, 203, 208; and reflex consciousness, 150, 163; and reflex inhibition, 16, 198, 203; and Russian reflexology, 162, 198–99, 203, 210; Sechenov on, 193–94, 198–99, 201; Stanislavski on, 208–9; Whytt on, 150–51
Reich, Wilhelm, 219
Rhetoric: *actio* (action), 30, 32, 52, 57; and antiquated acting style, 56–57, 79, 155; basis of, in pneumatism, 30–31; *deinosis*, 24; and eye-to-eye contact, 46–47, 155, 222; of the passions, 26–28, 218; *pathos*, 24, 25, 46; pervasiveness of, in seventeenth-century thought, 28–30; *pronuntiatio* (delivery), 32, 34, 57
Ribot, Théodule-Armand, 211; and James-Lange theory, 192, 201; on Lewes, 181; *Psychologie anglaise contemporaine*, 181; *Psychologie des sentiments*, 192, 201, 209; and Stanislavski, 201, 209–11
Riccoboni, François, 70, 83, 117, 196
Riccoboni, Luigi, 81, 83, 101–2, 117, 196
Riccoboni, Marie-Jeanne Laboras de Mézières, 135, 141
Richardson, Samuel, 98
Riley, Thomas, 41, 43
Rolf, Ida, 220
Roscius, 35

Rossi, Ernesto, 195
Rousseau, Jean Jacques, 76, 137
Rowe, Nicholas, 56
Royal Society, 60
Rubens, Peter Paul, 53–54

Sade, Marquis de, 102
Sainte-Albine, Pierre Rémond de, 110, 112, 117, 132; *Comédien*, 83, 98, 114; and Diderot, 120, 122; and John Hill, 100, 101, 110, 132; and Lessing, 83; on sensibility, 98–99, 101
Salvini, Tommaso, 195
Saxe-Meiningen Company, 153
Schlemmer, Oskar, 202
Score of the role, 151, 155, 188, 208; Artaud on, 223; Grotowski on, 225; Stanislavski on, 213–14
Sechenov, Ivan Mikhailovich, 193–94, 198–99, 201, 213, 214; and Lewes, 193, 214; *Reflexes of the Brain*, 193, 203
Sedaine, Michel-Jean, 119
Self-use systems, 162, 219–20
Semiotics, 57, 85, 87, 188
Sensibility, 16; and absorption, 155; Diderot on, 119–20, 121–22, 131–32, 135, 174–76; in eighteenth-century acting texts, 99–104; and eighteenth-century science, 96–98; Garrick on, 95–96; Haller on, 97, 131; John Hill on, 103–4, 112–13; meaning of, in English and French, 99–100; and mechanism, 94–95; as pathology, 98, 112–13; Sainte-Albine on, 98–99, 101; as theoretical problem, 110–11
Shakespeare, William, 59, 134, 172, 184; *Hamlet*, 32, 33, 37, 40, 44, 45, 52, 58, 81, 86–87, 112, 164; *King Lear*, 48, 141, 164; *Macbeth*, 37–38, 89–90, 111, 127, 145, 185–86; *Othello*, 46, 73–74, 102
Shelley, Mary, 164
Shelley, Percy Bysshe, 101
Siddons, Henry, 76–77, 106
Siddons, Sarah, 38, 173–75
Socrates, 46
Solon, 137
Sophocles, 103
Sothern, E. H., 193
Soul, 12, 25; Descartes on, 60, 63; Diderot on, 129–30; Garrick on, 95, 97; La Mettrie on, 66, 90, 97; Luigi Riccoboni on, 101,

112; as superstition, 112. *See also* Body: and mind; Descartes, René: interactive dualism

Spencer, Herbert, 181

Spontaneity, 16–17, 104, 109–12, 161; Artaud on, 222–24; as automatism, 150–51; Diderot on, 152, 221; Grotowski on, 226; organic theory of, 162–63; Quintilian on, 26; in self-use systems, 218–21; Stanislavski on, 194, 214; Talma on, 170–71; Wordsworth on, 163

Staël, Madame de, 166

Stanislavski, Constantin, 15, 161, 172; and adaptation, 206, 207; and Brecht, 197–98; and character biography, 172; and circles of attention, 208; and classical acting texts, 195–96; and Diderot, 204–5, 208, 214–15; and emotion memory, 209–11; and imagination, 209–10; his "magic circle," 179; his method of physical actions, 197–98, 211–15; and Meyerhold, 197, 202, 204; and Pavlov, 206–9, 210, 216; and public solitude, 155, 208; and reflex, 208–9; and relaxation, 208; and score of the role, 208, 213–14; and spread of the System, 215–16; and subconsciousness, 205–6, 207, 209, 210, 211; his System of acting, 194, 204–15; and Talma, 170, 171; and temporhythm, 212–13. Works: *An Actor Prepares*, 14, 205, 209, 211, 212; *Building a Character*, 205, 212; *Creating a Role*, 205, 213; *My Life in Art*, 217

Steele, Richard, 69, 81

Sterne, Laurence, 98

Sticotti, Antonio Fabio, 114, 132–33

Strasberg, Lee, 216

Sturz, Helfrich Peter, 95, 96, 102, 109

Suard, Jean-Baptiste-Antoine, 97, 127

Subconsciousness. *See* Unconsciousness

Swammerdam, Jan, 65, 94; *Book of Nature*, 94, 100, 107

Swanston, Eyllaerdt, 48

Tableaux, 69, 73–74, 87

Taglioni, Marie, 165, 168

Talma, François-Joseph, 162, 197; on acting, 169–73; on characterization, 172–73; Le-

kain, 169, 170, 189, 196; his plagiarism of Diderot, 169, 170

Taylor, Frederick Winslow, 203

Taylor, Joseph, 48

Thespis, 137

Tolstoy, Leo, 216

Toporkov, Vasili O., 215, 216

Torelli, Giacomo, 62

Toricelli, Evangelista, 65

Transitions, 42–44, 69, 73, 111, 152, 187–88

Treviranus, Ludolph Christian, 161

Unconsciousness, 96, 162, 164, 172; Darwin on, 179; and Descartes, 85; Diderot on, 146–47; Freud on, 179; Garrick on, 96, 108; von Hartmann on, 179; John Hill on, 108–9; Lewes on, 191; Meyerhold on, 203; Stanislavski on, 205–6. *See also* Diderot: on double consciousness

Vakhtangov, Eugene, 215

Vartanian, Aram, 121

Vaucanson, Jacques, 66, 91, 202

Vesalius, 33, 61, 64

Vibius, Gallus, 49, 144

Vibrations, 182; Diderot on, 147; Lewes on, 106, 186; as principle of nerve physiology, 104–7. *See also* Hartley, David

Visiones. *See* Quintilian: *visiones*

Vitalism, 93, 96, 100, 221–23; Diderot on, 121; and mechanism, 117, 152, 157, 161, 182–84, 223–26

Voltaire, 82

Walker, John, 76–78, 79

Watson, J. B., 198

Webster, John, 32

Whytt, Robert, 114, 150–51, 152, 163

Wilkes, Thomas, 70, 81

Willis, Thomas, 65

Wilson, Benjamin, 87–88

Wordsworth, William, 146, 163, 189, 215

Wright, Thomas, 32, 38, 39, 45; on gestures, 52; *Passions of the Minde*, 29, 31, 33, 105–6

Zakhava, B. E., 215